CHASING CATASTROPHE

MY 35 YEARS COVERING WARS, HURRICANES, TERROR ATTACKS, AND OTHER BREAKING NEWS

RICK LEVENTHAL

POST HILL PRESS

A POST HILL PRESS BOOK
ISBN: 978-1-63758-494-1
ISBN (eBook): 978-1-63758-495-8

Chasing Catastrophe:
My 35 Years Covering Wars, Hurricanes, Terror Attacks, and Other
Breaking News

Cover photo by Madelin Fuerste

This is a work of nonfiction. All people, locations, events, and situation
are portrayed to the best of the author's memory.

Post Hill Press
New York • Nashville
posthillpress.com

Published in the United States of America
2 3 4 5 6 7 8 9 10

To my wife, Kelly. I couldn't have written this book
without your love, encouragement, and support.
You've been with me every step of the way, feeding me,
inspiring me, listening to my stories, suggesting edits,
pushing me to keep at it, handling everything I couldn't
handle while I was filling these pages with my words.
You have changed my life for the better in
more ways than I can count and I will always
cherish every minute we share together.

TABLE OF CONTENTS

CHAPTER 1

9/11

Large pieces of flaky dust were drifting from the sky like some kind of strange summer snowstorm in downtown Manhattan, ashes slowly gliding down from the blazing towers, collecting on Church Street and covering everything on the ground: people, fire trucks, pieces of one of the jet engines lying across from me and our Fox News satellite engineer at the corner of Church and Warren, yellow caution tape already wrapped around the ripped metal and large gear on the pavement.

I saw what appeared to be federal agents taking photos of the plane parts, which were buried in the same layer blanketing everything else...a puffy gray powder that I could best describe as moon dust. The entire downtown area below Canal Street had become a massive crime scene, and we were standing right in the middle of it.

It was eerily quiet, except when it wasn't. The silence would be broken by the sirens of ambulances, police cars, and fire trucks rolling past. Then it was just the breeze and the plaintive cries of stunned survivors walking out of the smoky cloud like zombies, with chalk-covered faces and unrecognizable expressions, a mix of shock, confusion, and absolute horror.

And then, one minute before 10 a.m. on that beautiful crystal-clear September morning, we all heard the rumble of the first tower starting to fall.

I was with engineer Pat Butler, who'd parked the Fox News Channel satellite truck on Church Street near the corner of Warren, just five blocks north of Ground Zero, roughly 1,200 feet from the heart of the World Trade Center (WTC).

The producer and cameraman hadn't made it to our location yet, so Pat pulled some cables from the back of the vehicle and plugged in the truck camera and a stick microphone. He'd already dialed in our shot, but we'd lost communication with the studio. Cell phones weren't working, but as it turned out, our picture was live and we were recording all of it in the truck.

I grabbed the mic and he grabbed the camera, and I started narrating the scene, with no idea if the network was putting us on the air live, and just as I started describing what was happening around me, the first skyscraper started to crumble.

We heard what sounded like a freight train struggling on gravel-covered tracks, or a giant bucket dumping chunks of rock and sand from hundreds of feet in the air, as each floor of the South Tower pancaked onto the next, and the entire 110-story skyscraper became a massive pile of broken rock, twisted steel, tangled staircases, and victims' bodies. Close to three thousand lost souls were crushed and burned in the impact and explosion of the jet, the fires that followed, or the fall of the building itself, not to mention the jumpers who leapt to their deaths from above the impact zone rather than suffer an unimaginably horrible alternative.

Pat and I couldn't actually see the first tower fall, because of all the other buildings blocking our line of sight, but after the collapse we saw a huge dust cloud at least two hundred feet high rolling north up Church Street, right toward us.

Everything that happened next is recorded on tape.

I yelled at Pat to zoom in on the chaos behind me and started reporting again:

"There's been a huge explosion. Everyone is running in the other direction. We're on Church Street. We're not sure what happened."

Someone in the background yells in horror: "IT FELL DOWN!"

"There's been a huge explosion," I continued. "Everyone's running for their lives, literally. Police, media...I see a woman pushing a baby carriage. Here comes the smoke! Here comes the smoke. It's unclear what happened, if the tower collapsed or what."

Then I looked at Pat and said, "I think we getter get out of this mess dude. I think we better get out of this."

We ran to the truck, dropped the gear, and jumped inside to escape the cloud, unsure of what exactly had just happened and completely unnerved about what might come next.

The video goes to black as the camera is enveloped, but you can hear our entire conversation. Pat is coughing uncontrollably, choking on the smoke he inhaled outside. "Oh my God, Pat. Close that door dude! Oh my God, we might fucking die here together, you and me. You all right?"

Pat is still gagging and coughing.

"Where's Jonathan?" I ask, about the producer who's supposed to meet us to help with our live shots. Then I look out the small window in the back of the truck. "Holy shit. We can't see a fucking thing. Look at that."

"Oh my God. Oh my God," I continue. "Dude, this is not good. We shouldn't be here, should we?"

This was the most rattled I'd ever been in my forty-one years on Earth: "Everybody else fucking ran. The cops, everybody. I don't know what to do."

You can hear Pat in the background, frantically trying to dial the phone to connect with our Midtown office.

"Fuck," I say, "are we gonna die in this fucking satellite truck with no cell service?"

"Come on baby. Please!" Pat is talking to the phone. "COME ON!" He keeps trying. "Come on baby, WORK!"

"I think the fucking tower must have collapsed," I tell him.

"All those poor people, Rick. So many people in the building."

"Oh, I know" I told him. "This one cop told me he saw bodies on fire leaping out of the building from the one hundredth story or eightieth story."

The smoke is starting to clear now, and the shot from our camera slowly becomes visible through the haze, pointing at the street from below the truck.

"It's clear now dude. You wanna go back out there?"

Pat tells me, "I need a towel and water for my face!"

Then he gets his composure. "Wanna go out? What do you think, brother?"

"Yeah, I think we should go out," I said. "I just wish we could know if they're seeing our shot!"

We headed back out onto the street, where everything had turned a faded white, covered in ash. We'd been inside the vehicle for just under four minutes.

"I'll just start talking and you start shooting," I tell him.

What happened next was by far the most difficult challenge I'd ever faced as a reporter.

On a typical day, you have to turn people away who want to be on TV. Most people can't wait to share their opinions or mug in the background or try to tell you about some cause or project they're passionate about, but this was a day like no other.

I didn't even attempt to stop most of the people walking by because they were clearly in shock, stunned, or devastated by what they'd just experienced, their eyes blank and cold, and most of them barely noticed we were there.

I went back and forth between narrating the scene around me and interviewing anyone willing to talk, including a uniformed NYPD detective walking by, covered in dust, who'd been near the base of the first tower to fall.

"Everything just all of a sudden imploded," he told me. "I ran as fast as I could. Ran inside a building a block away, then it started filling with smoke. Then I came out and it looks like I'm in a surreal movie."

I asked if there were cops or civilians on the ground nearby, and how many were there.

"Where that happened, it was mostly police officers. Might've been 100, 150."

I didn't know what else to ask, or what else to say. This man might've just lost that many colleagues in the blur of the collapse.

The network was dipping in and out of our shot, with anchor Jon Scott narrating over live images of the smoking towers and a wider shot of the dust clouds over Lower Manhattan, as well as the developing scene at the Pentagon, hit by another hijacked jet, with flames and smoke rising from the iconic building and staff rushing past the camera toward safety.

When Jon tossed back to me, I was doing another scene-setter, as Pat zoomed in on the pieces of the engine on the ground.

"Pandemonium a short time ago, when the building did collapse or whatever it was that happened, it was a huge explosion, a huge rumbling cloud of smoke and fire, came across Church Street, and then started billowing this way, and all we saw was people, were people running in this direction, everyone. Law enforcement, a woman pushing a baby carriage..."

(I'd walked over to the parts of the airplane in the street, surrounded by crime scene tape.)

"This is actually, we believe, a piece of debris from one of the planes that hit one of the towers of the World Trade Center. The FBI is here, you can see this area is roped off, they were taking photographs and securing this area just prior to that huge explosion that we all heard and felt."

(Conspiracy theorists may take these references to an "explosion" to support a far-fetched version of events, claiming the towers were blown up by controlled demolitions after they were hit by planes, but I can assure you the word was used only because it was a quick way to describe the intensity of the collapse. There was no actual explosion, except when the planes hit the buildings and their loaded fuel tanks ignited.)

"We are trying to talk to some of these guys.... Can you tell me what you saw, what you heard?"

A bearded man with a Fire and Rescue hat on stopped to share his story.

"What did you see, what did you hear?"

"It felt like another plane coming, everybody took cover, we ran down into the subway..."

"Were there a lot of people on the subway?" I asked. That's how I'd gotten downtown, exiting at Canal Street and walking the rest of the way when the conductor was told the WTC-bound train could go no further.

"No, not that many because they already had evacuated before."

"Did you see people, anyone in danger?"

"Back there, yeah, but I was running, nothing you could do because we saw the thing coming right over..."

I started to ask another question and then trailed off because of a big muscle-bound cop lumbering past me, covered in dust. He'd clearly been wearing a protective vest and had taken it off after the collapse because you could see the outline of it on his shirt.

"Look at this guy, look at this guy," I said. "Unbelievable. Unbelievable."

I continued to narrate the scene:

"The streets have been shut down, there was very little traffic on the streets except for emergency vehicles going one way or the other, so there was not a lot of vehicle traffic in this area, but there were a lot of pedestrians on every single corner taking photographs and looking at the building which was still smoking and still on fire."

I turned back to my interviewee.

"Where were you when the explosion occurred, when a plane hit the building?"

"I saw it from my office on the Lower West Side and came here."

"You came here, what, to check it out?"

"No! To see if we could help but...[he looks around and shrugs.]" Clearly there wasn't a lot the man could do.

Just then a detective came walking past, gripping the upper arm of a woman covered in soot, clearly in distress.

"This poor woman," I said. "Wow." And then I stayed quiet as they hurried past, seeking some kind of medical attention, letting the scene speak for itself.

Just then people are running again, away from the scene, because of the sound of another plane overhead.

It was unreal. The sound of a plane was now a signal of danger in Lower Manhattan.

"It's our jet! It's our jet!" Someone yelled.

Apparently, it was a pair of fighter jets scrambled to patrol the airspace in case more hijacked planes tried to target the city.

"What are you guys doing right now?" I asked some motorcycle cops now on foot, still wearing their helmets, headed toward the scene. "What's your assignment?"

"Help people," one of them responded, not breaking stride.

I knew it was a dumb question. It was one of those times when I didn't want to bother anyone and didn't even know where to begin, beyond the basics of, "What did you see, what did you hear?"

Then a Black man wearing what looked like a doorman's jacket walked past, white from the soot from his head to his shoes.

"The dust is still thick in the air," I said as I resumed my narration. "What that guy is covered with is here," as Pat panned down to show my shoes shuffling through the layer of dust. "It's all over the street, just thick soot, ash, just came roaring down here in a huge cloud from the World Trade Center."

At this point I'd walked back to the center of Church, with the camera pointed south at me and the street beyond, still hazy with smoke, with first responders walking to Ground Zero and a few coming toward me, including another uniformed cop covered in dust, coughing and pouring water in his mouth and over his face and head.

"Are you able to talk, can we just talk to you about what happened?"

He answered while he walked:

"I was downstairs when it exploded," he said, with a frantic intensity in his voice. He'd been inside when the tower started to fall.

"You were right there at the building?"

"Yes. Lot of people trapped!" he half yelled, still walking away.

"Lot of people trapped," I solemnly repeated. Just then an EMT grabbed the cop by the arm and redirected him toward a triage area.

The network cut away to scenes of more smoke and flames at the Pentagon and a quick update from Washington, then came back to me.

"Our Rick Leventhal is on the ground in Lower Manhattan where these scenes of chaos and utter confusion are just mind numbing..."

"We were standing here," I began, "when there was some sort of collapse or explosion, and everyone started running in this direction, police officers, pedestrians, EMTs, everybody came running this way. I saw a woman pushing a baby carriage, running for her life, and right behind her was a huge cloud of billowing smoke and ash and debris coming this way..."

One of our engineers, Pat Muskopf, showed up and I started interviewing him, and the network picked it up mid-sentence:

"I looked up and I saw a huge plume of smoke and the tower was crumbling," Pat told me. "And it just turned into a huge ton of smoke and next thing I know there's smoke and one tower."

Another wave of survivors escaping the towers came walking past, as police vehicles with sirens blaring made their way north through the crowd.

Then I stopped a guy who had evacuated from the North Tower (One WTC), climbing down seventy-seven flights of stairs, reaching the sixth floor as the South Tower (Two WTC) collapsed next door.

"I was in the restroom, there was a big shaking, some of the ceilings collapsed, looked like there was a fire in the elevator shaft, and they brought everyone down and started bringing everybody down the stairs," he said.

"So you came down from the seventy-seventh floor?" I asked, incredulous.

"Seventy-seventh floor, down the stairs, yes."

"What was happening around you? Were people screaming?

"No, no, people were pretty calm.... When we got down to the sixth floor there was like another shake or another explosion, everyone started panicking, but [overall] everybody was really calm, and the police and firemen were very helpful."

They were still coming down the stairs when the South Tower collapsed next door.

"Which of the two towers were you in?" I asked.

"One. World Trade Center One."

"And when you got to the ground, then what?"

"It's just like, it's like rubble and dust like inches thick and like paper, paper [he's coughing] paper everywhere, and they just moved us out."

"How many people do you think were in the building on the floors that were affected?"

"I couldn't say," he told me. "I'm one office out of twenty on the floor so I have no idea."

"What's the first thing you thought when you heard it?"

"I had to call my wife."

"Did you? Were you able to?" I knew from very recent experience how difficult it could be to get a line out.

"I got through, I called her, I'm talking to you because I'm hoping she's watching so she knows I'm OK."

"What's your name?" I asked this incredibly lucky guy.

"My name is Matthew Garth."

I thanked him, and he walked off, presumably finding a way back to his wife.

The interviews in the street continued. A guy in a suit with a mustache and glasses who'd also escaped the towers after they'd been hit stopped and shared his experiences. Despite being in one of the towers, he was as uncertain about what had just happened as I was when I arrived on the scene.

"It felt like a bomb hit or a plane hit or something like that."

"A plane did hit," I told him.

"A plane did hit," he repeated. "We looked out the window, and all we saw was debris, all over the place. We thought the building was gonna topple over, it was going, shaking..."

"Well one of them did," I told him.

"One of them did," he repeated.

"We were in Tower One. We made it out."

"Well, you're a lucky man," I assured him.

"Thank you very much," he said, his voice breaking.

"Take care," I told him.

I turned to see a group of construction workers crawling past me, headed out of the dust cloud in a four-door pickup truck. A man named Artie Forman was driving, his window rolled down, and I will never forget what he told me, and especially the *way* he described what unfolded in front of him, in a thick New York accent:

"We were on the roof across the street, we see a big jet coming sideways—BANG! Through the middle of it, around the seventieth floor and then half an hour later we see the second one banging in—we're on the roof a block away!"

Searching for a question, I ask him: "What's going through your mind?"

"You see bodies flying out of the sky, and you can't do nothin' about it. You tell me! You tell me what you think. I mean, my heart's in my mouth. I mean, I pray for these people. There's no words to describe what's going on out there. I mean, you see bodies just coming out. A half hour later they're still coming out of the goddamn sky. Devastating. Devastating. I can't imagine anything worse than this."

Artie pauses for a moment, then continues: "I can't imagine. You know everyone on the plane must have died. The floor, I got friends of mine on the 104th floor, friend in other buildings. I just spoke to one of my friends a half hour prior to that getting ready to go upstairs to go to work. I mean, I've seen a lot of construction accidents, a lot of bad things happen, never seen a jet fly out of the sky, plow into a building, no less once but twice."

He shakes his head. "Devastated. Devastated. Overwhelming. Nothing can describe it."

Less than two minutes after I thank Artie, still stunned by the gravity and intensity of what he told me, we hear shouting and see more people running, and cops are yelling "BACK IT UP! BACK IT UP!" and we look up and see the top of the second tower, which had been visible just above the buildings in front of us, disappear from view, with that awful, familiar rumble shaking our feet.

"All right, here we go again," I say. "Here we go again. I don't know what's going on, but this, the second building is collapsing I believe."

"Here it goes, here it goes, here it goes!" I yell.

"We do need to put it down now, we need to put it down now," I told Pat, referring to the camera. I knew the drill now. We needed to take cover and would likely be able to come back out in a few minutes.

Pat put his camera on the ground for the second time, still wired to the truck, and we retreated to a side street a couple of blocks north.

The footage captured by his lens is as eerie as I've ever seen and still gives me goosebumps to this day—watching the second smoke cloud come rolling north, with the street gone quiet again, eventually engulfing the lens, the video slowly fading to black.

The network cut to a wide shot, apparently from a local news helicopter, showing the top of the second tower falling toward the ground, creating a black ring of smoke trails all the way down.

When the smoke cleared, we picked up where we left off.

I would spend every day and night for the next two weeks at Ground Zero, reporting on the search and recovery and the growing list of the missing, most of whom were virtually vaporized in the initial impact, the fire, or the collapse of the towers.

It was by far the most depressing story I'd ever covered. I felt intimately connected to it, and there was nothing but sadness, despair, and bad news followed by more bad news.

I forced myself to stay strong during my extensive coverage of the tragedy, doing my best to separate my emotions and personal feelings from the job at hand. It wasn't until my first day off, a Sunday, that I broke down and sobbed on the couch in my apartment on East 36th Street near Midtown when the weight of it all finally hit me hard.

I still have my reporter notebooks from the first days after the attacks, when just 233 dead had been recovered and 170 of them identified, and 5,422 people were still missing.

The first page of my notebook has a quotation from the New York police commissioner at the time, Bernard Kerik, who said: "We haven't changed from rescue to recovery, but with every day, every hour, and every minute that goes by, that hope diminishes. It's not looking good."

FEMA teams had poked fiber-optic cameras into the shopping concourse in the basement below the towers but found no one alive. More than one thousand two hundred firefighters and hundreds of police and corrections officers were helping with the search, and construction crews were brought in to deal with the massive amounts of debris that needed to be cleared.

There were two hundred thousand TONS of steel in EACH of the towers and many tens of thousands more tons of other debris carefully being scooped up and carted off in big dump trucks, and when they dropped their loads off, rescue workers were there to comb through the piles looking for human remains.

Here's a couple other statistics you can share with anyone foolish enough to float a conspiracy theory suggesting the towers would never have collapsed on their own and that for some convoluted reason, shadowy government figures rigged the buildings with explosives to insure they fell to the ground on 9/11 (I actually watched a "documentary" floating this infuriating and severely flawed argument). Tell them when Flight 11 hit the North Tower at 8:46 a.m., it impacted floors ninety-three though ninety-nine, with roughly forty-five thousand TONS of weight above the damaged, blown out section of building.

Flight 175 hit the South Tower at 9:03 a.m. between floors seventy-seven and eighty-five, with one hundred ten thousand tons above and flames burning rocket fuel and other debris in both buildings at a temperature of two thousand degrees.

The intense heat cooked the damaged infrastructure of the South Tower for fifty-six minutes before it could no longer hold the massive weight above, and the severely damaged North

Tower managed to sustain the smaller section of building above for one hour forty-two minutes before finally giving way.

That second collapse took all of eight seconds, registering 2.0 on the Richter scale.

Millions of cubic yards of concrete were pulverized into dust, which is what we saw coating everything on the ground around us. Subway stations below the towers collapsed, and some of the tunnels were pierced by steel beams. And the debris was creating roadblocks for first responders. A Marriott Hotel was also destroyed, leaving a six-story pile of rubble spread out in every direction, forcing workers to try and clear paths to get in.

I found a live shot script from one of those first days:

"Another day of digging, another day of fading hopes. More searchers are wearing 'Recovery' badges, meaning they're looking for bodies and body parts."

"233 dead have been recovered so far, 170 of them identified, but 5,422 are still considered missing, including 311 firefighters, 23 NYPD officers, and 37 Port Authority police, and with each passing minute, hope fades further any of the missing will be found alive."

I reported on the Federal Emergency Management Agency (FEMA) teams using fiber-optic cables but having no luck. There were voids in the rubble, but the heat was too intense for anyone to survive.

At that point, recovery workers had hauled off 60,000 tons of debris in 4,464 truckloads, but there was still an estimated 1.2 *million* tons of debris left.

We'd been pushed further and further back from the scene each day, until finally all media were moved to a large press area on Greenwich Street a few blocks north of Ground Zero, where every television network built platform "risers" for cameras and correspondents to report from. One day, Ben Affleck and Matt

Damon came by, just to get a look at what was happening. I think one of them had a place in the neighborhood, and I chatted with them for a few minutes.

Eventually, bigger machines were brought in, like bulldozers and heavy cranes, replacing the bucket brigade of dedicated workers and volunteers frantically moving rocks and other stuff off the piles, piece by piece, in a desperate search for survivors. It was estimated the cleanup would take six months because of the unimaginable sea of debris.

As the numbers of tons removed climbed, so did the number of bodies recovered, and we also began reporting on the wave of elected officials and notables allowed in to get a closer look at the recovery operations, including a delegation of forty senators one day and boxing champ Muhammad Ali, who told reporters gathered at a news conference that there are fanatics in every religion, and not all Islam is bad.

One day I wrote:

"I remember coming to the WTC towers for a press conference with the governor. There was tight security that day. Did those Port Authority police perish in the collapse?

"On the day of the attack, I came to the base of the North Tower, and cops told me to stay back. I identified myself as press, and they told me they'd arrest me because it wasn't safe to get any closer. Did *they* make it out alive?

"This used to be home to two of the tallest buildings in the world, representing strength, stability, and success, a landmark anchoring the bottom end of this incredible island.

"It's still hard to believe they're gone."

New York was a city that depended on tourism, but most of the hotels and restaurants and theaters were now empty. People were mourning. Authorities admitted there was no more than a very small chance of *any* additional survivors being found. Rescuers were narrowing the "hot zone", but fires still burned and would continue to burn for a hundred days after the attack. The work had to be done slowly and cautiously because of the human remains dispersed throughout the rubble, often in miniscule pieces.

At least sixty-three other countries reported citizens among the missing, including 250 from Great Britain, as many as 150 Germans, 91 from India, and 19 from the Philippines.

Police reported looting in stores in a basement plaza below Five World Trade that were still intact, including a Tourneau Watch store and a designer sunglasses outlet. Criminals pried open ATMs with crowbars. The crimes were committed with "speed and confidence," cops said.

A week after the attack, I was allowed in to Ground Zero with a camera crew, joining a group including then-Attorney General John Ashcroft, FBI Director Robert Mueller, New York Governor George Pataki, and Mayor Rudy Giuliani. Attorney General Ashcroft shook his head as he took in the sea of destruction, calling it "indescribable," and was clearly moved by it, speaking "strongly and passionately about reasserting the spirit of this country and using every resource to drive the largest investigation in the history of the U.S.," I wrote.

In the live intro to my package that night, from the riser we'd built blocks away, I told our viewers: "From here, the view is not dramatic. Up close, it's just plain horrific."

Two weeks to the day after the towers collapsed, when any hope of finding more survivors was gone, the largest piece of wreckage still standing was yanked to the ground. Crews attached three heavy cables to the eight-story or ten-story façade of 2 WTC and tugged on it for half an hour until it crashed down. A piece of it was later used as part of the memorial museum built on site.

We kept up our reporting daily and nightly, updating the number of confirmed dead and amount of debris removed, along with efforts to get the city moving again. Mayor Giuliani encouraged people to shop and go out for meals and drinks, reopening streets and tourist attractions. He even delivered the opening monologue on *Saturday Night Live*, flanked by his police and fire commissioners and a couple of dozen uniformed cops, firefighters, and Port Authority Police, delivering a somber tribute to the victims and first responders and people of the city, at one point telling the audience, "It's okay to laugh and cry at the same time."

The Yankees made it to the World Series against the Arizona Diamondbacks, giving New Yorkers something to cheer about again, and were up three games to two, needing to win just one more in Phoenix. It was a Cinderella story with a Hollywood ending until it wasn't. The Yanks lost games six and seven in an absolute heartbreaker for fans like me.

It was now early November. President George W. Bush visited the site for the second time, on the two-month anniversary of the attacks, delivering a message of strength and hope for the future and a resolve to never forget the attacks and the victims.

I was determined to do whatever I could to support my country, and when I heard a few journalists would be selected to join the first wave of troops headed to Afghanistan on the search for Osama Bin Laden, I immediately volunteered to go.

9/11 changed my life and my career, and I still get chills when I see *any* videos of the Twin Towers or read stories about the day. I definitely have some lingering PTSD, which is fine. I'd rather carry the effects of that day forever than forget it.

For me, "Never Forget" isn't an issue. It's ingrained in my soul and being and always will be.

CHAPTER 2

FIRST TO AFGHANISTAN

When I'm reporting on scene, my brain goes on auto pilot. I'm able to shut down my emotions and focus on the facts and make sure to get the best and most up to date information to the viewers. Once I'm done, I usually forget about the story and focus on other stuff: friends, family, football or baseball games, or a movie on TV.

But covering 9/11 from a decimated and depressed city was a completely different experience, rocking me to my inner core. Being a few blocks from the towers when they crumbled to the ground was the absolute most awful experience of my life, shading me with a darkness I couldn't escape, and I was getting antsy, weary of the daily numbers of the dead and missing we were reporting. My fear had turned to anger, and my uncertainty about what was happening around us had morphed into an intense desire for revenge against the mass murdering terrorists.

When I found out the Pentagon was offering to embed journalists, I met with John Moody, the boss of the news operation, just below Roger Ailes. I told him I was motivated and determined to embed with the Marines and cover the war on terror from the front lines. I remember him asking me if I was sure and if I realized the potential risks of such an assignment. I didn't care, I told him. This was a really important story, and since I couldn't join the fight, I could at least report on those brave souls who were.

He agreed to submit my name to the Pentagon, and before long I got the call to pack my bags and head to Bahrain, where a large group of journalists were gathering for daily briefings from the military and awaiting word on who would be in the final group of twelve selected for the small pool of reporters and photographers who'd be flown in to embed with the first wave of Marines already on the ground in the Afghan desert.

I was the only correspondent sent by Fox News Channel, but then Oliver North showed up with his senior producer. He was a highly decorated former Marine lieutenant colonel, a platoon commander in Vietnam awarded the Silver Star, Bronze Star, and two Purple Hearts, now hosting a series on Fox called *War Stories*. He became famous during the Iran-Contra affair in the late '80s for helping to support rebel groups in Nicaragua with proceeds from arms sales to Iran. I can still see him in his dress uniform, testifying before Congress on television. Did I really have to compete with this guy now to get into Afghanistan?

I liked and respected Ollie North but was pissed because he was vying for one of the spots in the embed, and we'd been told by Marine Corps Public Affairs that only one reporter from each network would be allowed to join the group. I remember confronting his producer about it, then calling back to New York and complaining to my bosses.

"He's not a real reporter!" I told them. "I'm here to cover the news. It's what I'm trained for and what you're paying me for. This is my story. He can't do what I can for the network. He's just here for his show!" They assured me I'd be going in before him.

After about a week, the Public Affairs office revealed the final short list of journos who'd made the cut for the embed, and my name was called, along with Alan Pizzi from CBS, David Wright from ABC, and Rob Morrison from NBC (he was a daytime anchor for WNBC in New York, where I'd once worked). One of our freelance shooters was invited to handle all the video (all the TV reporters shared him), and there were two still photographers from the Associated Press Television News and the Associated Press; scribes from Agence France-Presse, Knight Ridder, the *Los Angeles Times*, *The San Diego Union-Tribune*, and *USA Today*; and two AP dish engineers to feed all the material back to the states.

We were told to pack flak jackets, helmets, sleeping bags, and a limited amount of clothes and gear. Whatever we brought we'd be carrying ourselves.

For the TV guys, it was a bit of an unusual arrangement. We'd take turns each day filming live shots and packages. All of our reports would be pooled, meaning every network could use any correspondent's pieces. Even our live shots would be generic, reporting for any channel that wanted a hit from Afghanistan that day. It wouldn't be "In Afghanistan, Rick Leventhal, Fox News" at the end. It would be "Rick Leventhal with U.S. Marines in Afghanistan."

We'd be flown first to the *USS Kearsarge*, an amphibious assault ship carrying harrier jets and attack helicopters, deployed to the gulf ferrying troops back and forth to the fighting. There were thousands of sailors and Marines on board, and we'd be given opportunities to interview them and tell their stories before heading back to base and boarding one of their massive, lumbering, and loud C-17 cargo planes for what we were warned would be an "ugly trip" with "multiple stops in unidentified locations," loading freight along the way before the dangerous last leg to a remote compound in the middle of the Afghan desert.

I saved my reporter notebook from this trip, in which I documented our journey from late November 2001 until late December 2001.

> Eleven of us left the hotel at 1600 [military time for 4 p.m.] in a bus with a U-Haul trailer full of gear to an airbase in Bahrain. I had a double cheeseburger and waited 2 ½ hours, then brought our gear into a small terminal building, where they checked bags as you would in any airport. All went thru a heavy-duty X-ray machine, then were loaded onto a C-17, a big wide fat bodied 4 engine jet.

> After another two-hour wait, we walked onto the airfield and boarded the C-17. The inside looks like a hollowed out, wide body jumbo jet with exposed walls and ceiling, wires, hoses, and compression pipes visible, with rows of jump seats running along each wall.

> Parked in the center, a big hydraulic fork-lift for loading and unloading the palettes of supplies stored in the back. They opened the cargo door to back the aircraft out of its "parking spot."

Our final destination was forward operating base Rhino, a dirt landing strip and a series of stone buildings behind a wall, surrounded by long stretches of sand. We were told it was formerly used by drug dealers moving opium out of the country. Now it was in the hands of thirteen hundred U.S. Marines, who called it Camp Rhino.

There we met up with the 15th Marine Expeditionary Unit and Marine Task Force 58, led by Brigadier General James Mattis, who told us that ground forces intended to help to encircle the Taliban, block escape routes, and serve as a jump-off point for attacks by Special Forces and conventional troops.

The Taliban were believed to have Stinger missiles and other smaller arms, such as rocket-propelled grenades (RPGs) capable of bringing down the Marines' Cobra helicopter gunships, Huey Reconnaissance choppers, and troop transport helicopters. The base was "within striking distance" of Kandahar, the Taliban's political and spiritual capital. The days would be dry and hot, the nights near freezing. The terrain was sand and rock.

We were reminded of the strict rules we'd need to follow: no reporting of future military plans or operations; nothing on command strength, equipment, or supplies; no mention of specific locations, progress, numbers deployed, their positions, or downed aircraft during rescue operations.

The fighting was already fierce and deadly. Three Special Forces soldiers were killed, and twenty Afghans wounded, in a friendly fire incident, when a B-52 bomber missed its target with a two thousand pound "smart bomb," exploding within a hundred yards of American forces and a group of opposition fighters. The victims were flown to Camp Rhino, where the dead Marines were held in a makeshift morgue until they could be transported to ships and on to the base at Bahrain before being flown back to the states. The wounded Afghans were also flown out for medical treatment aboard the *USS Peleliu* and other locations equipped with medical facilities.

One of the Marine officers told us: "Seeing the wounded coming in, being aware of personnel killed in action, brings it home that it's no longer a game."

Our group of embedded journalists' home at the base was a stone warehouse designated the "press center," where we ate, slept, and wrote our stories. Every day began with briefings from the Public Affairs Officers (PAOs) who gave us the latest facts on the fighting and laid out our plans for the day. Most afternoons we were treated to another briefing from General Mattis himself, a tough-talking no-nonsense "man's man" who chomped on cigars and cussed and insisted that most of what he told us was off the record or on background, meaning we couldn't use it or couldn't quote him.

Our time at Camp Rhino was frustrating to say the least. It was completely unlike the embed I'd experience in Iraq fifteen months later, when we ate, worked, slept, and traveled with the Marines all the way to Baghdad and were part of every mission. On this first trip to Afghanistan, our movements were severely restricted. Every day we asked to join the Marines when they headed outside Rhino's walls, and every day we were denied.

Instead, we received briefings on what the Marines did, had to report on them without seeing or recording any of it, and took occasional field trips to tamer locations where the enemy had already been cleared and threats neutralized.

The base was growing by the day, as more troops and supplies were flown in, with massive C-130s delivering food, water, and supplies multiple times a day. We were assured that the base was well protected by "Stinger and Avenger teams," with a "strong defensive perimeter supported by a significant air defense."

We were safe, but we weren't satisfied. We could only watch as reconnaissance assets left the base, followed by armored, mobile hunter-killer teams in high-backed Humvees with anti-tank missiles and fifty-caliber machine guns, interdicting military targets and searching for mine fields.

We did get a tour of the base, including a mosque that had been taped off so Marines couldn't use it, "preserving the sanctity" of the building.

The Marines had their own satellite dishes for communications, a command post, officer's quarters, a maintenance bay, and a warehouse for vehicles and storage.

The 2.1-kilometer sand airstrip was smoothed and graded daily with a heavy roller, since it would get rutted by the landings, and we saw an outbuilding blown to bits during the fierce fight the Marines encountered when they seized the facility in a raid on November 25.

One day we were told of the first significant offensive ground operations, when U.S. Marine hunter-killer teams engaged enemy forces along road networks near Kandahar, killing seven and destroying three vehicles. The engagement started when one of the vehicles approached the Marines "at a high rate of speed," and after the Marines lit it up, they called in air support, and the fighter jets took out the other two vehicles and killed others fleeing on foot.

One night our base went on high alert, after recon units outside the walled compound spotted vehicles and more enemy fighters on foot, "probing the perimeter in more than one location." The Marines fired illumination rounds, mortars, and automatic grenade launchers in their direction, so-called indirect fire, thwarting any possible attack.

"They were probing to find defensive weaknesses in our lines," Marine Captain David Romley told us, "and I think they found out there are none."

There was also a helicopter crash. A Huey went down and burst into flames along the edge of the airstrip, apparently caused by the thick dust stirred up by the chopper's spinning blades. Two Marines suffered only minor injuries, one on board and one on the ground, and they were back at work the next day.

After a much quieter night, we got another briefing from Marine Captain Stewart Upton, who told us: "Things may look calm, but it could be the calm before the storm. A lot of Marines out there want to kill something," hunting not just for Taliban soldiers but also for identified terrorists, including Al-Qaida members, known to be in the region. The Marines carried the pictures of these terrorists on missions.

"We hope [the enemy] knows the war is over, lays down his weapons, and goes away. We are closing down and continuing to monitor all avenues of exodus for terrorists." Upton told us.

"The day of reckoning in regard to September 11th is close at hand. Those who haven't realized it yet will soon."

AMERICAN TALIBAN IN THE HOUSE

The biggest story I covered while at Rhino was the arrival of John Walker Lindh, the "American Taliban," who was temporarily held in a shipping container turned prison cell at Camp Rhino. He'd been captured earlier by U.S. forces during the invasion and held in a prison where a violent Taliban uprising broke out, leaving hundreds of foreign fighters dead along with CIA agent Johnny "Mike" Spann who was there to question Lindh when the riot started.

Lindh and some eighty-five other survivors took refuge in the prison's basement and were eventually recaptured; sometime in the middle of the night, Lindh arrived at our base, where our photographer snuck out of our building and captured some grainy footage of the helicopters landing and Lindh being moved to a shipping container on the base.

We were told he was being treated as an Enemy Prisoner of War, and the Marines refused to let us get video of him, since "parading" him in front of our cameras would be a violation of the Geneva Convention. We were told this could change if he was reclassified as an "illegal combatant." He was guarded twenty-four hours a day, given food, water, shelter, and medical attention, and while we put in daily requests for an interview or a chance for him to make a statement, we never saw him, and the Marines wouldn't let us anywhere near his metal box home. He was only there for a few days, and we also weren't able to see him leave. The Marines flew him to a ship and eventually back to the states to face charges and his trial.

We continued our coverage of ongoing Marine interdiction operations from our remote desert outpost, which was growing by the day with new equipment and reinforcements flown in. The hunter-killer teams were moving to new tactical fighting positions every day and night, blocking roads used by Taliban or Al-Qaida fighters.

"Unless they drop their weapons immediately, they'll die," the Marines told us.

One day a team rolled through a village and "got a lot of smiles" they told us, and the Marines handed out food, candy, warm socks, and other clothes to the villagers.

"It's a whole different world out there," one told us. "It makes you appreciate the little things in life, like running water, toilets, and a hot meal."

In two weeks, Rhino's airfield had eight hundred sorties by fixed-wing aircraft, almost exclusively C-130s, moving more than two million tons of cargo, over a million pounds of fuel, food, water, and almost four thousand troops in and out. Most of the takeoffs and landings were at night, which made sleep more difficult.

We had the same sleep challenges when we moved from Rhino to Kandahar Airport, where we staged for a few days and nights before heading back to Bahrain. It was far more uncomfortable than the building we'd just left. We were now eating, sleeping, and working in the airport's terminal, which didn't have a single window left intact. It was freezing cold at night, and we were barely able to sleep because of the constant takeoffs and landings of fighter jets and massive cargo planes on the runway right next to us. We also had no working toilets, so unlike the port-a-potties we'd used at Rhino, we now had to pee in designated holes outside and take dumps sitting on tires placed on boards over a ditch, three or four of them in a row, completely out in the open.

I remember one time struggling to take care of business and looking over to my left to see a Marine sitting right next to me doing the same thing.

"Hey what's up?" I think I said, trying to defuse the awkward moment.

My journey back was as uncomfortable as the trip in, but I wasn't dissuaded from continuing to cover the "Global War on Terrorism" overseas. I went back to Afghanistan four more times, and to Iraq four times as well, spending many months on the ground, with far greater access each trip to the brave souls doing the fighting, who were determined to deliver payback to those responsible for bringing terror to American soil.

I never wavered in my support of the soldiers, sailors, airmen, and Marines in service to our country. I was proud to tell their stories, and still am.

CHAPTER 3

HILLARY'S COLLAPSE AT GROUND ZERO

Because I was one of the first reporters at Ground Zero after 9/11, I was an obvious choice to cover the memorial ceremonies held at the World Trade Center site on September 11 every year since. I was only absent twice (once I was sick, and another year I was on assignment overseas) and considered it a duty and an honor to report on the events of the day, the ongoing heartache of the families of the victims, and the progress in clearing the debris and rebuilding Downtown.

It took years for the city, developers, and victims' families to agree on how to move forward, with lengthy debates over what would rise on the "sacred ground" where the Twin Towers had stood. I was there for the news on almost every update along the way, like the reveal of the plans for the memorial plaza and the planning and opening of the museum. I was also the first reporter to get a guided tour of the museum before it opened and highly recommend this incredibly moving and powerful tribute.

I covered the design changes and ultimate construction of the Freedom Tower (later renamed One World Trade), was there when it opened in 2014, and was there when the Observatory opened in 2015.

I had also been given a first-hand look at the still-unfinished skyscraper in early 2012, riding in a construction elevator to the highest level, wearing a hardhat on what would become the top floor before it was enclosed by walls and a roof. It was fifteen degrees colder up there than on the sidewalk below. We did interviews and got B-roll from this spectacular location, with ironworkers walking on beams 1,268 feet in the air, exposed to the wind and elements.

It made my legs weak to look over the edge, but the views were absolutely incredible in every direction, high above lower Manhattan, a helicopter-like vista of the rivers and bridges and all of the city, hundreds of feet above the peaks of the tallest skyscrapers around us.

It was a remarkable and exhilarating experience to stand on the top of what would become the tallest building in America and the Western Hemisphere, with only some orange nylon netting separating me and my producer and cameraman from the hard cement of the sidewalks and streets far below.

The September 11 ceremonies were incredibly somber affairs. Family members read the names of every person who died in the attacks. There were poems and prayers and tributes with songs and trumpets playing taps.

In the early years, survivors and family members and first responders would walk down into the pits where the towers once stood, where the waterfalls of the 9/11 Memorial Plaza would eventually be built. The press was always kept at a distance to give the families room to grieve. Strategically placed pool cameras shared footage with all the networks for live coverage, while the reporters and crews were positioned in a designated area nearby.

For a while, we all worked from a terrace of one of the buildings at the World Financial Center (now named Brookfield Place) across the West Side Highway from the WTC complex. Eventually we moved further down the road to a spot on the sidewalk of the wide promenade in Battery Park, next to the highway, with clear views of the tower in the distance.

On September 11, 2016, I was at this Battery Park location, hanging out in our satellite truck between the live shots I would do once or twice an hour. The fifteenth anniversary of the attacks was even more significant because it was less than two months before one of the most hotly contested and unlikely presidential races in modern times.

Builder, entrepreneur, reality TV star, and self-proclaimed billionaire Donald Trump rocked and shocked the political establishment by winning the Republican nomination, and Democrat Hillary Clinton, then a U.S. senator, was vying to become the first female President in the nation's history.

Both candidates were attending the memorial ceremonies at Ground Zero, along with dozens of other prominent dignitaries, including current and former governors, mayors, senators, representatives, fire and police commissioners, and more.

Some believe that what happened during the event that morning changed the course of the election and put Donald Trump in the White House. If that's true, I may have unintentionally helped to alter history by breaking a huge story, thanks to one of my best law enforcement sources who happened to be in a perfect position to witness what went down and called me immediately after.

I was truly fortunate to have developed strong, deep ties to a large number of officers and agents with numerous local, state, and federal agencies. I know that working for Fox News Channel helped me to gain their respect and confidence, because many of them appreciated the more conservative tone of the network.

It also helped that I spent so much time overseas with the nation's Armed Forces, since many who work in law enforcement once served in the military. Finally, I believe my solid, accurate, and reliable reporting gave me street cred. I was tough, focused, respected, unafraid, and known as someone who always protected his sources (except for one incident, when I failed to do so, that I detail in a later chapter on the Minneapolis bridge collapse).

Over the years, I developed strong connections with members of the FBI, the U.S. Drug Enforcement Agency, the U.S. Marshals Service, and the U.S. Secret Service. I had friends in the NYPD, from street cops to the commissioner's office, and great contacts with members of the New York and New Jersey State Police, along with officers and supervisors in other various local departments.

Many of these guys were members of the Joint Terrorism Task Force (JTTF), so when major incidents occurred, like a terror attack on a Jewish bodega in New Jersey or a bomb in a subway tunnel, I'd often hear about it from them because they were on the JTTF email chain.

Even if they weren't tasked with responding to the incident, they at least had the initial reports in their phones and computers. When shit hit the fan, I immediately went to the contacts tab in my phone and searched for the guys I knew in that jurisdiction, and then branched out. Sometimes I didn't even have to call because they called me first.

That's what happened on that Sunday morning in September 2016. Just after 9 a.m., a good friend and one of my best, most reliable, sources, a very well connected and experienced member of a New York-area law enforcement agency, called me on my cell phone.

I answered, "Hey pal! What's happening?" I loved talking to this guy. He always had great stories with good details and context, and he never steered me wrong, ever.

He asked, "Where are you right now?"

I was surprised by the question because I assumed he'd know. "I'm in our satellite truck in Battery Park, covering the 9/11 ceremonies. Why? What's up?"

"You're not gonna believe what just happened," he told me. "I just watched Hillary Clinton nearly faint. She just left with her protective detail. I think she's going to the hospital!"

"What?" I was incredulous. "Where? What did you see?"

He then described the series of events that unfolded in front of him. He was in uniform, positioned near the front of One World Trade, in a cordoned off protected area where dignitaries and elected officials arrived and departed in their motorcades. He told me he was surprised to see Hillary Clinton because no one was expected to leave for at least another thirty minutes or so, as the ceremony was far from over. He said he watched in amazement as she stumbled past, clearly in distress and needing help walking to the pickup area, white as a ghost and shaky on her feet.

He told me she had to stand and wait near the street for several minutes until her van and follow-on Chevy Suburban (for the rest of her security team) pulled up to the curb.

He told me she looked like she was in *really* bad shape and would have fallen had the agents with her not been holding her by each arm. When the van doors opened, she stumbled off the curb and almost *did* fall and had to be helped into the vehicle by the men holding her arms and a woman assisting from behind.

I was furiously scribbling his story in my reporter notebook, repeating some of the things he said and asking for more detail while my producer that day, Tamara Gitt, looked at me wide-eyed and curious. Tamara had followed Clinton for months during the early days of her campaign and knew everyone on her staff and was extremely skeptical of what I was being told.

When my source finished his story, I thanked him profusely, hung up, and looked at Tamara.

I shared everything my source told me and said, "This is incredible. I'm gonna report this."

She urged caution as she searched her computer for any confirmation of what I'd just learned.

"There's nothing on the wires about this," she said. "We need confirmation!"

"My guy would never steer me wrong," I told her. "He was right there and saw the whole thing! Just because no one else knows about this doesn't mean it didn't happen!"

She asked me to wait and then called her Clinton campaign contacts, but no one answered. She kept checking the wires, too, and suggested I wait. When I told her I didn't want to, she asked me to call my guy back, so I did.

"Dude, I'm ready to report this, but we're not seeing this story *anywhere*. Are you sure about this?"

I can still hear his voice in my head, answering the question.

"Buddy, I was fifteen feet away from her. She lost her *shoe* when she got in the van. One of the agents had to pick it up off the street and jump in the vehicle following her! This one hundred percent happened."

I went through the whole thing with him again, just to make sure I had his story straight.

This was a huge moment for me. One of the biggest rules of reporting is that you need at least two sources on anything. If one person tells you something, you need to find another person to confirm it. Relying on a single source can be very dangerous, because *if* that source is wrong and you report it, your credibility is shot when the real story emerges. Most news agencies don't allow stories to be reported unless they're confirmed, but in rare circumstances exceptions can be made, depending on the story and the journalist and the person sharing the information.

I was convinced this was one of those occasions. At that point I'd been in the business for nearly thirty years. I was seasoned, well-traveled, and extremely confident in my source.

I was staking my career on it, but I wasn't really worried. Well, I may have been a little nervous, especially because Tamara was really, really cautionary.

We didn't have another live shot scheduled until 10:10 a.m. and I wanted to break the news, so I did it on Twitter, posting three tweets to report what I'd just learned due to the 140-character limit at the time. At 9:37 a.m., I tweeted in a row:

> BREAKING: law enf source: Hillary Clinton just left 9/11 ceremony w/medical episode, appeared to faint on way into van, helped by security

> Source tells me Hillary Clinton "clearly having some type of medical episode" & had to be helped into van by her protective detail

> MORE ON #HILLARY per witness: "unexpected early departure"; she stumbled off curb, "knees buckled," lost a shoe as she was helped into van

The tweets spread like wildfire, my most-viewed by a long shot, with thousands and thousands of retweets and comments, including this one from "tenmountainman":

"If Rick says it. It happened. The man is a reporter, not a hack."

I later learned that my tweets were actually shared with the future leader of the free world *at the ceremony*. It started with former NYPD Commissioner Bernie Kerik, whom I was friendly with and who followed me on Twitter. He was sitting with New Jersey Governor Chris Christie, former New York Mayor Rudy Giuliani, and Donald Trump. I was told that Kerik saw my tweets and showed them to Christie, who passed the phone to Giuliani, who showed it to Trump who also read them, and the men exchanged looks. The story I heard is that the men raised their eyebrows and quietly celebrated the early departure of Trump's hated rival.

Then, at 10:10 a.m., I went live on Fox News Channel and broke the news to our viewers.

Anchor Jon Scott read his intro over live pictures of the ceremony and introduced me. He was expecting me to report on the ceremony itself and toss to a pre-recorded package I put together detailing the health issues suffered by first responders who were at the scene in 2001 and breathed the toxic air for days, weeks, or months after.

Jon Scott was also the anchor on air the morning of 9/11, and he watched the events unfold partially through the lens of the camera I was using on the streets near Ground Zero, where I was reporting almost nonstop that day just a few blocks from the smoldering towers.

"Our Rick Leventhal is in Lower Manhattan...he saw the attacks unfold fifteen years ago as well. Rick?"

I had no script. I just shared the story of what I'd learned:

> Jon, before we get to that I want to bring our viewers up to date on a story that is breaking right now, that I just learned about within the last fifteen or twenty minutes. As you know there are many dignitaries gathered at the scene including Republican nominee Donald Trump and the Democratic nominee Hillary Clinton, who was at Ground Zero, was there for the ceremony and left, unexpectedly left early because of what appeared to be a medical episode.
>
> I have a law enforcement source who was there, who was fifteen feet away from Hillary Clinton. He said she was standing on a curb with her protective detail waiting for her motorcade.
>
> They were surprised to see her because she wasn't supposed to be leaving yet so they had to wait for the motorcade two or three minutes... when it finally rolled up, my source said, she stumbled off the curb, appeared to faint, lost one of her shoes that wound up underneath the van... her protective detail I'm told helped her into that

van and then the van took off, presumably in the direction of a hospital.

They grabbed her shoe and flagged down the rest of her detail. Her shoe was given to that detail who was following the other two vehicles, and they left Ground Zero early, just moments ago, because of an apparent medical episode that Hillary Clinton was suffering. It's not terribly hot today Jon...warm, and it was certainly warm at the scene, but again, Hillary Clinton, my source was fifteen feet away said she appeared to be having some sort of medical episode, had to be helped into her van and left the, left Ground Zero early before this ceremony ended apparently because of a medical problem.

I then tossed to the report we shot and edited a few days earlier, and when it ended, I came back live and tagged with this:

One other note about the Clinton episode Jon, it happened in an area that was off-limits to the press...so the pool reporters that follow Hillary Clinton wherever she goes didn't see it, they didn't know about it, as far as we know there were no cameras at that location and as far as we know the Clinton campaign still has not confirmed that there was any problem with Hillary Clinton.

We still haven't gotten confirmation of why she left early, but we have confirmed with a second source she did in fact leave early and apparently, according to my source who was fifteen feet away from the former senator, Jon, she was clearly having some kind of medical episode, stumbled, and nearly fell as her knees buckled and she came off that curb and then was helped by her protective detail into her van and left Ground Zero within the last thirty minutes.

Now I was out there all alone on an island. Tamara and I kept checking the Associated Press wires and the websites of other networks, and Tamara kept trying to get answers from Clinton staffers with no success. It was like crickets.

No one else was reporting or confirming or adding to the story. It was like it didn't happen, and the more time passed without confirmation, the more nervous I got that maybe, just maybe, I'd made a huge mistake. I didn't *really* think I had, but at the same time I was thinking, "What if...?"

Clinton staffers remained quiet for what seemed like an eternity, even as they were getting hammered with calls from every news outlet following up on what I'd reported. At around 11 a.m., spokesman Nick Merrill released a statement saying, "Secretary Clinton attended the September 11th Commemoration Ceremony for just an hour and thirty minutes this morning to pay her respects and greet some of the families of the fallen. During the ceremony, she felt overheated, so she departed to go to her daughter's apartment, and is feeling much better."

As *Slate* pointed out that day, "The statement notably does not say whether Clinton received any medical attention at Chelsea's apartment, which is about a fifteen-minute drive from Ground Zero."

It wasn't until hours later, at 5:15 p.m., that the campaign admitted the candidate had been diagnosed with pneumonia on Friday, but her current health status wasn't made public. The campaign then quoted the candidate's doctor Lisa Bardack, who said, "She was put on antibiotics, and advised to rest and modify her schedule. While at this morning's event, she became overheated and dehydrated. I have just examined her, and she is now re-hydrated and recovering nicely."

Does anyone believe the campaign would have *ever* revealed she had pneumonia and was being treated for it or that she had an episode during the ceremony if I hadn't forced their hand?

CNN reported the story on "Reliable Sources," a show focusing on the press and coverage of major stories hosted by the network's media critic Brian Stelter. CNN tossed to its correspondent outside Chelsea Clinton's apartment after receiving the campaign statement, roughly ninety minutes after my tweets were posted and about an hour after I was live on Fox News Channel telling our viewers what happened.

From CNN's transcript of "Reliable Sources" on September 11, 2016:

> BRIAN STELTER (HOST): I do want to pause and go back to camera one and go to some news that Jeff Zeleny has. He's joining me I believe on the phone. Actually, he's on the line there in Washington.
>
> Jeff, tell us about Hillary Clinton, the news developing this morning out of New York.
>
> JEFF ZELENY, CNN SENIOR WASHINGTON CORRESPONDENT: Well, Brian, we do have a statement right now coming in just moments ago

from Nick Merrill, a spokesman for Secretary Clinton about her appearance at Ground Zero this morning. I will read the statement to you right now.

It said, "Secretary Clinton attended the September 11th Commemoration Ceremony for just an hour and thirty minutes this morning to pay her respects and greet some of the families of the fallen. During the ceremony, she felt overheated, so she departed to go to her daughter's apartment, and is feeling much better."

So, again, this is coming on the heels of what's been really unfolding in New York for about 90 minutes or so, Brian.

STELTER: Right.

ZELENY: She was seen by some law enforcement officials leaving abruptly. And then, we were not told exactly where she was. The statement now coming out from the Clinton campaign, from Nick Merrill, again, I'll repeat to you. He said, "During the ceremony, she felt overheated and departed to go to her daughter's apartment."

So, she is at Chelsea's apartment in the Flatiron neighborhood of Manhattan. That's where she is now, Brian. Of course, this is all, you know, being discussed. There have been questions raised by her opponents about her health and other things.

But she was seen this morning leaving Ground Zero and the statement out from Nick Merrill saying she was fine, she was just feeling over-heated this morning. We also have some other reporting from our other colleagues here.

Let me look at this right now, Brian. It says she left the 9/11 event because she was not feeling well. Secret Service agents were helping her into her van in the motorcade. Someone saw that happening, a law enforcement official is telling CNN as she was helped in her van at Ground Zero and she was taken to Chelsea's apartment, and she is at her daughter's apartment right now in New York, Brian.

STELTER: Very worrisome news to hear, ob-viously, Jeff. As someone who covers the Clinton campaign, what can you tell us about how fre-quently Clinton may have any health issues, be-cause obviously for years, there have been cons-piracies online promoted by conservative web-sites, saying that she is secretly ill. The campaign has denied that. And her physician has said she is fit to serve as president.

ZELENY: Indeed, her physician has said she is fit to serve as president. She's released much more medical information than her rival has, of course, but still has not released all records as others have over the years. Now, this, certainly, is going to prompt and renew and raise more questions about her health potentially here.

She is 68 years old. She will turn 69 in October, before Election Day. It has, you know, we have seen it a lot over recent weeks, you know, some selected images and pictures and video of her stumbling.

STELTER: Taken out of context.

ZELENY: Taken out of context. Yes.

And I can tell you, Brian, after, you know, I cover her a lot day in and day out on the campaign trail. Her schedule is very aggressive. We heard Donald Trump often saying, oh, she is taking a nap in the middle of the day. That's not true. She has a very rigorous campaign schedule.

On Thursday, for example, I flew with her all day as she left the airport there in Westchester, you know, around 10:00 a.m. after doing a press conference, and we returned at 11:00 p.m. She had a couple of different campaign stops, a couple of different fund raising stops, and working along the way. So, she's definitely keeping up a rigorous pace here. But there are going to be questions about her health.

In this incident, this episode, the situation this morning in Manhattan is just the latest example of that. But the fact of the Clinton campaign putting out this statement this morning saying she felt overheated at Ground Zero and was taken to her daughter's apartment is the information we have right now at this hour—Brian.

STELTER: Jeff, thank you very much. Appreciate it. We will stay close to you and check back in.

Let me turn back to our panel and ask David Zurawik a question about this.

David, full disclosure, this news happened earlier in the morning on Twitter, a FOX reporter reported this according to one law enforcement source. We and other news outlets have been waiting for confirmation, of course, reaching out to sources in the meantime. That's how it should work in the news business.

I want to ask you what you think the media and the political implications of this are, especially how a story takes root online, how rumors spread before facts actually catch up.

ZURAWIK: Yes, let me tell you what I actually thought in my heart of hearts sitting in the green room when I found out about this and it was only FOX reporting it. It looked like it was one source, then it was a little fuzzy about the second source. But I thought, wow. They better be right about this because if they're not, the possible implications of what they are reporting, if they are wrong, this is awful.

My feeling was, you—on something like this, Brian, you wait until you have at least two sources you are comfortable with. This is not something you go out there—it was also reported with details, alleged details I should say about the physical appearance of the candidate and as she got to the van.

I don't want to repeat those because I don't know they are confirmed and I never would.

STELTER: Let me give you an example of that. Let me give you an example of that, David. Full disclosure to our audience, people are saying she is at the hospital, which is not true. CNN's Dan Merica is outside the apartment building where Hillary Clinton is with her daughter. So, it's a sample of misinformation that could happen.

ZURAWIK: Yes, and this was textbook, the careful way it was reported here. Only what they confirmed.

Look, if it's worse for this, there's time for it. But you wait until it's confirmed with something that is this, possibly volatile in terms of this election, this close to the election. You go with extreme caution. I was surprised to see anybody reporting it without confirmation. Certainly not online and social media, but elsewhere.

Later, Vox published an article about the reporting of the incident and interviewed Brian Stelter. I don't know if they reached out to the media relations department at Fox News, but I never heard from anyone at Vox. The article gave much credit to Twitter and gave Stelter a chance to bash me. It read, in part:

When it comes to breaking news, the speed of social media can be hurtful—think Reddit users falsely identifying who bombed the Boston Marathon in 2013. But sometimes, social gets the story first *and* gets it right. That has big consequences for professional journalists, CNN's Brian Stelter said on this week's episode of "Recode Media with Peter Kafka." He said a tweeted video of Hillary Clinton's pneumonia-induced stumble on Sunday, following an unscheduled departure from a 9/11 memorial ceremony, had a huge impact on the media and underscored weaknesses in the Clinton campaign's media strategy.

"This was a 'pictures or it didn't happen' sort of situation," Stelter said. "I wouldn't call it 'citizen journalism,' necessarily—I think the phrase 'citizen journalism' is kind of complicated—but it *is* eyewitness video, and that eyewitness video changed the story."

The "Reliable Sources" host was preparing to go live just hours after the story broke online. He said he and his team treated an early tweet from Fox News' Rick Leventhal with "appropriate skepticism."

"He was relying on a single law enforcement source," Stelter said. "And he didn't witness it himself and he hadn't heard back from the campaign yet. Fox made an interesting choice to go with the information without hearing from the campaign first."

But I had been right. The information had been completely accurate. And if I hadn't reported it at the time, the truth of the day would likely have been buried.

I met Stelter once at a book party. He was nice enough to me and definitely didn't bring up this event, but if he had, or if I'd remembered it, I would've had some choice words for him.

All that my guy told me happened *did* happen, and his description of the candidate matched the video that emerged later that morning from a witness who recorded a short clip of her wobbling and almost falling on her way into the van. If I hadn't gone on the record with it all, I doubt CNN would've even mentioned it, since the video didn't come out for another half hour or so, just after 11:30 a.m.

That video saved my rear by confirming what I'd reported. It was shot by Zdenek Gazda, a former fireman in the Czech Republic who had moved to the states in the early 1990s. He later told news outlets that he made it a point to visit Ground Zero every year on 9/11 to honor the first responders who died that day, and after taking a bunch of pictures and videos he was getting ready to leave when he saw Hillary leaning on a pillar near the curb.

He did *not* see her being helped across the plaza like my source did, but he was able to shoot twenty crucial seconds as the van arrived and she stumbled toward it, almost falling before her guys caught her and held her up. He then stopped recording.

He later told *Newsweek* that he stayed to take pictures of Donald Trump and then posted the Clinton video to Twitter on his way home to New Jersey. This was the only physical evidence of her early exit, and when I saw it, I knew I had nothing to worry about.

I obviously understand the significance and importance of sourcing material and getting confirmation, and there are exceptions to every rule. Again, my biggest issue with the criticism of my reporting is the failure to recognize that if I *hadn't* shared the news, the only evidence of her medical issue would've been the firefighter's video, lacking context and perspective.

He wasn't a journalist, and his post could have been dismissed as "doctored." Zdenek Gazda (the firefighter who shot the video) could have been dismissed as a Republican operative with an agenda. The campaign could have released a bland statement about her leaving early and going to Chelsea's apartment, and that most likely would have been the end of it. Any follow ups I did at that point could have been dismissed as biased reporting from a conservative news network.

I did get some credit for breaking the story, including from *The Washington Post* under the headline "News media kept in dark on Clinton's health and whereabouts" by Paul Farhi on September 11, 2016:

> Hillary Clinton's campaign left reporters in the dark for a full 90 minutes about her health and whereabouts on Sunday after she unexpectedly left a 9/11 memorial event in New York. It took most of the day to disclose that Clinton was diagnosed with pneumonia nearly three days earlier and wasn't simply "overheated," as the campaign's initial statement on Sunday said.
>
> The campaign's limited and confusing disclosures frustrated reporters who cover Clinton and seemed to play into health rumors that have been promoted by her Republican opponent, Donald Trump, and his surrogates and touted in conservative media outlets.
>
> Pool reporters—those who follow the Democratic nominee into restricted spaces and provide

reports to other reporters—never saw her leave the commemorative event at the World Trade Center complex in Lower Manhattan and then apparently collapse into a van. The pool was confined to a media pen out of sight of Clinton's location. Footage of her halting departure was captured by a bystander, Zdenek Gazda, who noticed her being helped to the vehicle.

The news appears to have been broken Sunday morning on Twitter by Fox News reporter Rick Leventhal. Citing an unnamed source, Leventhal tweeted at 9:42 a.m. "Hillary Clinton 'clearly having some medical episode' & had to be helped into van by her protective detail at WTC."

Shortly thereafter, Leventhal, citing a law enforcement source, tweeted that Clinton "appeared to faint on way into van" and that she "stumbled off curb, 'knees buckled," lost a shoe as she was helped into van." He said his source "watched it happen."

Leventhal's reporting was initially met with skepticism by people who suggested it might be a continuation of inflated claims about Clinton's health pushed by Trump and conservative media sources, such as Breitbart News. But Leventhal's reporting was accurate.

It wasn't until about 90 minutes later that Clinton's spokesman, Nick Merrill, released a statement saying that the candidate felt "overheated" and went to her daughter's apartment in Manhattan.

The statement made no mention of pneumonia.

There are many ways of setting yourself apart from other reporters. Being smooth and composed on camera is terrifically important. So is being a great writer and storyteller. Being diligent about getting facts straight and being able to digest and quickly share information in a cohesive and entertaining way will make viewers appreciate you.

One of the things that can *really* make a difference is having truly reliable and well-connected sources. This isn't something that can be taught. It's more something you earn by your performance and track record. People need to get to know you and trust you before they'll share stuff that might get them in trouble if anyone finds out they gave it to you.

Being able to earn that trust is huge, and I always appreciated the support I got from people doing work most of us aren't trained for and couldn't handle. I have deep and profound respect for law enforcement, and this story wouldn't have made the headlines it did if not for one of those guys telling me about it.

One thing I find frustrating and curious to this day is how my own network handled the reporting of MY reporting that day.

Instead of celebrating the scoop, they seemed to bury it. It barely got mentioned on our air, except by Jennifer Griffin, who was at the time working as our National Security Correspondent at the Pentagon.

The day after Hillary's collapse, Monday, September 12, 2016, Shepard Smith did a timeline of the events on his 3 p.m.

newscast, detailing what happened at Ground Zero, her exit, and the campaign's handling of the breaking news.

He made no mention of me breaking the story almost two hours ahead of everyone else.

Without my reporting, the story might never have seen the light of day, and if it had, it would've likely been a very different account of what happened, with far less detail and far more uncertainty.

I knew the story wasn't about me, but I felt strongly that it was at least worth mentioning that we brought it to light.

When I watched the show and saw our reports had been omitted from his "tick tock" of events, I texted him with something like, "Dude WTF? Why wouldn't you mention that I broke that story hours before anyone else??"

He wrote back something to the effect of, "I had no idea. I don't watch news on the weekend."

This was ridiculous on so many levels. The event itself happened on a weekend. He had a staff of writers and producers who helped put the show together. Surely some of them were aware of my reporting. It seemed obvious a decision was made to not mention me, but to this day I don't know who made that call or why.

CHAPTER 4

THE EARLY YEARS

I definitely didn't follow a traditional career path to become a senior correspondent and anchor for the most-watched cable news network in America. In fact, I could just as easily have wound up dead of a drug overdose or been a drywall mechanic my whole life. I took lots of missteps as a teenager and young adult, but I was fortunate enough, and I guess smart enough, to avoid going too far down the wrong path and eventually found the motivation and drive to search harder for what I was destined to do, and I found it.

I grew up in Silver Spring, Maryland, in the coolest house on the block, a big red-brick home with a long driveway on an acre of property at the end of the street. It had belonged to a local church and served as the pastor's home until my parents bought it in 1968 for something like $43,000, spending another five grand on the addition of a fourth bedroom upstairs with a screened porch below. My older brother Scott won the new, nicest bedroom in a coin flip.

I was the middle child and had the middle bedroom, with my younger sister Leigh next to me and our parents across the hall.

When I hit my teen years, I started hanging with the kids my parents warned me about, and by the time I got to Montgomery Blair High School as a tenth grader in the fall of 1975, I was smoking pot and doing other drugs, and my grades took a nosedive.

When I brought my first report card home the following January, my parents flipped out. I had more than a dozen unexplained absences from almost every class and all C's, D's, and F's.

My sixteenth birthday was two weeks later, and I was super excited to get my driver's license, but my parents immediately took the air out of my tires.

"You're not getting your driver's license until you get better grades," they told me.

"But I'm sixteen!" I yelled, angry and disappointed.

"We don't care how old you are. YOU NEED TO GET BETTER GRADES BEFORE YOU CAN DRIVE!" they yelled back.

That was all the motivation I needed. I quit doing drugs and applied myself, focusing on my schoolwork. When my next report card arrived just before summer, I had straight A's and shortly after, got my license.

That next school year, I stayed clean and continued to do well, joining the school newspaper *Silver Chips* as a reporter and making the morning announcements over the archaic PA system. I decided to run for senior class president and won, and that, plus my rising GPA, was just enough to get me into Lafayette College in Easton, Pennsylvania, but only because my dad had gone there and vouched for me.

DROPOUT TO DRYWALL

When I got to Lafayette, though, I backslid big time. I was away from home for the first time since summer camp and took full advantage of my freedom. The school had eighteen fraternities and every one of them had at least one party every week, which meant there were at least three parties every night, and freshmen were welcome since the frats were rushing for pledges. This meant free beer and grain-alcohol punch in the basement, a pool table and HBO on the main floor, and bong hits upstairs. I would partake in all of the above and wind up getting sick later, oversleeping and skipping classes the next morning.

After my first semester, the school sent a letter to my parents suggesting I not come back for the spring because my attendance and grades were so bad. I apologized tearfully and assured them I'd get my act together and make them proud. But when I got back to Easton, I quickly lost interest in my classes and started partying even harder, and after pledging a fraternity, I de-pledged just before hazing, knowing I'd be dropping out at the end of my freshman year. I was "one and done." I wasn't happy at Lafayette, wasn't motivated, wasn't focused, and clearly wasn't cut out to be a Lafayette Leopard.

When I got home, my parents told me if I wasn't in school, I'd need to find a job, so I went to work for my buddy Butch's dad's drywall company, hanging and finishing sheetrock in custom homes in the suburbs of Washington, D.C.

One of the neighborhoods we did a lot of work in was Potomac, Maryland, which coincidentally would later become the setting for a *Real Housewives* franchise on Bravo TV, the network employing my wife Kelly when we met.

Being a drywall mechanic made me appreciate what hard work really meant. We carried the eight-foot and twelve-foot sheets two at a time off Butch's dad's big truck into unfinished homes and grabbed the sixty-two-pound buckets of mud and hauled those in two at a time as well. We had to be on the job site at 7 a.m. and were done at 3:30 in the afternoon, when I'd hustle to beat the awful D.C.-area rush hour traffic home, exhausted and covered in spackle.

After a year of this, I decided to give college another try and enrolled at the University of Maryland in College Park, about twenty minutes away. I signed up for some business classes but quickly realized they weren't my speed either and dropped out before the first semester was even over.

My cumulative GPA from a year and a half of higher learning was 0.27, a number I'm very proud of to this day, because it represents just how low and lost I was and how far I was able to climb.

ON MY OWN

I went back to drywall full time, going to work early and partying with my friends till late, still living at my parents' house and, I guess, driving them nuts, because as my twenty-first birthday approached, they told me they were kicking me out. I'd need to find a place of my own.

When the day came, they handed me my Bar Mitzvah money they'd been holding for me, about three grand, and said goodbye, and I think I didn't talk to them for at least a year after that.

I rented a room in the home of Mickey Welch, a friend of one of my drywall buddies, in Wheaton, Maryland, just up the road from my parents' house. Mickey, an auto mechanic at a local dealership, was also renting out his finished basement to a tow truck driver named Ricky, who eventually wound up in jail. Ricky loved to party and blasted Bob Seeger on the stereo constantly. I wasn't a fan of the music, but the rent was cheap, and it was definitely a fun place to live. I also saved money every time my car broke down. Once or twice, Ricky towed my old T-Bird (for no charge) to Mickey's garage, and he just made me pay for parts.

When one of my high school buddies got a second job as a doorman at a live music venue in Georgetown in Northwest Washington D.C. called The Bayou, he suggested I apply too, and I was a bit surprised when they hired me. I was probably the smallest guy on staff at 5'10" and 185 pounds, but I was in shape, could handle myself, and was smart and a good talker, so the manager usually put me at the front door to check IDs.

It was a great way to meet girls and hear awesome live music a couple nights a week and get paid for it at the same time. I saw Joan Jett perform right after "I Love Rock 'n' Roll" came out. I worked nights when Bryan Adams performed, as well as Wendy O and the Plasmatics, The Ramones, Gregg Allman, and some excellent club bands like Southside Johnny & the Asbury Jukes.

I also worked the door at a sprawling bar/restaurant near Georgetown called Deja Vu and at another popular spot called Rumors at the corner of 19th Street and M Street, but I was fired after I failed to notice a fight going on behind me on the back patio. I was standing on the landing by the front door watching the crowd in front of me, and someone came up and asked, "Do you work here?" I proudly said, "Yes!" and that person said, "There's a fight going on back there." I was mortified. By the time I got there it was basically over, and the guys who broke it up were super pissed at me for not being there sooner to help out.

A couple of years later I wound up working at Rumors again as a DJ, and it's where I met my first wife.

BACK TO SCHOOL

At some point I realized I didn't want to stare at unfinished walls the rest of my life. The turning point came when we were sitting around on empty mud buckets at lunchtime, and Paul, the oldest guy on our crew (probably in his mid-forties at the time), was complaining about his back. I think I was making six bucks an hour, which was good money then, and he was probably earning twice that, but I didn't want to be where he was when I reached his age. I hated the cold mud on my fingers and the monotony of using a blade to spread and smooth the spackle over nails and joints. It was mindless grunt work, and I just felt like I was destined for bigger and better things, so I signed up for some classes at Montgomery County Community College in Rockville, Maryland, where I soon discovered my true calling.

I registered for a "Careers" class, which basically involved taking surveys every week on what interested us most and what our dream job might be, and I realized I really wanted to be a big-time sportscaster, like Bob Costas or Brent Musburger, covering the Super Bowl and the World Series every year. I loved to write, and I loved sports! How great would that be? And then I looked in the course catalog and saw a two-year program in Broadcasting & Communications Technology, and a big bright light bulb went off over my head.

Why hadn't I thought of this before? In high school, I'd worked for the school newspaper and did the morning announcements. Growing up, I was always a class clown, and even acted in school plays through junior high. This was my eureka moment. I'd discovered my destiny at twenty-three.

I did really well at Montgomery County Community College, earning mostly A's, while anchoring the college newscast and working part time as a cameraman at local city council meetings. I graduated with my associate's degree and convinced American University (AU) to accept my credits on my way to a bachelor's in broadcast journalism, which I didn't have to pay for because my dad worked at AU for years as director of the Counseling Center (he was a clinical psychologist).

I was one of the older students on campus, and my real-world experience really paid off in the classroom. I had to take freshman English for the fourth time as a twenty-five-year-old, because every school required it, and I had a huge advantage over seventeen- and eighteen-year-old freshmen, handling material I'd seen over and over again. It was a breeze.

Being older also gave me an advantage when I auditioned as anchor for AU's college newscast at the campus station

WAVE-TV, a well-run outfit with excellent equipment, much of it donated by local network affiliates.

I kept working as a cameraman at the city council meetings and got a second job as a club DJ (which brought me back to Rumors a few nights a week) and also got an internship in Washington at WTTG television, Channel 5, which at that time was part of Metromedia.

When my internship at Channel 5 ended, I applied for every part-time position that became available and after four or five attempts got hired as a weekend chyron operator. The chyron was a machine that put the words on the screen during the newscasts, which TV people often referred to as "lower thirds" and "upper thirds."

The lower thirds listed the names of the reporters and the people being interviewed, and the upper thirds listed the dates and places. It was terrific hands-on, real-life training for what I'd be doing later. I definitely learned more in the newsroom than I did in the classroom, and I worked with some broadcast legends, including Maury Povich, who was the main anchor there at the time. I even interviewed him for a class project.

One of the reporters was a tall Texan named Brian Wilson, whom I'd later work alongside at Fox News Channel. Former NBC anchor Brian Williams was a freelance weekend reporter at the time, sitting right behind me in the newsroom. He'd type out his scripts, hand me a copy, and I'd "put his chyrons" in the system, as we called it.

Years later, I saw him on the back terrace of the Los Angeles County Superior Court where we were both covering the arrest of O.J. Simpson. I said hello and reminded him that we'd worked together, but I got the impression he didn't remember me.

One Wednesday night at Rumors, working my regular shift at the DJ booth behind the bar near the front doors, I saw Penny Daniels walk in. She was a reporter and anchor at WJLA, the local ABC station, and I recognized her right away. We made eye contact, and a short time later she came up to me to request some music. I could tell she was interested in me, so after a few minutes of chatting I put on a long song and danced with her.

I got her number and we started dating, but she didn't want anyone to know, since she was well established and I was five years younger, still in school and working as a DJ in a bar. I probably should have seen the writing on the wall, but we spent ten months in a secret relationship and continued it long distance when I got my first reporting job in Columbia, South Carolina.

When I graduated from AU, I'd just turned twenty-seven and went from being a part-time to a full-time chyron operator, even though I'd almost been fired once for misspelling "Tennessee."

In the meantime, I was sending letters to news directors at dozens of TV stations, primarily in the eastern half of the United States, pitching myself for on-air news or sports jobs and asking if they'd be interested in a resumé reel.

I must have sent at least sixty-five letters and received a handful of respectful rejections and two or three requests for a tape. One of those stations, WOLO-TV, the ABC affiliate in Columbia, was interested. The news director called me, and I answered in the kitchen of my parents' house where I'd moved back to save money.

"Hey, this is Bob Moore. How are you?" he said. "Would you like to come work for us?"

I was a bit confused by the offer over the phone.

"Don't you want to fly me down for an interview?" I asked.

"No, we really like your work and think you'll be a great fit here!" he told me. "The job pays $250 a week."

The car payment on my almost-new Mustang GT five-speed convertible was $251 a month. This would eat up about half my take-home pay. But it was my only offer, and I really wanted to get started on-air, so of course I said yes.

He gave me a start date less than a month away, so I got my stuff together, packed what I could fit in my car, and took the roughly five-hundred-mile drive down to Columbia, where I would be shocked to see what WOLO-TV looked like.

When I pulled into the gravel parking lot at the top of a hill, I thought I must be in the wrong place. I figured it must be the transmission facility and not the actual station, since the building was so small, with a tin roof, at the base of the station's transmission tower.

But when I walked in, a receptionist greeted me, and I met the general manager, a super nice guy with an office right by the front door. After a warm welcome, he led me back to the newsroom where I met Bob Moore in person in his small office with cheap wood paneling on the walls. The adjacent newsroom was equally spartan, with a bunch of desks with manual typewriters and carbon paper stacked alongside.

I then got a tour of the studio, and I'll never forget looking at one of the guys and, talking without thinking, asked "Where's the *main* studio?" And the guys kind of laughed and assured me this was it: a small cheap-looking set with a bamboo-wall backdrop.

"Welcome to the big leagues," I sneered to myself, not realizing just how challenging the next year, one week, and one day would be, which is exactly how long I worked there.

I did it all for Newscene 25—carrying the heavy gear, including the massive recording deck and bulky tripod, shooting my own interviews and standups, writing my own scripts, editing my own packages, submitting my own graphics, and anything else required to get my piece on the air. I also became the main anchor just three months later when Bob was fired after one of the female reporters accused him of sexual harassment. When he left, and the general manager asked me if I could fill in on the anchor desk, I asked if I'd be getting a bump in pay.

"No," he said, "but if you don't want to do it, I can ask someone else."

Of course I wanted to do it, and said yes, and continued to report and anchor until they hired a replacement about three months later.

WOLO only had one newscast a day, at 6 p.m. Monday through Friday. It aired re-runs of *The Beverly Hillbillies* at 11 p.m. and was number one in that time slot, so it had zero incentive to expand, especially since the newscast didn't fare well and ranked a distant third among the three stations in the market. WOLO also had no weekend news, which actually worked in my favor since I went home almost every weekend to visit my future wife.

The job sucked, though. The station was super cheap. Pay was low; we had no microwave truck, so I got zero experience going live; and the gear was terrible. So the resulting product looked and sounded bad, which hurt me every time I sent out resumé reels, which was pretty much every week.

There was only one photographer, shared by half of dozen reporters and two sports guys, which meant that most of the time I had to wait for the only other set of gear and only other vehicle to shoot my own stories. Sometimes reporters paired up so we could shoot each other's standups and interviews. One day, I was with another reporter, about to shoot her standup in front of some elementary school:

"Why don't you try a walk and talk?" I asked. Walking while talking was a way to add movement to the piece—when the reporter starts in one place and delivers the lines while walking to another spot a few feet away. It can be an effective way to show what happened at an accident scene, or to reveal something on the landscape, or just to make a story a bit more visually interesting.

She looked at me, confused, and, I swear, said: "You want me to walk *and* talk, *at the same time*?!"

I said yes and tried to explain, but she couldn't do it, so I just shot her standing still. To this day I have to say she was the absolute worst reporter I've ever seen on television.

Another time I came to work early and saw that both of the station's news vehicles were gone.

"Where are the cars?" I asked someone when I walked in.

One had been in an accident, and the other blew an engine, I was told.

"Aren't you gonna rent another one?" I asked.

"Our insurance won't cover it," was the response.

"Well, how are we supposed to shoot our stories?" I asked.

"You can use your own car!"

The last thing I wanted to do was put all that old heavy gear in my new Mustang convertible with leather seats and a tiny trunk.

"What if I don't want to use my car?"

"We just won't cover the news today!"

I used my car.

MY BOY BRETT

When Walter, our only shooter, found a better gig, we were left without a cameraman for month after month. I kept asking when they'd be hiring a new guy and kept being told they were looking but having a hard time finding someone, so I called my high school buddy Brett Abbott back in Silver Spring. He was the biggest guy I knew, six foot, six and a half inches and about 250 pounds, a brawler who never backed down from a fight. He'd played basketball for our high school, which had a great team (they won state championships in '75 and '77) but quit because he hated the coach yelling at him.

I knew he wasn't working and figured he might like a TV gig.

"Hey Brett, want to be a cameraman?"

"I don't know how to do it," he told me.

"I can teach you! It'll be cool. You're so tall you'll tower over everybody and won't even need a tripod!"

"How much does it pay?" he asked. He'd be making what I made, about $6.50 an hour, I told him.

"OK," he said, and he moved down to Columbia, and I trained him, and about a month later he left when he got a better offer from Harvey Cox, a news director known for his screaming fits at WSPA-TV in Spartanburg, about ninety minutes north on I-26. When I last spoke with him, Brett was still living there, buying and selling used cars from his own lot.

I reunited with Brett when I also took a job at WSPA in Spartanburg, even though I knew I'd be moving to South Florida in a couple of months. Penny had gotten hired at Miami's WSVN-TV, but when Harvey Cox offered me a gig for a bit more pay, I figured I might as well take the extra money and gain some experience in a bigger market, where they had live trucks and multiple shows a day. But the story selection wasn't much better.

One day I covered the Mighty Moo Festival in Cowpens, South Carolina. I can't remember most of my other assignments at WSPA, but I do remember my most embarrassing moment there, freezing on-air in the middle of the second live shot of my career, when I forgot the name of one of the bands playing at the festival and just stopped talking. It was a terrifying few seconds of TV, and it would be at least another year before I was comfortable going live.

MIAMI MOVE

The day I left Spartanburg for the long drive to Miami to meet Penny at her new job was the same day the station lost its NBC network affiliation. The owner, Ed Ansin, was a very wealthy and quirky guy who'd been in an extended battle with NBC over the costs of carrying network programming.

Ansin wound up telling NBC to pound sand and gave his news director, a sharp visionary named Joel Cheatwood, the green light to go wall-to-wall news. Right then and there on that very day, the station announced it'd be expanding every newscast to fill seven hours of programming, with a three-hour morning show, an hour at noon, a two-hour block from 5 p.m. to 7 p.m., and another hour at 10 p.m.

Penny, hired for the noon show, was quickly promoted to more hours, and I applied for a reporting gig but was told I was still too green for the Miami market, which was top twenty, so I started freelance editing there instead. I considered a job as a shooter but wound up getting hired a couple months later at the powerhouse NBC affiliate in West Palm Beach, WPTV Channel 5, where I was the first reporter to man the new bureau in Boca Raton.

I'd drive there from Miami every day, about an hour each way, and started getting more comfortable with live shots and storytelling. Then came my biggest assignment, covering Hurricane Hugo in Charleston, South Carolina (where I overslept and almost got fired, detailed in Chapter 8), and not long after that I got my shot at WSVN, earning more money freelancing three days a week than I did working Monday through Friday at WPTV.

In a few months I was promoted to full-time reporter in the Broward bureau, near Downtown Fort Lauderdale, and was at the courthouse almost every day for one wild case after another, including the obscenity trial of the hip-hop group 2 Live Crew, the murder trial of Elvis impersonator Michael Conley (who sang for me in the courtroom during jury breaks and was later convicted), and the prostitution trial of Kathy Willets, the wife of a Broward sheriff's deputy, who was accused of turning tricks in the marital bedroom while the deputy hid in the closet with a video camera.

I got exclusives with all of them. I became very aggressive as a reporter, constantly pushing for more, learning how to write fast and on the fly, going live numerous times a day.

I also started doing more fill-in anchoring, especially on the weekends, and even hosted a few hours with my wife as Hurricane Andrew came barreling toward the South Florida coastline. I remember looking over at Penny as the satellite image of the massive storm filled the screen, wondering "Who's going to secure our house with both of us sitting here?"

She wound up taking our baby daughter Veronica to the news director's home in Weston to hunker down, while I braved the storm from the beach in Fort Lauderdale where Andrew was initially predicted to make a direct hit. Instead, the Cat 5 storm took a big left turn at the last minute, slamming into Homestead well to our south, where I spent most of the next few weeks and months reporting on the damages, aftermath, and cleanup.

While I wasn't happy in my marriage, work was going really well, and we had a great house on a canal with a pool and boat lift in the back yard. When Penny got a lucrative job offer from WBBM, the CBS-owned-and-operated (O & O) station in Chicago, she really wanted to go. I was reluctant for a number of reasons, including our lifestyle and the weather, my blossoming career, and the fact that once taxes were factored in, we wouldn't be making that much more money. She also didn't get a good feeling about her potential future colleagues during her job interview there.

WBBM was old-school Journalism with a capital "J," and Penny's former co-anchor, who had been hired a couple of months earlier at the same station along with some producers, was having a tough time. The general manager in Chicago was trying to overhaul the tone of the station's newscast by bringing in some of Cheatwood's best talent, but the folks in the newsroom were calling the fresh imports "the Miami mafia," turning up their noses at the attempted change in direction and resisting efforts to adapt to new ways of covering news. But Penny was from the Chicago area, and it was her dream to be an anchor in her hometown, so I quit my job for the second time, and we packed up and moved to Highland Park in May 1993.

It snowed the day we moved into our rental house by the lake. In May. And I knew right then that this wasn't going to be my happy place.

My wife didn't want me to work. She wanted me to be available to run errands for her and help us get settled in, but after three months I was going stir crazy and convinced her to let me look for a job, and I quickly found one at WFLD, a Fox O&O where two of our former WSVN colleagues were now in charge.

I quicky became WFLD's star reporter, earning the nickname "A-1," because I almost always led the 9 p.m. newscast (the A block was the first block of news, and A-1 was the top story). It was a fun job, but I absolutely hated working in the cold. One night it was at least thirty below with the wind chill, and after a long but ultimately successful argument to report from *inside* instead of *outside* a homeless shelter, my crew and I were sent last minute on breaking news to an apartment fire on the city's south side, arriving to find the building in flames.

It was so cold that the spray from the fire hoses froze on anything it hit, resulting in thick layers of ice on trees and vehicles below. Firefighters struggled just to get the hydrants open, and three of our cameras froze up and had to be swapped out. I wound up doing my live shot with my fur-lined hood drawn so tight you could barely see my face, since any exposed skin could be frostbitten in a matter of minutes.

MY FIRST EARTHQUAKE

I did get to travel for some compelling stories while I was in Chicago, including to Los Angeles to cover the Northridge earthquake. It was a powerful shaker registering 6.7 on the Richter scale and had done significant damage to the region. It was also January during Chicago's coldest winter in a hundred years, with wind chills reaching fifty below at home. I was thrilled for the hundred-plus degree swing and sunshine in Southern California but astounded by the widespread damages.

I remember two incidents clearly:

My cameraman and I were standing on a guy's lawn, interviewing him after we drove past and saw that his chimney had crumbled to the ground. Just as I asked him if he'd felt any aftershocks, we felt a 6.0 rumble beneath us. It was like a giant bowling ball rolling just beneath the ground we stood on.

Another day, early in the morning, we talked our way past a police roadblock onto the closed I-5 freeway and took an eerie ride north, with absolutely no other vehicles in sight, to reach the Newhall Pass Interchange, where LAPD motorcycle officer Clarence Wayne Dean was killed when he drove his bike off the edge of a collapsed stretch of roadway, dying instantly when he landed far below.

He hadn't been able to see that the elevated ramp was no longer there and hadn't been able to stop in time. When the Interchange was rebuilt and reopened a year later, it was named in the former Marine's honor.

MJ TRADES HIGH TOPS FOR CLEATS

Of course, Chicago at that time was Michael Jordan's town, and I was there when the absolutely stunning news broke that he was retiring from basketball and would be pursuing a baseball career with the Chicago White Sox.

The news was so unreal that most didn't believe it at first, and then all sorts of conspiracy theories started popping up, such as that it was somehow related to his father's strange and seemingly random murder while he was pulled over on the side of a North Carolina highway, or that it was a deal Jordan made with the National Basketball Association (NBA) commissioner because he'd supposedly been caught gambling, taking a year off voluntarily instead of being suspended.

While Jordan was a known gambler, we couldn't confirm any of these theories. In the meantime, just a month after escaping the brutal Chicago winter in California, I was dispatched on another week-long journey in the sun, this time to Sarasota, Florida, for MJ's spring training debut.

This was an absolute dream assignment, and on our last day there, I was walking through the players' parking lot and saw Jordan sitting in his Corvette with the door open, surrounded by a group of Japanese journalists who stopped him for autographs before he took off. I just happened to have a batting-practice ball in my hand that I'd just picked up, and I walked over and patiently waited for the group to leave before I approached the superstar.

"Hey Michael, could I get one too?" I asked, holding the ball in my hand.

"You know you're not supposed to do that," he said to me, annoyed. Members of the press were not allowed to get autographs from the players. It was printed on the back of our credentials.

"I know but they all did it..." I said, trailing off, and he reluctantly took the ball from my hand, scribbled on it, and handed it back.

I thanked him, turned, and was immediately confronted by the head of White Sox Public Relations, who had his hand out:

"Give me the ball."

"Why?" I asked.

"You're not allowed to get autographs and you know it. Now give me the ball."

"They all got one!" I protested, gesturing toward the quickly departing group of Japanese journalists.

"Give me the ball, or give me your credentials," he said, even more sternly.

The credentials hanging around my neck, issued by the team, gave me access to the field, the locker rooms, and most other areas at the complex. Without them, I'd be stuck outside the gates. But, since this was my last day, and all we had was one more live shot scheduled that night, I plucked the creds from my neck and handed them to him.

"Here you go!" I said, and walked off, the ball firmly clutched in my hand.

I still have the ball in a box somewhere, but I don't think anyone would ever believe, or be able to decipher, that it actually has Michael Jordan's signature on it.

NEW YORK: NEVER SAY NEVER

After just eighteen months in Chicago, Penny was approached to be the next anchor of the tabloid show *A Current Affair*, which had made Maury Povich a household name. Penny's tenure at WBBM was stressful and not going well. She was disliked by many of her colleagues and failed to get the promotions she was promised, before the general manger who had hired her moved on to another station.

Even though Penny and I had just moved into a house we bought and had spent hundreds of thousands of dollars and several months gut-renovating it, we were both ready to move on to greener (and warmer) pastures, so I quit my job for the third time for her career, and we packed our stuff, expecting to move to L.A. The original plan was to have her co-anchor with a guy in New York on a split screen. We found a house to rent in Brentwood and were about to sign the lease when Penny got another call telling her we needed to move to Manhattan instead.

I always swore to myself I'd never live in New York. Both my parents grew up on Staten Island, and I had relatives there, in Manhattan, and on Long Island, too, and my family and I would visit there once or twice a year. I'd also been there numerous times for work, and while I knew it could be a fun place to visit, I couldn't imagine dealing with the traffic and the trash and the crowds and the crime on a daily and nightly basis.

We didn't have much of a choice, but after three days living in Manhattan, I never wanted to leave again.

I loved New York. I loved the vibe, the energy, the non-stop action, the fact that you could order anything at any time of day, and it would be at your door within minutes. I loved Central Park and the museums and the shopping and the bars and the restaurants. There was always something to do and somewhere new to go.

Penny, at this point my soon-to-be ex-wife, still didn't want me to work, so I took another eight months off managing our lives, and during that time we finalized the adoption of our second daughter Shoshana, whom we picked up from an orphanage in Colombia, South America, when she was just four months old.

Meanwhile I was getting antsy about not working and started looking for news gigs. I reached out to some of the local stations and was quickly hired by WNBC to be a full-time freelance morning reporter for its (very) early show *Today in New York*.

It was a great gig with terrible hours. I had a desk in the WNBC newsroom at Rockefeller Center with a view of the skating rink. I could walk down one flight of stairs to the *Saturday Night Live* studios and use the same bathroom John Belushi used (which I often did), and I shared the halls and airwaves with legendary local broadcasters, including Sue Simmons and

Chuck Scarborough. Al Roker and Matt Lauer also worked with me before they moved from local news to *The Today Show*. I was friendly with both of them, even sharing a cab Uptown with Matt after work one day.

I kept getting raises until I was making $500 a day, which was almost double the minimum union rate set by the American Federation of Television & Radio Artists (AFTRA). The worst part of the job was having to get up at 2:45 a.m. to get ready and rush to the office so I could hop in the live truck with the crew and race to our first location to go live at 5 a.m., and usually a few more times until 7 a.m. The best part was being done after the noon show and having the rest of the day to do whatever I wanted or needed.

But when a new news director was hired, I got screwed. She bumped me back to the minimum pay and had her Assistant News Director suggest I start looking for work elsewhere. She wanted to bring in her own people, and without a contract, I was the first to go, even though I believed I was one of the best reporters on staff. It turned out to be a blessing because after short freelance stints working for old colleagues in Boston at WHDH, and a few weeks back in Chicago at WFLD, I got an offer from the fledgling Fox News Channel. The network had just launched a few months earlier and was getting "goose eggs" (zeroes) in the ratings. No one was watching, but I had faith the start-up could succeed—in part because of the deep pockets of its owner Rupert Murdoch and because I'd seen the success the Fox Broadcast Network had over the past decade. In fact, when I first read about the pending launch of the news network about a year earlier, I asked my agent at the time to submit a tape, and he said, "Fox News Channel? They'll be off the air in a year." I never worked with the guy again.

The first job that Fox offered me was in its Chicago bureau. I really didn't want to move back there, but the money was good and I needed a job, so I agreed, but kept reminding them that I would prefer to stay in New York. And on the day on which I was due to sign my contract, fate intervened. A New York–based correspondent quit, and I was asked if I wanted to fill his slot instead.

My marriage had been troubled almost since the start, and we split up around the same time I started working for Fox. Penny moved with the girls to Spokane, Washington, taking an anchor job there, and I spent the next twenty-four years at Fox News Channel. They were some of the best years of my life, and some of my favorite assignments and proudest and craziest experiences are highlighted in this book.

CHAPTER 5

IRAQ EMBED: VOLUNTEERING FOR WAR

In late 2002, as the U.S. geared up for what appeared to be an inevitable invasion of Iraq, we learned that the U.S. military was planning an embed program to bring roughly 500 journalists along for the ride.

To me, being a war correspondent was about as good as it gets. There are few stories more compelling, meaningful, powerful, and important than armed conflicts with citizens and soldiers risking their lives for cause and country.

During my first embed in Afghanistan in 2001, the journalists had been confined to a building on base, allowed off base only for tame field trips. We didn't witness any fighting.

This deployment would be a true war experience. We would ride *in the vehicle* with the soldiers or Marines, go where they went, face the same dangers they faced, eat what they ate, and sleep where they slept. We'd be attached to a battalion, company, and crew for the entire journey from Kuwait to Baghdad (or wherever the unit we were assigned to started and finished).

The Pentagon adjusted its posture toward the press dramatically. We would no longer be "handled," "escorted," or "managed." Instead, the Pentagon opened its doors to us, removed restrictions on access to the grunts, and emphasized allowing interviews to demonstrate the courage of the troops and use their dedication and commitment to win the hearts and minds of the American public and build support for the mission.

The Pentagon allowed unparalleled access, and it was a game changer for my reporting and our coverage, not having to ask permission to talk to the guys, who were far less nervous and cautious about sharing their feelings and experiences. They provided the character and color and emotions, humanizing the war.

Signing up to cover Operation Iraqi Freedom turned out to the be the most remarkable, incredible, and meaningful experience of my career. Dangerous, physically demanding, and exhausting beyond comprehension, it was personally and professionally challenging and ultimately, wholly rewarding.

I lost eighteen pounds in seven weeks. I rarely shaved and didn't shower for thirty-one days. We also never saw a real toilet, mastering the art of pooping through an ammo box or perched on a shovel blade. We learned to sleep for minutes or a few hours at a time, usually in the dirt or sand, sometimes on a mat or in a sleeping bag, but often just splayed out on the ground or leaned against a tire in the shade of our armored vehicle or crammed in the back. Sometimes I leaned over to rest my helmet on the interior wall of the back seating area. We were so exhausted we could drift off within seconds, despite the ridiculous conditions—heat, cold, wind, dirt, no pillow or cushion of any kind. I fell asleep standing up at least once.

We discovered that war could be boring. We'd often joke with the captain about finding us some action: "Captain! Let's go shoot something!"

And when our company drove into an ambush at dusk on a desolate stretch of desert highway, we endured close to an hour of nearly non-stop cannon and machine-gun fire, a full-on firefight that was equal parts frightening and exhilarating.

When I first heard about the embed program, I asked for a meeting with one of the top bosses at Fox at the time, John Moody. I told him I really wanted to be a part of it. I desperately wanted to cover our troops in Iraq.

I don't think he was surprised, but he asked me a bunch of questions. He was thoughtful, thorough, and perhaps a bit concerned.

He asked me why I wanted to go, whether I was *sure* I wanted to go, whether I understood the dangers involved, whether I realized I wouldn't be paid extra and might not come home alive, whether I talked to my family about it, and more. I told him I considered this the epitome of reporting and that it was a natural evolution for me, having covered 9/11 and then traveling to Afghanistan. Following the so-called war on terror to Iraq made perfect sense. I told Moody I was serious, highly motivated, and ready to roll.

He thanked me and said the network hadn't yet decided whom to send or submit to the military as candidates but that he'd add my name to the consideration list. When the time came, I got the call and couldn't have been more excited and maybe a bit nervous.

My daughters were very young at the time and didn't live with me, and I traveled for work a lot, so as far as they knew, this was just another business trip. My girlfriend at the time worked in news and was supportive, but when I told my parents, they were *not* happy about it. My mom and dad are both very liberal and didn't support George W. Bush or his efforts to root out terrorism in the Middle East, and they certainly didn't want me going to Iraq to join up with a bunch of Marines heading into battle in the desert. But I was a grown man and didn't seek their permission or approval. There would be no stopping me from this incredible journey.

GETTING READY

One of the things that stands out about the Iraq embed was just how much training we had before we stepped off. There were boot camps run by the military for journalists and technical staff who'd been accepted into the program, and counterterrorism and situational awareness seminars organized by Fox for smaller groups of reporters, engineers, and cameramen headed overseas.

We learned how to spot signs that a vehicle had been tampered with, suggesting a possible booby trap or car bomb. We learned how to vary our behavior and routines to avoid being followed or targeted. We were taught basic first aid and tricks for handling more severe injuries, like how to stop the bleeding from significant wounds using tourniquets made from basic materials.

We learned how to exit a vehicle when under attack and what to do when we hit the ground. We received more first aid tips from the military at the seminar it organized at Fort Dix, New Jersey that included classroom lessons and exercises in the woods, but it was so cold that week we had to severely limit our outdoor activities. Later, in Kuwait, just before our actual embed began, we had more lectures to remind us of military protocol, the 101s of each branch (including ranks in order from private to general, for example), basic survival techniques, what was expected of us, and what we could and couldn't report on during our embed.

The primary rule? You could talk about what happened yesterday or earlier that day or even what was happening right then and there (if we were live), but you absolutely *could not* disclose your exact location, what was about to happen, or what was planned for the near or distant future. This was basic operational security. You don't tell the enemy where you are or where you're going, who you're going with, or what you plan to do when you get there for the obvious reason you'd be tipping them off and putting yourself, your crew members, and the service members at risk. I learned to be vague about certain things, especially my current location, when going live. The focus of our reports was on what we'd witnessed, the progress of the mission, and the morale and backstories of the Marines around us.

Not revealing our location and future missions was critical, and the importance of the rule was drilled into us. This was the most important thing we were taught by the military, and we had to agree to abide by the rule before we loaded on to buses with our gear and carted off to the base camps.

It was Gospel, and it was ironclad. A violation of this rule meant immediate expulsion from the embed program.

And it's the rule my old friend Geraldo Rivera broke when he embedded weeks after we did. Geraldo didn't go through the seminars or training programs because he was Geraldo and didn't have to. Someone gave the green light for him to helicopter in and join a unit after the invasion launched, and, sure enough, at some point he drew the infamous map in the sand and talked about where his guys were headed, and some generals at the Pentagon nearly had a meltdown.

Geraldo downplayed the significance of what he'd revealed, saying it was completely vague, but the rest of us were pissed because he didn't have to go through what we all went through before heading off to the desert, and then, sure enough, he made us look bad.

I for one supported the initial calls to expel Geraldo from the embed program, but he somehow managed to convince the brass to let him stay, and he continued reporting on the war until, I guess, he decided he'd seen enough and bounced.

We spent close to three weeks in Kuwait City, waiting for the Marines to call and let us know that war was imminent and our embed would begin. We covered what we could from our hotel workspace, rooftop live position, and from the streets of the city, including how locals were preparing for the possible conflict, the latest from allied partners in the region, and whatever news of the day it made sense to report.

We also spent time prepping our gear, testing the satellite dish and sat phones, buying supplies, and getting in shape. One day when we had some free time, a bunch of us went to a go-cart place and went a bit wild, smashing into each other and tearing up the track. The guys who worked there kept yelling at us to stop hitting each other. I don't think we got kicked out, but we didn't stay long.

Some days we'd take trips to the temporary base camps the military had built in the middle of the Kuwaiti desert, miles from civilization. The camps provided food, shelter, sanitation, and other support services for tens of thousands of soldiers, sailors, and Marines.

We visited Camp Commando, home to Marine Expeditionary Force (MEF) headquarters, and Camp Matilda, headquarters for the 1st Marine Division, hosting final combat staging and rehearsal operations for more than twenty thousand Marines and sailors.

We shot interviews with arriving troops and commanding officers about what they expected, how they were feeling, how prepared they were, and what they hoped to achieve. We also frequently asked how the Marines felt about the antiwar protests back home, and they must have gotten media training before they arrived because every single one of them told us they didn't mind it, that they were fighting for Americans' rights to free speech and free expression, and that the demonstrations wouldn't deter them from their mission.

At Matilda, we got critically important briefings from a variety of military officers on a variety of topics, which I took copious notes on in a skinny spiral reporter's notebook with a camouflage cover the Marines gave us as a welcome gift. Reading through it brought back a flood of memories.

"GAS GAS GAS" were the first words I wrote atop the first page. It was the warning that the Marines yelled in the event of a suspected chemical or biological weapons attack. We would hear the warning one day when we reached Camp Ripper, the base where we linked up and lived with the 1st LAR for the last week before the launch of the war. We all frantically strapped our masks on as a Marine ran by yelling, "THIS IS NOT A DRILL!" scaring the crap out of us. And yes, in fact, it *was* a drill, but the point was made. We needed to be on guard at all times.

They'd issued us all camouflage chemical suits with charcoal lining, NBC (for nuclear, biological, chemical) suits also known as MOPP suits (for Mission Oriented Protective Posture) consisting of long pants, a jacket with hood, rubber boots, rubber gloves, and a belted pouch designed to carry our gas masks, extra filters, and atropine kits. We were told the filter would last twenty-four hours in a contaminated environment, and that symptoms of exposure could include runny nose, drooling, headache, trouble with vision, tight chest, or difficulty breathing.

The suits were good for thirty to forty-five days, and we'd need to wear them at all times, even when sleeping, to protect ourselves from nerve gas or biological or chemical weapons. We wore shorts and T-shirts underneath and were told to shave daily so the masks would have a clean fit and seal on our face.

They showed us the Atropine pens we'd carry in kits strapped to our legs, with a long needle you'd jab into your thigh and hold for ten seconds before pulling it out.

"If you come up on someone in need, in trouble," my notes said, "administer all three sets, one after another. If the person is convulsing, give the final shot."

Saddam Hussein was known to have deployed nerve and blister agents in the past, including VX and Sarin, Anthrax, and other toxins, and we were warned to assume that *any* incoming artillery is a chemical attack, and we were assured that should we be injured, we'd be medivacked with the same priority as Marines.

We also learned about the different levels of suit protocol: MOPP LEVEL 1 meant in the suit, but no boots required. MOPP LEVEL 2 meant suit and boots. MOPP LEVEL 3 was suit, boots, and mask. MOPP LEVEL 4 was suit, boots, mask, and gloves for *total encapsulation*. Scared yet? I was. The gloves came with inserts you put on first, then the rubber, which you'd cuff at the end.

Should we get "chemmed," we were to be moved to a containment site for decontamination procedures—though, fortunately, this never happened.

"SNOWSTORM" meant any indirect fire, such as mortars or artillery. "LIGHTNING" was a scud missile alert.

They issued us Cipro pills in addition to the Doxy pens and told us to take both if exposed. They spent lots of time on medical guidance, CPR, first aid, and hygiene, including gems like "Do what the Marines do, except when they're playing with dangerous animals!" And "Drink what they drink, eat what they eat, and wash your hands...it's very important to maintain personal hygiene!" which was laughable, since once we got to the desert, we didn't shower for more than a month, and when we bothered trying to clean up, we'd be dirty from the dusty desert in a matter of seconds.

The Marines talked confidently about dominating the battlefield, "preparing for the worst, hoping for the best," insisting that if Saddam attacked, the Marines' response would be "extremely violent" to the point that "he would never do it again."

"Marines will fight dirty if necessary," but they also joke that they "fight dirty all the time, because they don't *want* a fair fight, they want to win."

This kind of confidence was reassuring. If they were trying to make me feel more comfortable with this incredibly ridiculous situation I was putting myself in, it was working.

In another briefing, we learned that Marines operated on Zulu time, which is Greenwich Mean Time, and can be very confusing. It was three hours behind local time and also different from Eastern, Pacific, or any other time zone. So, for example, if someone said, "our next briefing will be at 1400 Zulu," we'd look at each other and say, "OK, that's 1700 [5 p.m.] local, so minus eight, it's 9 a.m. ET, or noon PT..." and we'd often get it wrong.

The most anticipated briefing (for me at least) was from Major General James Mattis; Mattis was commander of the 1st Marine Division and would lead the invasion of Iraq and the war itself and would later spend two years as Secretary of Defense under President Trump.

I really liked and respected General Mattis. He was at Camp Ripper in Afghanistan when I was embedded there in late 2001, and I always looked forward to his daily afternoon visits to our media housing, when he'd go on the record, give us stuff on background, and then go off the record.

The off-the-record stuff was always the best, of course, and we'd always try to talk him into letting us use some of it. He was a hard-core dude, blunt and salty and no-nonsense, usually chomping on a cigar and saying some variation of "fuck" almost every sentence. He was a Marine's Marine, not afraid to spend a night in a fighting hole with the grunts.

At Camp Matilda, General Mattis told the large group of assembled journalists: "You're welcome here."

"There never would've been an Iwo Jima statue of the flag raising if there hadn't been pictures of it," he pointed out, and then told us he was hoping we'd spend most of our time with the youngest Marines, who deserved the attention for their bravery.

"Conditions will go downhill from here," he warned. "Your comfort level will be on par with a lance corporal infantryman."

"We're out to do a noble deed here," he said. "The ground you sit on is free because of these types of guys [pointing at the Marines in the room]." Mattis told us he led the invasion into Kuwait, his ninth deployment to the region. "The last time, easy rules of engagement. See a guy with a gun, you shot him. This time, lots of innocent people," so the Marines would need to be more careful.

"We're expecting much of Saddam's regular army to surrender," he said, and would "funnel them to the rear, get them out of the danger area. We need to keep them safe, get them food, water. Follow-on units will address those issues."

As for timing of the invasion, he told us: "Once the political decision is made, we can move very, very quickly. Our vehicles are in formation for a reason. We have an execution matrix... can't go into detail, but we're thirty to forty miles from the border and these boys are from Southern California and they're fast on a freeway."

He threw some more one liners at us, including how the Marines were looking for "brilliance in the basics."

"We never stop the planning."

"Iraqis are moving all the time, and we watch 'em."

"These are the best ambassadors from America," he told us about his troops. "We have no problem with Muslims, we have no problem with the Iraqi people. What we have are a lot of people who've been victimized. We want to show them when *this* army comes to town, it's a whole new ball game. Marines will use their brains before they use their weapons."

"Marines have been training for urban combat for years, preparing for a fight, focused on tactics." As for their relationship with the Army, "we're in this together. The 3rd

ID [Infantry Division] is a great outfit, and we're happy to be fighting alongside them."

He warned us that sandstorms are a big problem and that they'd use ground medivac if necessary. "Highly qualified surgeons will be an hour away, but we can't fly through most of this."

He also warned about friendly fire, "a constant danger on the battlefield since General Stonewall Jackson was fired on by his own troops. The number one way to overcome it is through training and situational awareness, engage the brain before the weapon."

He said the Marines were warning Iraqi civilians to stay away from Iraqi military gear. Saddam was parking his tanks, rocket launchers, and other equipment next to hospitals, schools, and mosques to make it more difficult for coalition forces to target them. Mattis said the Marines were also telling Iraqis to get off the roads.

> We'd rather go around a city than through it, and if fired on we will try to fire back without hitting innocents. Bad things happen in war. We'll try to avoid it.

> If we're hit by chemicals and we're on the move, we'll probably pull off straight away, self decon, and wait for a down unit to get there. But if we're locked in the middle of a firefight, we'll continue to fight dirty until we can break contact and the unit can be replaced. Then we'll get cleaned up and get back into the fight. They've been training for this, wearing suits in California for days at a time, gotten shots, etc. His troops are in more danger than ours.

We're all a product of our experiences. It's mostly
a battle of willpower. We need to maintain our
spirits and discipline at the highest level. We've
fought some of them before...and we know they
don't want a rematch.

We're not the least bit worried about Iraqi forces.
We'll take out any that remain loyal to Saddam.
Our primary goal is to get everyone back safely,
in one piece. We don't want to lose *any* of them.

He also proudly said of the Marines: "They're looking forward to the brawl! This is an infantry division with young soldiers, very determined. Experience is valuable, but training is more valuable."

He finished by bragging about the Marines' superior air power.

"Aviation has become so much more capable. It used to be we asked, 'How many airplanes will it take to take out a target?' And now we ask, 'How many targets can our aircraft take out?' Total reversal in thinking."

Someone asked if he was worried about the harsh weather ahead. "We're an all-weather force," he replied proudly. "We can fight any old time."

Finally, he was asked: "What about Saddam? What will you do if you find him?"

His reply was classic Mattis: "He probably won't enjoy the encounter."

LAR BATTALIONS

When the embed assignments were first issued, I was told I'd be reporting to an Army unit the Pentagon was planning to stage in Turkey and then move into Iraq from the north. I spoke to some buddies in Public Affairs who highly encouraged me to request a shift to the Marines and not an infantry unit. "L-A-R" (for Light Armored Reconnaissance) was the way to go, they assured me.

For one thing, riding in the back of a troop transport was incredibly uncomfortable, hot, and crowded. For another, Marines were cooler than soldiers, they assured me, and I'd definitely see action and have a better overall experience.

LAR Marines called themselves "the tip of the spear" because they'd be out in front, alone and unafraid, probing the enemy for weaknesses, determining his posture and capabilities. Their primary mission was recon and security with limited offensive and defensive missions in support of the division commander.

They'd "go out and find stuff" from their mobile platform. The battalion drove light armored vehicles (LAVs) that looked like small tanks, except they had eight tires instead of tracks like tanks or infantry personnel carriers, which made them far more comfortable to ride in by comparison.

Covering the war with these guys was definitely the best fit for me, I assured my boss, reminding him I'd spent quality time with Marines on previous assignments in Albania and Macedonia during the Kosovo war and again in Afghanistan in 2001. I had contacts and connections there, and it helped that the LAR Marines really wanted me to join them for the march up.

I was actually surprised that my boss agreed and put in for me to switch to a Marine Corps embed and move another correspondent, Greg Kelly, to the Army's 3rd ID. Greg was a former Marine captain and pilot (who once crashed a jet off a carrier), and he was *not* happy about being reassigned to the Army, but I had seniority and my boss appreciated my reporting skills and apparently wanted to keep me happy.

The Pentagon made the switch, and I think in the end, Greg and I both had meaningful and highly successful experiences. He made it to Baghdad first and got lots of attention for a wound he suffered on his nose during a firefight when he got cut by a piece of shrapnel, and I had the most amazing journey of my life and career.

The LAV-25, an eight-wheeled LAR vehicle in which we'd spend the next few weeks, was made by General Motors of Canada (now renamed General Dynamics Land Systems Canada) in London, Ontario, in the 1980s. The "25" variant was named for its motor-driven twenty-five-millimeter chain gun, protruding from what looked like a tank turret, albeit a bit smaller. It fired high explosive armor-piercing rounds that resembled hand grenades, considered "very effective" by our USMC hosts. There was also a .762 caliber machine gun mounted on top, which I test-fired one day. When I released the trigger too soon, the gunnery sergeant taught me to hold it for as long as it took me to say "die motherfucker die." Seriously.

It was called a light armored vehicle for a reason: The armor was actually lighter than that of other fighting vehicles, which put less load on the tires and made it faster and more maneuverable. It weighed fourteen tons, which sounds like a lot but not when compared to an M1 tank, which weighs seventy tons. The LAV armor could shield vehicle occupants from small arms fire, but *not* from tank fire. It could operate on two-, four-, or eight-wheel drive and get 250 miles per tank of fuel.

The LAV-25 had a number of portals for Marines to stick their heads out of while on the move. There was one for the driver up front, another for the captain in the center, and another for the guy firing the machine gun. The gunnery sergeant had a chair he sat in as part of the base for the chain gun.

The gunnery sergeant constantly spun from side to side, scanning the horizon for threats by looking through a scope. The noise of the motor as he spun around drove us crazy. (They found a way to make it quieter in newer models.)

There were more portals in the back for the infantrymen that the journalists shared with them. There were two bench seats back-to-back in the rear of the vehicle, just long enough to lie down on if you bent your knees, with very thin pads on top for a minor improvement in comfort.

I'd sleep back there when I could, and one of the Marines would sometimes sleep on the floor next to me. My cameraman Christian Galdabini had played college football as a lineman. He was huge, about 6'5" and 250 pounds, and he had a much tougher time getting rest, scrunched up on the other side.

When we were driving, we'd always try to pop our heads out of the holes since it was so hot inside and the breeze felt good, even though we'd also be sucking in desert dust. We'd wear cloth masks around our faces, twenty years before we'd all be told to do it because of COVID-19.

Each company also had anti-tank-variant LAV-ATs, equipped with a tube-launched, optically tracked, wire-guided (TOW) ballistic missile system. We watched the Marines fire one during weapons training in the desert one day. It was wicked, like you'd imagine a missile firing would be. Really loud, and superfast, and it did significant damage to its target.

There were logistical-variant LAV-Ls, carrying water, food, and extra gear for the Marines, as well as a recovery variant LAV-

R, a maintenance vehicle equipped with a crane and welding kit. This was the Marines' tow truck of sorts, and we'd watch them at work in the Iraqi desert, freeing another LAV stuck in the mud after a horrific sandstorm.

There were LAV-Ms, the mortar variant with eighty-one-millimeter mortars hidden by doors that opened on the roof, and a LAV-C2, for command and control, a truck equipped with radios and antennas that handled communications with higher command.

WAR PARTY

Between day trips and live shots, I spent a *lot* of time in the hotel gym, bulking up. I gained a bunch of weight while prepping for the war, tipping the scale at 205 or 206 the day before we left, which was the heaviest I'd been in my life, but I didn't keep it on for long. I dropped eighteen of those pounds over the next few weeks, thanks to a shortage of MREs (meals ready to eat), and lots of calories burned thanks to the extremely long hours and extremely tough conditions, sweating in the sun and working through the nights.

Our staff also bought an old Land Rover while we were in Kuwait City and had it painted a desert sand color. We'd had many discussions with the PAOs about bringing our own ride. We had a *lot* of gear, and they were limiting us to three cases on the LAVs (also a constant battle and point of negotiation), and we wanted and thought we really *needed* our own truck to carry the rest of our gear (including the satellite equipment). We could also use the truck as a separate workspace, a place to write scripts, edit, eat, or sleep.

We figured our engineer Dusty Grubish could drive it and follow our convoy and we wouldn't have to leave any of our equipment behind. The Pentagon resisted at first, then reluctantly agreed to let us and other networks bring our own vehicles, but (as the story goes) as soon as General Mattis saw our whip just before we stepped off, he told his underlings something to the effect of: "There's no fucking way that piece of shit is coming with us," and the extra vehicle allowance was rescinded.

We were ecstatic (and a bit nervous) when we finally got the call informing us that our embed would begin the next day. We were told to be curbside with our gear at 5 a.m. for our bus ride to a hotel where we'd get our final briefing and unit assignments and head off to a base camp in the desert.

This meant only one thing: time for one last party! We knew there would be no alcohol during our adventure with the military and this might be our final chance for fun for a very long time, so someone got a bunch of bottles of booze (not easy in Kuwait), including some cheap whiskey, and we had a rager in our hotel workspace. We were slamming drinks and dancing to music from a colleague's iPod.

At one point, as Christian reminded me, I saw some Brit in the hallway wearing a camouflage elastic bandana (the circle kind that you can wear around your head or neck), and I gave him $20 for it. I wound up wearing that thing almost every day of the war.

Anyway, I drank *way* too much and yakked multiple times when I got back to my room at 1 a.m. or 2 a.m. I yakked again when I had to get up three hours later to pack and head downstairs. I was *really* sick and wasn't sure I could even make it. I kept throwing up, hoping it was the last time.

At some point I knew I couldn't wait any longer and sucked it up and headed down to the lobby, but when we boarded the bus to meet up with Marine brass, I realized I was gonna have to puke again. My stomach was still doing flip flops, and once we were on the road, I spent every moment trying to talk my body out of any more purging, but it was hopeless.

Christian told me he was completely hung over too but hadn't gotten sick, and when he got on the bus, he closed his eyes and just tried to chill for the long ride ahead. I, however, was in a really tough spot.

There was no bathroom on the bus, and there were bars on the windows. I could slide the window open but couldn't stick my head out, so the only way I could get sick again without getting it all over me or the floor was to get off the bus and take care of business in the bushes somewhere.

I was also really embarrassed because there were many people on our bus, including former Marine Lieutenant Colonel Ollie North, a Vietnam war veteran famous for his role in the Iran-Contra affair in the 1980s involving the illegal sale of weapons to the Khomeini regime to secure the release of American hostages being held in Lebanon. North then used proceeds from the arms sales to support rebel groups in Nicaragua.

I knew him well because he joined Fox to host a program called *War Stories*. Seated next to him was his good friend Bing West, a former Marine infantry officer, Vietnam combat vet, and former Assistant Secretary of Defense in the Reagan Administration. Bing was writing a book about his embed experience and would write a few more about his return trips to Iraq and Afghanistan in the coming years.

I'd spoken with Bing a few times in Kuwait. He was a fan of Fox News and respected my work, but he was also a bit intimidating, and I knew he'd have little tolerance or sympathy for my current condition. But this was happening no matter what. When I couldn't fight it any longer, I carefully made my way up the aisle and asked the driver if he could pull over so I could get off.

The driver was reluctant at first but then he got stuck in traffic; I told him it was urgent so he opened the door and I jumped out, ran to the culvert along the side of the road, and vomited out all I had left. When I was done, I had to double time it to catch up to the bus, still creeping along in traffic.

Feeling slightly better, I sheepishly climbed the steps and did the walk of shame back to my seat. I'll never forget the disgusted looks on Ollie's and Bing's faces, shaking their heads at me as I walked by.

CAMP RIPPER

When we got to the Hilton Hotel where the PAOs were coordinating the press, we got another briefing and were told to pile our gear in designated areas of the parking lot. We wound up sitting there for hours, and at one point, I shot what we call a "show and tell" standup, wearing my last civilian (but quasi-military) outfit, including green pants, a brown T-shirt, a green and black jacket, my "desert floppy" USMC hat (which became a signature of mine during the embed), and my press credentials on a lanyard around my neck, holding the Fox-flagged microphone and smiling:

> We've been waiting three weeks and a day for
> this and finally the time to embed has arrived.
> We're outside the Hilton Hotel outside of Kuwait

City with hundreds of journalists and all of our stuff, waiting to join the United States Marine Corps out in the desert somewhere. I'm gonna show you our kit...this is my photographer Christian Galdabini's bag and his chem suit, we got three hard cases here, this is my chem suit, this is Galdo's (my cameraman's) helmet, this is my pack [I pick it up], pretty heavy, probably weighs about 75 pounds [I may have exaggerated just a bit], got a tent, sleeping bag, sleeping mat [then started showing stuff on my belt], got my gas mask, my canteen, GPS, satellite phone, we're ready to go.

Eventually, Christian, Dusty, and I boarded another bus for the ride to Camp Ripper. Christian told me he was still hurting during that final forty-five-minute bus ride, and remembers driving through a windstorm and being very uncomfortable.

"I remember feeling, 'This sucks! What did I sign up for?'" he told me.

When we got to Ripper, we were shown the large barracks tent we'd be living in the next week. The tent was equipped with a heater and power plugs and had a plywood floor, on which we laid out our rubber mats and sleeping bags. The tent housed dozens of Marines who completely ignored us at first, which puzzled Christian and me.

For some reason we expected a warm welcome, excited greetings, and handshakes. We were Fox News! But no one seemed to care. They put us in a corner and a logistics officer gave us the rules we'd need to live by, and we got a tour of the facilities.

We were told to always carry water and our gas masks. The mess tent was a bit of a hike, and there was always a *long* line, but it moved pretty quick. Morning chow was from 0600 to 0800 hours, and evening chow from 1630 to 1900 hours (4:30 p.m. to 7 p.m.). After dark, we were allowed use flashlights but only with red lenses.

I used a red sharpie to make mine compliant. Light discipline was *very* important, we were warned. We were shown the hygiene area, with twenty-five port-a-potties and eight shower trailers, and buckets and a clothesline where we could hang our laundry after hand washing our clothes in a bucket.

We could use the shitters anytime but were only supposed to shower every other day. No smoking or eating was allowed in the tents, and lights had to be out at 2200 (10 p.m.). I washed my underwear, T-shirts, and socks one day, washing the clothes by hand with some cold water and a handful of detergent in an ammo can, wringing it out and hanging it on the line. Christian got video of it, and as I was laying some socks on the rope, I looked at the camera and said: "They say war is hell. Now I know what they mean."

Eventually, we met our commanding officer, H. Stacy Clardy, the man in charge of the 3rd LAR Battalion during Operation Iraqi Freedom, who became a very good friend of mine and whom I still talk to today. Stacy Clardy was a lieutenant colonel at the time and has been regularly promoted in the years since. As a one-star general, he took charge of 29 Palms, the sprawling Marine base and war training facility in the California desert, and eventually, as a three-star he ran the entire Marine

3rd Division from Okinawa, before retiring from the Corps in early 2022.

When we met Stacy, he was all business, as you might expect, ready to lead an entire battalion of nearly one thousand Marines to war. He'd been battalion commander for twenty-one months and admitted that not all of his marines were "squared away and locked on." Part of his job was trying to make sure that they were when it came time to engage the enemy. He told us his was a mechanized unit in an industrial environment with a high risk of injury and death, and we all needed to be careful. He warned us that Mission Control (MCON) could and would be putting restrictions on our ability to communicate from time to time.

It turns out that Stacy was a huge advocate for the media joining the Marines for the march up. I spoke to him recently while working on this book and asked him if he was ever reluctant to allow press into the inner circle, since this wasn't typically how Marines roll.

"I was unusual in that I was actually eager for the embeds," he told me. "I spent two years in Public Affairs as a major and felt strongly about the importance of having a close relationship with the media, so we could tell our story to the American people, and I was really happy to have you with us."

I then asked how important a role we played.

> From a selfish perspective, our families back in the states were following you very closely and relished the opportunity to hear stories about what we were doing.... You were with the lead elements of the 1st Marine Division, and it was a compelling story, and you were the right people to help tell that story. You personalized it and made the Marines real for the American people.

They wanted to hear what our armed forces were doing. We represent them [the American people], and having you there telling their story was beneficial to us and the Marine Corps as a whole.

One person who apparently *wasn't* happy was Alpha Company Commander Jon Custis.

Stacy told me that when he told Custis we'd be joining his unit, he declared: "WHY?? They should be with you!"

"He was not happy about that at all," Clardy said. "Most military, even junior Marines, don't have trust of the media as a whole, but you proved them wrong. And that's good."

We filed stories and did live shots every day at Camp Ripper, and slowly the guys in our tent started to come around. I think it took time for them to get comfortable with the idea of us being there, and once they saw the kinds of stories we were doing and how laid back we were, they warmed up. We started making friends and learning more about them, which led to some pretty compelling interviews before we stepped off.

We would also share our satellite phone when we could, which was a *great* way to make friends. Every Marine had loved ones back home worrying about him, a wife or girlfriend he missed, a milestone event he couldn't be part of, so when we had some down time, we'd try to give the guys at least three minutes each to call the states.

This could be challenging though, because we'd typically draw a crowd, and sometimes there would be dozens of Marines lined up. I remember one day one young jacked-up dude got on our phone and got into a huge fight with his wife or girlfriend and was screaming at her in front of a pretty-good-sized crowd all waiting their turn.

He burned through his time and kept yelling at her, and I kept trying to give him a signal that he needed to wrap up the call, but he kept ignoring me. I think he might've even come back after hanging up to cut the line and call her again to continue the fight. Eventually he hung up and stormed off.

One day I did a show-and-tell chem suit demonstration for the camera:

> We have rubber boots that fit over our shoes, we have these pants that have Velcro straps to tighten them around your ankles, we have these jackets that fit over our flak jackets, we're wearing T-shirts and gym shorts underneath. We have gloves that I'm not wearing, and then of course we have our gas mask which I'm supposed to be able to put on in six seconds. [Here I pull the mask out of its canvas pouch, grab the rubber straps, yank my hat off, and pull it over my head, then grab my hood. Then the hood, the hood fits over the top [I pull it over my head], attach the Velcro underneath [I secure the strap], and we should be protected.

I pose for the camera, fully dressed, with my gas mask completely covering my face and camouflage covering me from the top of my head to the toes of my rubber boots. We would soon live in the suits 24-7 for weeks on end, and I still have mine in a cabinet at home.

We also met some of the other battalion commanders, including Colonel Steven Hummer, in command of Regimental Combat Team Seven (RCT-7), a big bad group of mechanized Marines whom he called "one of America's most important natural resources." They'd be attached to the brigade as a combat element "on a very short thread," he told us. "We need to be ready to move in a very limited amount of time. He called it "strategic mobilization."

"We're eager to get this thing going," he said. "Heat is a factor. Everyone is here and we're ready." They were used to living in the desert and used to sand, but it was more humid in Kuwait and Iraq than at 29 Palms, so there would be some adjustments.

He assured us that "we're not here to destroy Iraq," and said that one of the things they'd be doing was distributing humanitarian rations to the locals, similar to military MREs, but tailored specifically to the culture.

A DEATH AT CAMP

One day at Camp Ripper we heard a gunshot. It turned out to be a Marine who killed himself with his rifle in one of the port-a-potties. His reasons weren't clear, and while networks as a rule typically don't cover suicides, the circumstances of this death were significant enough that my bosses back in New York and D.C. decided to at least shoot a story on the incident and feed it in, and they could decide later whether to air it.

The Marine Corps Public Affairs Division was reluctant to say much about the death except to confirm that it happened, that he died from a single gunshot wound in an apparent suicide. We were told that the incident was under investigation, and that next of kin hadn't yet been notified, so per protocol his name wouldn't be released, just that he was with the 3rd LAR Battalion. (We had his name and that he was a staff sergeant but wouldn't use it in the story.)

Then I spoke with Colonel Clardy.

"Sure, this is affecting every Marine here," he said. "Anytime there's a death it affects everyone around, including the entire 1st Marine Division."

He told me that he spoke to the men to give them the facts and minimize the rumors. "It's an absolute tragic event. Everyone has a hard time understanding it," and it pissed him off personally. "I came over here with the full intention of bringing all of them back, and that won't be the case. I wanted to ensure their safety," he said, "and I want to make sure it doesn't happen again. We're a family. Any problems, they should talk to me. Most Marines are more concerned with letting their buddies down," he told me. "We're part of a team and a brotherhood and are concerned with not failing. Most soldiers fight for the man on their right and left," he said, shaking his head.

He told me they'd give everyone the opportunity to talk things out and meet with the chaplain, and they'd be holding a company level memorial service the next day but said the best thing for them to do was to get back to training and routine and stay focused on what they're here to do.

"Each Marine handles things differently, but I want to avoid them sitting and thinking about it too much." Clardy said it was the first time in his career as a Marine that he'd been associated with a suicide. "Other deaths I can explain," he said. "This one, I can't."

He told me they sent the dead Marine's info to the Pentagon, which then contacted the Marine's local Marine Corps office, which would send a team to knock on the door of his home and let his family know what happened. They'd normally wear their dress Marine blue uniforms and bring a chaplain. The Marine's body would be flown back to the states for burial there.

I found the script for the suicide story in my notebook:

> It's been a tough couple of days here at Camp Ripper, home to the 1st Division's 3rd Light Armored Reconnaissance Battalion. Punishing sandstorms have been whipping thru the base... winds last night easily topped 50 miles per hour... conditions are rough and will only get rougher if and when they move North.
>
> And this morning, a young Marine with the 3rd LAR apparently took his own life, with a single round from his rifle.
>
> The Battalion Commander, Lt. Col. Stacy Clardy, called the 100's of Marines in his unit to formation to give them the facts of the incident, calling this a tragedy, the loss of a brother, one of their own, something they feel deep in their hearts, but the Colonel told me it also makes him angry.
>
> LT. COL. STACY CLARDY: "I came over here with the full intention of bringing all of them back, and that won't be the case. I wanted to

ensure their safety and I want to make sure it doesn't happen again."

"The Marines will be given time to grieve. A memorial service will be held Friday morning, but then they'll go back to work."

The Colonel says the best medicine in this case is to get the men refocused on what they're here to do.

With the 3rd LAR in Kuwait, Rick Leventhal, Fox News.

We fed the piece, but the bosses in D.C. opted not to use it, which was fine with us. Meanwhile, another reporter embedded with our unit, a print guy, filed a story on the suicide for his paper, which ran it on the front page with a big headline above the fold.

The Marines were pissed, and he was moved to another unit soon after. He was overweight and had trouble getting in and out of the LAVs (and could barely fit through the hatch) so that may have had something to do with it, but I can't say for sure.

THE GUNNER

One of my favorite Marines I met during the buildup to war was Chief Warrant Officer Tim "Gunner" Gelinas, a fifty-five-year-old Vietnam vet who'd retired twice and come back, most recently at the request of Colonel Clardy, who needed the Gunner's help in training the younger Marines on weapons. Gelinas chewed Red Man tobacco non-stop and cussed like a—well, like a sailor. He was from Woonsocket, Rhode Island, and was believed to be the oldest active-duty Marine deployed in Kuwait.

We spent a day with him at the Udairi Range Complex in the desert as he taught tactics and procedures on a variety of weapons systems to a big group of troops with advice like "Keep your head in the game!" and "Don't shoot at anything that's not your target!" Among the weapons on display that day were M-16s, TOW rockets, the twenty-five-millimeter Bushmaster chain guns, the .762 caliber mounted machine gun, and a .50 caliber Sasser sniper rifle.

The targets positioned among the sand dunes were the hulks of old armored vehicles destroyed during the Gulf War along with some assorted cars and stacks of tires. Everything was super loud. We spent three hours on the range, and I wrote in my notes "I'm glad I wore earplugs."

Interviewing Gelinas was a treat. He was full of one-liners, and I kept having to remind him he couldn't say "shit" or "fuck" because we'd have to edit it out. He lived out near 29 Palms and was teaching phys ed and handling security at a local high school after he retired for the second time and told me, "Every time I'd drive by an open space in the desert, I'd say to myself 'God it would be so nice to be out here with a group of Marines blowing something up!'" When his good friend Stacy confirmed that his services would be welcomed, he didn't hesitate to go back to the Corps, with his wife's permission of course.

"What are you doing here?" I asked him during our interview.

"Training Marines in the deployment of weapons in both offensive and defensive situations," he said rapid fire, almost like he'd rehearsed it.

"Hang on a second, you're fifty-five years old! What are you DOING here?" I asked again, encouraging him to be a bit more candid—and he was.

"I don't know, boy that was a hard decision I had to make. I was retired a little over two years and there was a shortage of Marine gunners in the Marine Corps and I called a friend of mine and said look if you guys need me, give me a call and that kinda started the wheels workin'…"

"But most guys your age are out playing golf right now," I said.

"Oh, I really don't know how to play golf," he replied with a smile. "Matter of fact, the last time I played golf I only went to see if I could hit anybody with the golf ball, see how my aim was."

"So your mind is in a slightly different place?"

"Check! It's on target engagement."

"There are some people on the other side of the border who are good people and we're gonna try and take care of the good people," he told me. "But anybody who fires a shot in our direction, I'm telling you we're gonna flatten 'em. It's that simple. We're gonna flatten 'em. We're gonna run 'em over."

I loved his confidence. It made me feel better about heading into battle.

ON THE BRINK

The next day was a Sunday, and the guys were given some time for R & R, so they improvised equipment to play horseshoes and softball flag football, and that night we spent $800 on Fox's credit card to buy them forty pizzas from a Pizza Hut in town as a thank you for their hospitality.

When I asked how they were going to keep the pies hot, the Marine handling the logistics looked at me with absolute disbelief at the idiocy of my question.

"Hot? They're not gonna be hot!" I then realized not only was it a dumb question, no one would care. It was pizza, and they scarfed it all down.

We also got our vehicle stenciled that day. The battalion's nickname is The Wolfpack, so we got its wolf emblem spray-painted on the hood of our Range Rover, which ultimately never crossed the berm. We had to leave it behind in the Kuwaiti desert, still holding all of the gear that Christian couldn't fit in our LAV, and he was shocked when he found out weeks later that the vehicle was recovered by Kuwaiti police, who returned it along with all of Christian's equipment to our Kuwaiti office.

Instead of driving our truck, Dusty loaded the satellite dish and as much of his equipment as he could fit into another LAV, and we saw him every two or three days after the war started, when we'd have a chance to feed material and do some high-quality live shots, far better than the primitive videophone we had to use without him.

On Monday, March 17, I got a haircut from one of the Marines (high and tight of course) while sitting on a box in the sand, and we received our second anthrax shot.

In a diary entry in my notebook, I wrote:

> Didn't hurt too bad going in, but burned after a few minutes and I'm told the second day is worse. My arm is sore now in the area but no big deal. It's really hot here today, maybe even

warmer than yesterday when I played football [with the Marines]. Been sweating quite a bit and our shower day isn't until tomorrow. I hear regular booms out in the desert. Sounds like they're firing heavy weapons and there have been multiple flyovers of fighter jets, too many to count. Presumably they're heading to the No-Fly Zone, possibly taking out targets before they come back.

Had our Company photo day today. I took pictures with about 10 different Marine's cameras handed to me. They all lined up in front of and on top of four LAVs, then broke down into platoons for smaller group shots. Me and Christian took pics with the 1st Sgt and Gunny and also with all the officers, and then one of the platoons called us in and loaded us up with weapons. I was holding a SMAW [shoulder-launched multipurpose assault weapon] rocket launcher over my shoulder, had an M-16 in my left hand and Barretta pistol in my right [and I really wish I had that photo!]. Christian was holding a modified M-16 with a grenade launcher and had a K-bar knife between his teeth. Very fun.

Lt. Noble just told me the Colonel wants to meet with us at 2000 tonight, after chow. May be to discuss the logistics of our push forward.

Still not sure if we're going live tonight. Our amplifier broke AGAIN yesterday, right before a scheduled live shot for Sunday's Fox & Friends, so now New York isn't even booking shots, waiting for us to tell them if and when we can go. It's very frustrating because we have great stories to tell out here, one after another. So many Marines, each with an interesting background or specialty. Today I'm hoping to have a live demo of the chemical casualty decontamination team in action, showing how they'll clean people up who've been slimed. We watched them rehearse earlier...pretty cool stuff.

We were in our tent and a group of Marines were in there going over battle plans. I walked up saying "Is this something I can listen in on?" And the one Lieutenant quickly covered the map and said "No!" And another Marine joked "He plays football with us a couple times and thinks he's one of the guys!" We all had a good laugh and I said "hook a brother up one time" and they laughed some more and I walked out.

Dusty managed to get the equipment working and I did a live shot for my buddy Shepard Smith's *Fox Report* show, saying:

Another long hot day for the thousands of Marines and sailors here at Camp Ripper. These guys have been spending their days doing last-minute training and packing, making sure their armored vehicles are stocked with ammo and supplies and their kits are ready to go.

And they've been doing chemical weapons preparedness training as well. Earlier they set up a chemical-casualty decontamination site, and specially trained Marines put on their chem suits and rehearsed how they will treat victims of a chemical attack, decontaminating the victims' MOPP suits and masks, cutting the suit off with scissors, moving the men to stretchers, washing them with sponges and bleach and then carrying them to an ambulance, which can hold up to four victims at a time, to be transported to a landing zone, and time, of course, is very, very crucial.

[Here I inserted a soundbite from a Marine about the importance of moving fast to decon after exposure, then my script continued]

The decon teams will travel not far behind the combat units, and their goal is to get any victims cleaned up within the first hour, known as "the golden hour." We'll be wearing the same suits, and if we get slimed—their term, not mine!— we'll get the same treatment. Shep, back to you.

During the photo session that day, we also celebrated the birthday of Lance Corporal Craig Carlucci, who turned nineteen at Camp Ripper.

Craig was one of the scouts who would ride in our LAV for the next several weeks, and I was crushed to learn that he died in a motorcycle accident shortly before the tenth anniversary of the war, when we'd traveled out west to interview him and some of the other Marines we'd shared all that time with.

As the launch of war moved closer, we were warned it could be a matter of hours, not days, when we got the call to roll out, and we were also warned there'd be a forty-eight-hour black-out period when we left the base, during which we couldn't transmit, report, or make any phone calls whatsoever. Things were tense. Christian and I went to Colonel Clardy's tent to see if we could learn more about our immediate future. We knew there was only so much he could share on camera, and sometimes I'd mess with him by asking questions he wasn't allowed to answer.

"What marching orders have you been given?" I asked. He gave me a hard stare, and in his best deadpan, said "left, right, left, right..." and we all cracked up laughing.

We soon learned that President Bush had given Saddam Hussein and his sons forty-eight hours to get out of Iraq, putting us at Camp Ripper at the MCON Alpha state of readiness. As President Bush was telling the world, "We are now acting because the risk of inaction is far greater," every Marine vehicle was already being loaded up and every Marine and sailor had already packed his kit and moved out of his tent. The LAVs were staged and ready to roll, and we were told we'd be heading north at first light.

We listened to the President's address on a radio in Colonel Clardy's tent, with him and a few other Marines. I sat on the floor, taking notes. It was an eerie experience, knowing we were about to step off, part of the invasion the President was so calmly and forcefully explaining to the world. We didn't know exactly when we'd be heading off toward the Iraqi border, but it didn't take long to find out. At 2 a.m., we were awakened and told we'd all be rolling out at dawn. I don't think I got much sleep after that. I was nervous and excited and scared and unsure. Would we see action? Would we be gassed? How long would we be gone and how fierce would the fighting actually be? Would we make it back alive?

The next morning, before we left, we did a few interviews, including one with Corporal Cody Nelson, who told me, "I don't want to die, but I'm willing to do it right now. I wake up every morning thinking there's a chance I might not wake up the next day, and I think that's how every Marine out here feels, and that's why I know we're going to win."

"Nobody's better than the U.S." he continued. "That's worth dying for, for me. I got friends back home who don't want to come over and do this kind of thing, well hey, I'll do it for them."

STEPPING OFF

We were awakened at 2 a.m., two hours before the President's speech, and told we would not be allowed any satellite communications until further notice. The Marines were already packing and were pumped with nervous energy, loading their vehicles with nicknames like Gut Truck, Gravy Train, Roach Coach, War Pony, Redneck Express, Lucky Strike, and Battle Cat.

"March 18th, Game Day," I wrote in my notes, along with highlights from a candid and graphic motivational speech we witnessed from one of the 1st lieutenants to his platoon before heading out of Ripper for the last time: "Fucking kill every fucking thing that fucking moves! You guys have been trained, you don't need me to fucking tell you what to do. You see some fucking farmer who doesn't have his hands up, fucking SHOOT HIM."

The LAVs were all staged in predetermined rows and positions, like a NASCAR race about to begin. Everyone was fully dressed for combat, including the embeds. With our hearts pounding, we secured our spots in the back of the LAV, and we rolled out into the open desert.

After we stepped off, I wrote: "We're driving west on Highway 80. The toughest part is not being able to call anybody...so many people I'd like to talk to right now and share the experience with but it's forbidden."

Our vehicle was commanded by Captain Jon Custis (originally from Bridgeton, New Jersey) who was also the Alpha Company commander.

Sergeant Bill Gwaltney, a big, tall mid-westerner from Kenosha, Wisconsin, was our gunner, who'd spend most of the next few weeks seated in the turret, constantly rotating back and forth as he scanned the horizon through his viewfinder, looking for threats.

Sergeant Michael Timmons, from Amarillo, Texas, was our constant companion in the back of the LAV.

Corporal Craig Carlucci, from Chicago, the one who'd turned nineteen just days earlier, carried his girlfriend's picture in his breast pocket. He survived the war only to die in a high-speed motorcycle crash near his home in the Pacific Northwest ten years later.

Corporal Jason King, our driver, hailed from La Porte, Indiana. He was the quietest of the bunch and would later suffer from PTSD, which he talked about candidly when we did a "where are they now" follow-up to the war in 2008.

We would spend the next month with these men, sharing one of the craziest, dirtiest, and most challenging rides of our lives.

After almost two hours, we reached our assembly area on a desolate stretch of sand, and the Marines parked the LAVs in a 360-degree protective formation.

The landscape was barren. There was nothing on the horizon in every direction. It looked like we'd landed on the moon. Then we were ordered to put on our chem suits, including our ballistic vests underneath.

Sergeant Timmons jumped off our LAV, slung his M-16 across his neck and shoulder, screwed his folding shovel into place, and began digging. He dug a long trench, carefully shoveling the dirt to the front, then marked out borders along the sides, creating a three-sided rectangle. He dug along the edges to mark the area, then settled in for the real work.

"You gonna dig that whole thing out?" I asked. "Yessir," he answered. "Gotta make a fighting hole, give us some protection in case we're attacked."

"How long do you think it'll take?" I asked.

"A few hours, but that's ok. It's part of my job. It's what I get paid for."

After a few minutes, Captain Custis, Timmons' boss, came over and corrected him.

"I only need two skirmisher trenches. Skinny ones. You don't need to dig this whole thing."

Then, while Timmons refocused his digging, the captain lined out a second hole to match the first, got on his knees, and went to work.

Timmons and countless other Marines would dig hundreds of these holes over the next few days, which I imagine were eventually filled by the blowing sand in the days and weeks that followed.

I made notes about the abundance of bugs. Big blue flies, smaller house-type flies, even smaller gnat-like bugs, and some that look like bees but apparently don't sting. We decided that the bugs were confused about all the fresh company but thrilled to have so many people show up in their remote patch of desert.

Later, in the shade of our LAV, Captain Custis gave us a briefing:

> We'll be securing an airfield just over the border for a resupply point, giving the rotary wing a place to land. There may be border guards and militia. The other part of the battalion is seizing an oil field.
>
> H hour, when we cross the line, we go through the berm and over the ditch, it's 60 kilometers to Iraq. At H plus 20 hours, we'll link back up with Battalion for a follow-on mission to the north.

He told us a key part of the Marines' job was to find the enemy "so bigger dogs can clear 'em out.", meaning fellow troops with heavier weapons and air support would take out opposition forces once the 3rd LAR identified the targets.

The Rumaila oil fields to the west were also on their radar, considered strategic objectives: "We don't want Saddam to blow them up."

The captain told us cuts had already been made in the southern berm, electric fence, and wire.

While we were parked in the northern Kuwaiti desert, the Marines kept busy, cleaning and lubing their guns and digging more fighting positions, preparing for the possibility of an assault coming our way. They concealed their vehicles with camouflage nets and kept their eyes on the horizon. They also put fluorescent-colored panels on top of the LAVs so they could be spotted as friendlies from the sky. We were told to transition to MOPP Level 2, which meant putting on our full suits and boots, and the doc passed out doxycycline, telling us to take one pill per day to fight off malaria.

The next morning, March 19, we learned of some potential issues. The thermal-weapons-sighting display was going out of focus, and our gunner couldn't switch from wide to narrow. Radio communications were spotty, and some LAVs had left camp with empty water cans, which the captain wasn't happy about. Meanwhile, according to intelligence gathered, the Iraqis had moved a hundred armored personnel carriers near Safwan Airfield, apparently preparing for a fight.

At 10 a.m. we started slowly moving north, at about five kilometers an hour, carefully creeping through the desert toward the border. The engine on Delta Company's C2 crapped out, with no power to the radios. The captain told us there were ways to compensate, including moving radios to different LAVs.

We linked up with Colonel Clardy, who gave us a detailed breakdown of the battle plan, with the understanding that we couldn't report any of it until after the fact. He told us where the different Marine regiments would be headed: RCT-7 would maneuver through Safwan and attack the Iraqis' 51st Mechanized Infantry at the town of Al Zubayr, while RCT-5 would seize the southern and northern Rumaila oil fields, and RCT-1 moved around the left flank to seize control of Route 80, also known as the Highway of Death.

Iraqi border guards were dispersed along the southern border with Kuwait, and the colonel warned us we'd be in range of the Iraqi's artillery tubes. The guards also had AK-47s, T-55 tanks, and armored personnel carriers (APCs) and troop carriers with machine guns.

The battalion planned to cross the berm five kilometers south of the border, breach the concertina electrified fence, climb over an eight-foot berm, and then roll through a twenty-foot-wide, ten-foot-deep ditch dug at the border. Then we'd be in Iraq.

On the way back from our briefing we stopped and picked up a crate full of grenades.

"Four of us in the back of the LAV," I wrote, "so we wedged the crate of grenades behind me on the seat, and I'm leaning up against it for the ride back to our staging area."

We were reminded once we started broadcasting again not to give any specific locations, including where we are or where we're going, why we're going, or what's going to happen, and the captain warned us that first contact with the enemy would likely come at our position (and he was right), telling us to expect artillery and small-arms fire.

We made our way to the northern berm to protect bulldozers preparing to cut through fencing, and we saw Iraq with our own eyes for the first time. I did a standup from the back of the LAV on the way there as part of our video journal, which wound up in Christian's "Embed" documentary:

> It's Wednesday morning and we're now rolling toward the border. Just a moment ago we had to jump in the back of the vehicle and close the hatches to cries of "lightning, lightning, lightning" because of missiles fired toward Kuwait. The

start of war could be moved up because of this latest offensive action by the Iraqis.

At 3:30 p.m. that day, I wrote:

We've reached the first electrified fence, about one click [kilometer] from the border. We can see with binoculars a bus and about a dozen Iraqis milling about. Scouts report they're waving white flags. We can't handle any surrenders... Kuwaiti soldiers will be responsible for them at this location...and we can't tell if they're soldiers or civilians yet.

A bit later, I wrote:

Game-day for real? H-hour is supposed to come tonight, right over our heads. One of the first targets in the war is right in front of us: Safwan Hill. It'll be pounded by air assets, including fighter jets and Cobras along with ground artillery. We should be just a click and a half away, between the berms at the border. Another sandstorm today, blowing while we waited for the order to move up. Christian and I fell asleep on the sand, getting some shelter from the tires of the LAV. I woke up with enough sand in my ears that it literally poured out when I turned my head to the side. Meanwhile Timmons just named our LAV "The Gypsy Wagon" and we picked up a Brit who'd be riding with us across the border, Flight Lieutenant Mick Morley, who turned out to be entertaining as hell.

We moved back from the border and settled in for the night. I rolled out my mat on the hard desert sand and slept on top of it in my sleeping bag, and we were up again at 5 a.m., traveling back and forth between the fence and other positions. We got resupplied with food and water and then went to the Brit's camp so that Captain Custis could re-coordinate the liaison movements with the Royal Air Force (RAF) regiment. We got word that the air war began overnight which was disappointing for us since nothing was really happening yet where we were, and we remained under orders not to broadcast or make any phone calls.

The next morning was more of the same. Rolling near the berms, meeting up with other platoons, coordinating plans, frustrations with radios, constantly scanning the horizon for trouble.

We knew this thing was about to kick off, which made every minute and every hour seem interminable.

The new battle plan was set for that evening, with our guys deploying along the northern berm while the air assault on Safwan unfolded. Then they'd be tasked with clearing any Iraqi barracks or other targets of interest that the air power wasn't able to neutralize. When a scud missile was fired toward Kuwait, we went into our full gas mask drill, and when a second scud was launched, we went to MOPP Level 4, which meant not just our suits and mask and boots, but also our hoods on and secured tight, and we then had to sit in the cramped space of the vehicle with virtually no air flow, sweating profusely. I wasn't completely claustrophobic, but when they told us we'd have to put our gloves on for a complete seal, I started to lose it, and that's when we were given the all-clear.

I wrote, "I want to go to war already! Enough of this BS. Tired of sitting and waiting and so are the Marines."

We didn't have to wait much longer.

It came without warning. We'd been sitting for a while near the border, and Christian and I had been lulled into a false sense of security, not fully paying attention since there wasn't much going on. And out of nowhere we were rocked by the incredibly loud and jarring "BOOM BOOM BOOM" of our chain gun.

Sergeant Gwaltney was firing what are believed to be the very first ground shots of the war. Captain Custis spotted what he called "hostile activity" at one of the border guard posts and made the snap decision to take them out.

It was one of the Iraqis' objectives, and he wasn't going to wait for them to initiate contact. Gwaltney triple-fired repeatedly, and other LAV-25s joined in. Christian poked out of the back hatch when he could, capturing some of the action on his camera, and then we took off in a hurry, flying down the dirt road to meet up with other companies, and I got the green light to call in and report on the historic first shots fired by Marines.

Along the way we saw Iraqi soldiers fleeing another post to avoid certain death.

Meanwhile, the captain's prediction proved true, with Iraqi artillery landing dangerously close at one point, flying right over our heads, hitting maybe a hundred yards or so past our position. It was close enough that Christian and I heard it, felt it, and freaked out maybe a little. Marines near us returned artillery fire, and it was clear we were now at war, or at least on the brink, and experiencing it from the actual front lines.

WAR BEGINS

That night was the full-on assault on Safwan Hill, and we watched it unfold from our front row perch at the top of the berm. Located just three kilometers north of Iraq's southern border, Safwan was the highest peak in southern Iraq and provided the Iraqis a continuous line of sight into the Kuwaiti desert. The Iraqis had built several observation posts there, along with a signal intelligence gathering facility, which they might have used to calibrate our position for the mortars fired in our direction a couple days earlier. Coalition forces lit up Safwan in spectacular fashion, like Fourth of July fireworks on steroids, with Cobras armed with Hellfire missiles, TOW missiles, Sidewinder missiles, 2.75-inch rockets (for personnel and soft targets), and five-inch rockets, along with twenty-millimeter three-barrel cannons capable of firing 650 rounds per minute. The Cobras were joined by fighter jets and bomber aircraft carrying more powerful and dangerous munitions, including napalm and a massive two-thousand-pound bomb.

It was an amazing scene that lasted for what seemed like hours. At some point I called in to report on what we were witnessing, lying just below the crown of the southern hillside of the berm so I could see over the top.

After the assault was over, we pulled back to get some rest, and the next morning we crossed the berm into Iraq for the first time.

Our first stop was the border post our guys destroyed a couple days earlier. The place was absolutely leveled, but a rickety flagpole was still standing, with an Iraqi flag at the top. Sergeant Timmons hopped out, climbed up the pole, and snatched the flag. Our first souvenir.

Then we headed toward the Rumaila oil fields, where the Iraqis had set fires, either to try to interfere with U.S. military operations or to prevent America from getting its hands on the Iraqis' most valuable resource. We got so close to the burning rigs, we could feel the heat and were breathing the smoke, so we put on protective masks the Marines had given us in anticipation of this event.

As we made our way north, I wrote a story about what we saw, using a standup open I'd shot earlier, showing the vast environmental impact of the Rumaila fires and smoke, filling the horizon in every direction as far as we could see:

> We have an amazing vantage point of these oil fires, you see on the horizon there where the smoke starts, and then just walk with me as we pan the horizon there [I began walking in a big circle around Christian, who stayed in one place and panned the camera to follow me].

> ...thick black smoke like a blanket all the way as far as you can see across the horizon [pointing], you can see flames off on the horizon of another fire burning, it just keeps going past all those light armored vehicles there [the LAVs are in the foreground close to us, the smoke is miles away] and if you want to come back this way, believe it or not there's another source of smoke over here that goes in this direction [I'm now walking the other way and Christian is panning with me to the right] and again, blankets the horizon as far as the eye can see.

We passed more than a dozen oil fires as we traveled north, some of them with flames several stories high, and saw hundreds of camels, most in large packs but one young one all alone.

We passed empty guard posts built on overpasses and men dressed like farmers who the Marines suspected were soldiers who shed their uniforms.

And we got a flat tire and watched our guys change it with lightning speed.

I did a standup on camera about it that didn't make air but *did* make it into Christian's "Embed" documentary. I'm standing, poked through the back of the LAV, with my sunglasses and yellow helmet on, looking hot, disheveled, and exhausted, saying: "We're on the road toward the Euphrates River and we may have a flat tire, which is a problem because we called Triple-A and they said it's gonna take them at least six weeks to get here—so we're not sure what we're gonna do next."

The tire change took twelve minutes, and we hit the hardball again.

We passed Iraqis walking along the highway, and clearly some of them were soldiers, with military pants and boots under their robes. I was surprised the Marines were leaving them alone and was told they weren't concerned with anyone who wasn't shooting at them or actively opposing them. The military objectives were ahead of us, and they'd only pause and shoot to clear out obstacles along the way.

Christian and I recorded anything and everything of interest, including the guys walking on the road, the camels, the sheep and their herders in the fields, the traffic jams of military vehicles, the attack helicopters buzzing overhead. We'd feed material or file stories when we could, when our company would pull over to discuss plans or pause for resupply of fuel, food, and water.

My next standup was a bit cryptic:

> The 3rd LAR is on the move. We will be hitting the road north to once again serve as the eyes and ears of the 1st Marine Division in a critical mission focused on strategic positions. Because of the sensitivity and importance of this mission and because of our proximity to enemy forces, I will not be able to file reports for probably the next eighteen hours.

On March 23, my dad's birthday, we were up at 5:30 in the morning, and I shaved for the first time in days. We hit the road early for a trip north across the Euphrates and beyond, joined by the 1st and 2nd LAR and the 18th Army brigade and other assets.

"Nothing but U.S. Military on the highway," I wrote in my notebook,

> and today we're supposed to take the lead. Alpha and Bravo companies are heading to another river crossing providing security and recon to insure follow on forces can move safely towards Baghdad. They won't let us transmit or even do phoners [a live shot on the air over the phone, without video]. Everyone is expecting trouble or some kind of resistance. Passed a graveyard

of smashed up shells of vehicles on the side of the road, plus several spaced out in the median of the highway, every 50 feet or so. MRE boxes, bags and empty water bottles litter the shoulder of the road.

Then I wrote down a conversation I overheard between Custis and Gwaltney, the gunner.

Capt: "Hey, you know your weapon's on 'fire,' right?"

Gunner: "How'd it get like THAT?" And he starts laughing.

We passed a destroyed Humvee where two U.S. soldiers were killed by an RPG and stopped near an airfield taken over by coalition forces and renamed Air Jackson. We watched massive C-130s take off, and helicopters circle overhead.

At some point some Special Ops guys stopped us, asking for help. They'd been worried about an ambush from mortar fire from a building off in a field and were outgunned, so a platoon from Delta Company went in, found an anti-aircraft weapon and one thousand rounds of ammo and some mortar pits and detained a bunch of guys. We hung around for an hour or so providing security.

I believe this was also the day that my man Christian took his first dump in twelve days.

It was the strangest thing. I had no problem going. I was *very* regular, squatting on a shovel or an empty ammo box every day. Other guys might have had issues from time to time, but longer than two or three days was unusual. Christian hadn't pooped since before we left Ripper and confessed to it after about a week. It then became a daily topic of conversation and word quickly spread. Marines kept giving him their home-brewed remedies. Extra coffee. Extra hot chocolate. Tabasco sauce, which came in the MREs in tiny bottles. It became a running joke among our crew and even with other companies and platoons, and the efforts to get him cleaned out ramped up, with no success. Christian was setting records in an unlikely category and becoming a legend.

And then, nature finally called. It was midday and we were paused for a bit, parked somewhere in the sand, and he told me he felt something brewing, so I grabbed his camera and recorded him reaching for a couple of half-used rolls of toilet paper stashed in the back of the LAV, then watched as he grabbed the empty ammo crate we shared as a toilet seat and headed off to a spot behind the closest dune.

A few minutes later, he returned with a grin.

"We had an effort. Not the herculean, all-clean effort I expected—but it's a solid start."

The drought was over. His bowels were back in action, and he began taking care of business on the reg like the rest of us.

As so often happens, the laughs would be short lived. We'd crossed the Euphrates earlier that day, so we were now in Mesopotamia, the historic region between the Euphrates and Tigris Rivers. "The crossing," I wrote, "was anticlimactic. Heard so much about it, thought it would be heavily defended but just a small pocket of resistance. Marines had already secured the bridge we crossed, and the river itself was more like a stream, not very wide and not very impressive."

The LAVs were parked along the roadside every two hundred meters or so, with their turrets pointed across the desert farmland, and I wrote, "all quiet so far."

Colonel Clardy called his company commanders together and told them we weren't done for the day. We'd be making a run to the Tigris, despite the approaching darkness. I did a standup, looking rough and tired:

> We just had a roadside briefing with the Lieutenant Colonel, who told us he senses an opportunity and wants to push forward and seize the bridge at the Tigris River, and push across and secure the road there and hold it for follow on forces. He said we still can't broadcast though, and I asked why, and he said because we'll be all alone up there and if the enemy finds out where we are, they'll gas us.

There was no complaining. The Marines were tired, but this was their job and there would be time for rest later. That night was our first major contact with the enemy, when we drove right into an ambush.

AMBUSHED

It was the scariest and hairiest experience of the entire war, caught up in a full-on firefight that lasted close to an hour. The sun had gone down. It was unusual for us to be traveling at night, but we were with the entire battalion, with roughly 250 vehicles and one thousand men. We were somewhere near the rear of the convoy when we started hearing shots, and our vehicle rolled to a stop.

It was strange and eerie and incredibly unsettling, hearing the shouting and gunfire creep closer and closer to our position, until all of a sudden it was a full-on firefight, with every Marine engaged and every gun blazing on our rig.

The opposition was at brigade strength, many of them moving on foot, popping up and down like whack-a-moles from behind sand dunes to fire on the Marines. Christian and I couldn't see them, but we later learned there were hundreds of enemy fighters, some as far as two thousand meters away, others advancing within thirty feet. One Marine told me he saw seven Iraqi tanks and saw one of them taken out by an air strike.

Sergeant Gwaltney barely let up on his chain gun, and our machine gun was getting heavy use, too. Christian and I stayed crouched in the back for most of it, but he occasionally popped up with the camera to try to record footage, which was difficult because it was so dark. He managed to capture some tracer rounds, and you can hear the captain yelling. I also popped out to get a look but was primarily focused on trying to get permission to go live on our hand-held satellite phone.

"STAY DOWN!" He yelled over the constant weapons firing. Cannons, machine guns, more machine guns, more chain guns, tracer rounds lighting up the sky, explosions in the distance, more gunfire, on and on and on.

Once I'd gotten over the shock of what was happening, I realized I needed to call New York and get on the air, but because of embed rules, I wasn't supposed to report live without letting the captain know first, but getting the captain's attention was nearly impossible, because he was shooting at enemy fighters.

"Captain!" I yelled. "CAPTAIN!" He ignored me, for obvious reasons. "CAPTAIN, CAN I DO A LIVE SHOT?" No response.

After a few minutes, I decided there was zero risk in my broadcasting, since the enemy *obviously* knew where we were. I wouldn't be revealing any secrets, so I called in and they put me right on the air.

I described the scene, my words often drowned out by the explosive rounds fired from our guns. The anchors were breathless, and at times I just held the phone up toward the hatch so the audience could hear what I was hearing.

The enemy fired mortars, small arms, and at least three RPGs our way, moving in on our flanks, fully aware that we were coming because they apparently saw us from an observation post they fled as we approached.

My sister later told me that she was driving on the Long Island Expressway in New York, listening to Fox News Channel on Sirius XM Radio and heard my report and had to pull over to the side of the highway because she was crying so hard and scared for my life.

I was scared, too, probably the most scared I'd been up to that point, wondering if it would get worse, if the enemy would reach our line, if any minute our LAV would get hit by a round it couldn't deflect, if we were all destined to die that night on a stretch of highway many miles from Baghdad.

It wound up being a very one-sided battle. The only casualty the battalion suffered was a Marine hit by shrapnel, a vehicle commander who'd been popped up in the turret. Fortunately, he was just bruised. His flak jacket protected him from greater harm.

When the firing stopped, we all turned around and drove south, but only for a few minutes, and turned into a field and parked. I was incredulous.

"We're stopping here? Seriously?" I couldn't believe it. We'd just been attacked by hundreds of enemy fighters, and while the

Marines killed a bunch of them, I knew they couldn't have killed them all, and yet here we were, still in what was basically their back yard, now staging for the night.

"Are we just gonna stay here???" The answer was yes, and the funny thing is, I was *so* exhausted, I still got out of the LAV and put my mat and sleeping bag on the ground and crawled inside to crash. "Fuck it," I said to myself. "I need the sleep."

Our battalion commander Clardy, who retired in 2022 as a three-star general, admitted to me during the writing of this book that the ambush was a surprise to him and his men, but says the push to the Tigris was the plan all along, directed by General Mattis.

"We were tasked to get to certain locations ahead of Division, conducting move and contact operations, and we knew we might get contact along the way. We operated a lot at night," he told me.

> Our battalion trained for it, but we didn't know the enemy was there, we weren't expecting it. The lead company was hit by a volley of RPGs and before long, the whole battalion was in contact. Up to that point we were under the belief if we ran into an Iraqi unit they wouldn't stay and fight, they'd take off. The fact they stayed and fought was very much a surprise to me.

Clardy told me that when the firefight was over, "We were gonna keep pressing but Mattis didn't recommend it. He thought there was more enemy ahead of us, and there was, and they [other Marine units] ended up fighting with them for three or four days."

The next day, March 24, we returned to the battlefield and found all sorts of spent munitions, destroyed enemy vehicles, and some dead Iraqi soldiers on the ground.

I interviewed some of the Marines involved in the fighting. One of them, a gunner on another LAV-25, told me that he saw several Iraqis setting up a mortar, and he killed them all with one shot. He said they all just evaporated when the twenty-five-millimeter explosive round hit them, and that his heart "was beating a thousand miles an hour."

Another Marine told me it was his birthday that day. "Quite a birthday party," I said to him. "Not what you expected?"

"Well, we're here so I expected it, I just didn't want to die on my birthday," he told me with a smile.

Another Marine told me he was so excited after seeing all that action, he jerked off when he got back to the staging area.

I chose not to report the most lurid details:

> Marines in the 3rd LAR have spent this day refueling their vehicles, stocking up on food and water and recharging their batteries, preparing for the next battle.
>
> They need rest, after last night, when we wound up in the middle of a fierce firefight in south central Iraq.
>
> Traveling along a dark road headed for a strategic objective, the 3rd LAR came under attack from more than three hundred Iraqis, firing rocket-propelled grenades, mortars, and small arms.

The Marines immediately fired back from their light armored vehicles, with twenty-five-millimeter chain guns, machine guns, and other weapons.

Many of the Iraqis dismounted their vehicles and began running toward our convoy, using sand dunes for cover, popping up and down to get shots off, but the Marines won this battle.

Well over 50 Iraqis were killed. The Marines suffered zero casualties but were surprised at the level of resistance they face.

I closed the piece holding a live rocket-propelled grenade in my hand: "This is one of the RPGs the Marines discovered when they went back to the scene today. If one of these seventy-three-millimeter rounds had hit one of the LAVs, it could've done serious damage."

In an entry in my notebook that day, I wrote:

Exhausting night. Couldn't get comfortable wedged in the back of the LAV. Went live all day on the phone, then with the dish, reporting on our battle the night before. We fed in video including a group of POWs detained near our assembly area. The Lt Col looks exhausted, so do captain and crew, but everyone's hanging in and pushing forward tonight. Much of RTC-7 pushed past us today. Higher command wanted tanks and artillery up front because of the resistance we faced and don't want Marines getting killed, but we're gonna catch up to an artillery unit and provide security for them and may see even more action this evening. Before we left, the Colonel said "it's gonna be a long night!"

We moved forward and parked in a field somewhere and saw more artillery fire and machine guns in the distance. We see flashes and explosions. Finally got to sleep around 12:30 and woke up at 5 feeling a bit better, the first solid four hours of sleep in days.

Tuesday March 25, another log entry:

Convoy at a halt because of fighting up ahead. Small arms, number of different positions, trying to clear out now with heavy artillery to prepare for assault. I look to my left and notice several figures in dark clothing moving across a sand berm and behind a wall. The Captain notices them too, stops the LAV, swings the turret and we surveil for at least 30 minutes. Then he decides to move in for a closer look. Other units pull ahead, scouts dismount, set up on berms surrounding some mud house, we roll up and park and sit for a while, the Captain directing ops with binoculars to his face. It seems incredible that 4 or 5 guys could stop the progress of an entire company but that appears to be the case.

Our convoy continued north, clearing ground along the way, finding wounded Iraqis who became enemy prisoners of war. Massive howitzer rounds regularly shook us to the core from hundreds of meters away. We found culverts packed with explosives, either to cut the road or kill Marines as they passed. We stopped at a farm and heard more rounds of artillery fire, but soon there would be an "operational pause" because of brownout conditions. Massive sandstorms were hitting our area and were expected to last another forty-eight hours.

"More shelling. The thuds shake the door of the LAV I'm leaning against, vibrating my flak jacket," I wrote.

Then, during a phone call to the states, I learned that my reporting was getting a lot of praise, and I wrote that down, too, sounding like an asshole: "Everyone is apparently talking about me back home and what a great job I'm doing and how I'm the hottest thing at Fox. Highlights of my reporting on *Access Hollywood* and *Inside Edition* and *Good Day Live*, and Rush Limbaugh was talking about me on his radio show. Very gratifying. Hope I can make it home safely to reap the benefits."

Then, the "blackest night we've ever seen."

The next morning, my notes continued:

> Rough night to say the least. The sandstorm got progressively worse till visibility was about ten feet. I walked to the nearest LAV and chatted with Staff Sgt Wilkins, he was like "oh my gosh, maybe the Lord is trying to tell us something! I ain't never seen nothing like this before!" One Marine got lost after doing security on post and wound up on the highway, needed an escort back. We sat in the LAV all night, all 7 of us. No one could sleep outside cuz it started pouring

rain. Told stories and swapped gossip for a while, good time, but sleep was painful and difficult.

I shot a standup before the storm completely blacked us out. The video is eerie: yellow and orange and hazy. I'm wearing my full camouflage suit with my helmet, plastic protective goggles, and a bandana covering the rest of my face, holding the Fox microphone:

> We're in the middle of the worst sandstorm we've ever seen. It's gotten progressively worse throughout the day. Early this morning, the wind was blowing a little bit, visibility was several hundred meters, then it got to one hundred, then fifty, then twenty and now you can only see a few feet in front of your face. The wind is gusting well over fifty miles per hour, perhaps sixty, seventy miles per hour. The conditions are just awful. It's like you're taking a bath in dirt out here. They were firing mortars earlier in the day, but we haven't heard any in a while and it's easy to understand why: You cannot see anything out here. But perhaps more incredible than the weather is that a Marine can actually sleep through this. That's Carlucci down there.

Craig Carlucci was curled up on the ground, next to a tire, completely out. At some point the captain told us to wake him up and get him inside, and I swear it took about two minutes to shake him from his slumber. We were all exhausted, and when we actually fell asleep, it was hard and deep.

The next morning, we woke at dawn to another surreal scene. As dirty as we all were, and as dirty as our vehicles had been up until that point, we'd discovered a whole other level of filth. Sand and mud were caked to and covering every inch of everything. Any zippers or pockets left open were now full of dirt. Everything needed to be shaken out, brushed, and scrubbed.

From my notebook:

> Woke up 5-ish. Wind stopped blowing. LAV is a mess. Guys spending the morning cleaning out the vehicle and cleaning their weapons and gear, taking wire brush to the machine gun, etc. Right now, King and Timmons are loading 25 mm shells for the chain gun. Got 'em stretched out on the bench I usually sleep on. We slept with an extra M-16 in the back last night and this morning I was playing with it and posing for pictures, checked it when Galdo handed it to me and it was set on SEMI instead of SAFE. Woke up during the night to an extended barrage of artillery. Awesome sight. The flash, the streak and then a rocket kicks in and boosts the shell, and a delayed boom like a loud clap of thunder.

The scene unfolding around us could best be described as an absolute shit show. Our field had turned into a swamp thanks to the heavy rains that followed the near-hurricane force winds, and some of the other LAVs in our company were in trouble. Two of them were firmly stuck in the mud. One blew a radiator hose while trying to get out and the other almost flipped.

First, Marines tried to pull one of the LAVs out with cables but couldn't because it was stuck too deep in the mud, so they brought in an LAV-R (equipped with a recovery winch). The engines roared and whined, and at some point, I looked over to see a battery of howitzer cannons right next to us, one of them about thirty to forty yards away. We didn't know we'd slept that close to them because we couldn't see anything. The howitzers were by far the loudest big guns the Marines had deployed, and if they'd opened fire it would've been extremely painful!

Meanwhile, the LAV doing the pulling also got stuck, so a third was positioned to help out the others, and before this particular mission was complete, a fourth LAV had to be brought in to help rescue the others. After much tugging and maneuvering, one by one the vehicles were pulled free, and we all gave the men a round of applause.

We met up with Dusty our engineer later that day and fed tape and were getting ready for a live shot when the captain rolled up shouting, "We gotta go!" He got a frag (for fragmentary) order to move north to help out Bravo company, which had come in contact with the enemy using machine guns and mortars.

"Moving closer now," I wrote.

> Pulled off to talk to another unit, convoy of artillery rolls by, troops in 5 & 7 tons with sandbags and machine guns and Humvees with every Marine pointing his rifle out the window. Haze is thick, visibility poor. Conflict continues… Bravo suffers 2 casualties, not serious. Got some Iraqis cornered in a building, trying to get Arabic speaking Marine up front to talk them out and Gwaltney says "blow em up!" Nine more EPWs surrender. Finally drive north to battlefield (from

the 23rd), see two dead Iraqis, at least one in uniform intact, looked like vintage WW2. In fact, the whole scene looked like WW2, with thick haze all around and EPWs in a pen ringed with concertina wire, 30-40 of them.

As we moved up the highway, we got an eyeful:

Spent shell casings and TOW tubes litter the roadside. 100s of vehicles: LAVs, tanks, APCs, Humvees and thousands of Marines, many dug in to fighting positions on berms on both sides of the road. Now passing a large building complex behind a high sand wall, bombed or damaged during battle, the scene of the Bravo Co. contact. The Capt says it was blown up during battle.

Now seeing trucks, pickups and two personnel carriers, heavily damaged and burned, no sign of casualties. Mortar tubes, and boxes of shells in piles.

Watched a convoy of Abrams M1 tanks roll by along with the big beastly APCs and heavily armed Humvees. Very comforting to see the infantry and tanks moving ahead of us. The M1s have a great rep...Marines say NOTHING can stop them.

So after night falls, we roll off to follow the convoy but they're way out in front and it's so dark literally you can't see your hand in front of your face and these guys can't use light, because it would give up their position to the enemy who are likely hiding behind dunes or mud huts or

God knows where else within striking distance. So we're crawling along, inch by inch, the gunner helping to guide the driver, both with NVGs [night vision goggles], the gunner also with thermal sighting and somehow we wind up off the road and on a patch of sand and it feels like we're gonna flip, so now the gunner has gotten off to try and guide King back on the road and may have to use a chem light, cuz otherwise King won't be able to see him anyway and I hear Captain Custis say "Dude, we're in a lot of trouble. We gotta unfuck ourselves before we roll this bitch!" Instead, we back up a 50 meters and park it for the night and Gwaltney says "What a fucking nightmare."

The next morning, I wrote: "The sun is finally shining again and we hope the weather stays clear so we can push north. The Captain tells us today's mission is to guard an airfield along Highway One."

All of the company commanding officers (COs) bring their maps and gather around the front of our LAV. I write in my notes how dirty they all are. You can't imagine just how poor conditions had been and how impossible it was to get clean. Mud was caked on their faces, hands, and clothes, but hygiene seemed to be way down the list of priorities at this point.

Captain Custis told them: "We need to get stacked up on the road right now. You guys don't have time to brief your people! You're gonna have to brief them on the move."

From my notebook:

We hit the hardball, rolling north on Highway One. We pass an abandoned pick-up truck with dead body next to it on the highway, then we see a road sign for Baghdad.

We pass another artillery battery and are now doing a slow cruise scanning the horizon. Captain Custis rides with one hand on his machine gun, the other holding binoculars, wearing green gloves. Now he's unhooked the gun. There may be a threat in the weed covered dunes. The Captain has his plastic covered map propped in front of him in the turret, talks on his headset with a pistol strapped to his vest. Now seeing lots of villagers, farm houses, mud huts, cows and sheep. Many homes lining the road side, small square flat roof buildings made from mud or clay. Galdo says it's a "National Geographic special rolling right by our face."

First Battalion 5th Marines Bravo company out of Camp Pendleton is providing security and their CO is barking orders.

This is not the Lido deck. I don't want people tanning drinking smoking talking, I want those people to think we're professional killers. They take us seriously the sooner we get the job done. We're heading north so pay attention!

Then we moved to an airfield where Cobra helicopters fly over with low air support.

Marine infantry line the roadside. We pass Iraqi sandbag bunkers along the road, now 78 miles from Baghdad. Captain Custis just took us back a couple clicks to retrieve Staff Sergeant Brian's yellow Power Ranger, his son's favorite toy. The kid threw it to his dad as he was leaving for this trip and Custis promised he'd put it on his vehicle when he crossed into Baghdad, so now he has it in his hand. The Power Ranger is missing an arm "but he's still kicking!" says Custis, who's now attaching the toy to one of the antennas with black electrical tape. [I realize this is hardly breaking news, but it's an example of how these warriors stay grounded, with reminders of normal life back home kept close.]

Now we're back on the move, but at a snail's pace. There's heavy shelling up ahead. We see air cover nearby and a big smoke cloud. We pass tanks with nicknames painted on their gun tubes including "Boob Tube," "Boregasm," and "Big Johnson." I just love how in your face these guys are and how well protected we feel. It's like having a gang of your biggest, toughest friends surrounding you wherever you go.

At 3 PM, after all the moving and excitement about heading north, we get word we were involved in a feint (trying to deceive the enemy by going in a different direction). Don't know who did what because of our fake-out but now we're heading south again to where we started this morning! It's so frustrating. The whole crew is pissed and antsy. We don't get back till near sundown, after another two-hour delay on the highway. Some threat off in the distance caused the entire convoy to come to a halt. [This would happen often and was one of the most annoying things about the journey. It felt like it took forever to get *anywhere*.] We get back, find a dry spot in the mud, I roll out my mat and sleeping bag and then deal with power issues with Dusty and New York until late.

It's crazy how you find energy when you have to, even when you're completely spent. In the wee hours of Friday, March 28, we got woken up *twice* to calls of "GAS GAS GAS!" I was fast asleep both times, war weary and more exhausted than I'd ever been in my life, but the threat of a painful death is a powerful motivation.

Each time I scrambled to get my mask on, grabbed my shoes, and ran into the back of the vehicle. Once I had to wake Sergeant Timmons who was still asleep in the dirt next to me. We went to MOPP Level 4, which was the worst part, because we had to put on our boots and hood and gloves and then sit there for twenty minutes or so until someone gave the all-clear. The second time Galdo had to wake me. He told me he called my name three times and then shook me awake and says I finally sparked up as soon as he said, "GAS GAS GAS." I couldn't find my socks, so I put my boots on with bare feet. It was also freezing outside, by the way, very uncomfortable. Both times we thought it might be the real deal. In my notes, I called the experience "very unsettling."

The second time we got the frantic warning, we all packed ourselves inside the LAV, and Captain Custis realized Carlucci wasn't there. Gwaltney asked permission to open the hatch, jumped out, and yelled his name from inside his mask but got no response, so the captain told Timmons to go out and check Carlucci's skirmish hole. We all pictured him dead out there.

Timmons was sitting to the inside of me, so I asked if he was ready, and when he said he was, I popped open the door, jumped out, let him by and jumped back in, closed the door and latched it, and slid over to make room, worried the whole time I might've been slimed. A short time later, Timmons came back with Carlucci who seemed dazed but fine, and of course, there was no gas attack.

We crashed again, and I woke at 4:50 a.m. for a live shot, only to find out they didn't need me till later, so I wrote in my notes: "I take a leak, do 75 crunches and 30 push-ups, pack my stuff and we roll."

Later that day, Colonel Clardy gave another briefing to his team, which I noted "was one of his best and most inspirational addresses during the march up. Part informational, part motivational."

"I don't think you're tired!" Clardy told the men. "I look in your eyes and I think you're getting enough sleep. We're out here to kill the enemy and accomplish the task. You guys can get it done. You guys are kicking ass and taking names. This is a good organization, fucking great organization, and I'm very proud to be a part of it."

He breaks down the Iraqi troop strength:

Seeing forces north of Baghdad. The city is crawling with Republican Guard, special Republican Guard and retired leaders coming back to make sure the men fight. We've collected (not even trying) twenty-one 82-millimeter mortars with 800+ rounds, over 20,000 .762 rounds, over fifty gas masks, 84 RPGs with hundreds of rounds, 54 machine guns, 42 record books, 12 ID cards, one passport, hundreds of grenades, many pounds of C-4. All troops here carrying gas masks. We've traveled 386 kilometers, roughly 142 to go. No clear number of dead but they're dragging off the victims. Found a grenade with orange powder inside, inspecting it to find out what it is. Iraqis fighting in onesies and twosies [yes, he actually said that], sometimes with tanks. Progress: thought it would take two weeks, we're fine timewise.

Colonel Clardy says he's:

satisfied they're fighting. We are combat troops. If we're going to war, let's fucking do it. Gotta keep our guard up, don't get complacent! I have no doubt we'll accomplish the mission we're assigned, but my goal and your goal ought to be to keep these Marines alive. The enemy is organized and persistent but can't shoot for shit. The threat is primarily in the northwest. We have to be prepared to the east also. More conventional as we head north, more armor, more artillery. Use your thermals. See them at two clicks and bomb the shit out of them! Our strength is our weapon systems. We gotta be able to use them. I'm exceptionally proud to be here with y'all. My Marines are handling themselves with discipline and have the capability to work on the fly. I'm comfortable pushing you out to work independently. Very proud of the way you're handling yourselves. The leadership is exceptional. Trying to spread out missions and let everyone gain experience. These lessons will pay off in the long run.

Clardy said he believed that as we moved north, the threat to the south would disappear.

"The Intel from translators is that the Iraqi civilians want us here. Fuel, water, and ammo are no concern but chow is an issue," he said, and we all knew it, since we'd been forced to cut our intake down to one MRE a day.

From the start we were limited to two meals a day, which wasn't a problem since each bag had two thousand total calories with a variety of stuff inside. There was a main meal with a heating bag you'd activate with water, there were crackers and a pouch of cheese or peanut butter or jelly, along with random other items and some kind of dessert.

It was like opening a prize to find out if you'd gotten Skittles, or M&M's, or Starburst, which was my least favorite. We often made trades to get what he wanted. I actually gained some infamy in the battalion for apparently being the first to mark bags of MREs with a sharpie. I preferred the chicken noodle or chicken with rice, and when I'd find one, I'd set it aside for myself and write "Rick's Chow: Don't Touch!"

This apparently violated USMC ethics. The guys told me you were supposed to reach into the box and pull one out and eat whatever you grabbed. You weren't supposed to cherry pick, and you *definitely* weren't supposed to write your name on them, and more than once Gwaltney took the bags I'd set aside and ate them himself. In my notes, I wrote, with mock outrage: "Gwaltney is a glutton and a thief!"

In any event, we'd gotten far ahead of our supply chain, so the captain informed us we had to cut back. It wasn't a huge deal for us, but we *were* kinda hungry, and I reported on it because it kept it real, and it was part of what was happening.

But the Pentagon didn't like that angle, especially after getting calls from families upset that their Marines might be starving while fighting for their country. Marine brass reached out to division headquarters, and former General John Kelly, then the division commander, got in touch with Clardy, who pulled me aside and asked me to stop mentioning our shortage of chow.

When I spoke to him recently, he told me he remembered that call.

"I wasn't able to hear your broadcast specifically but apparently you were complaining about the lack of food and John Kelly got me on the radio, asking me to ask you to tone that down a bit."

"Did he use saltier language than that?" I asked.

"Yeah, it would've been something more like 'I need you to do me a favor. Tell Rick Leventhal to stop talking about food,'" with a couple expletives along the way, Clardy told me, saying that Kelly told him, "It's not helpful to hear from the Pentagon that people are upset our Marines are hungry."

But this was one time I didn't comply with the colonel's request. I told him I was sorry, but I was there to report on what was happening, and this was one of the things that was happening. I agreed not to dwell or focus on it, but if an anchor asked me about it, I would answer honestly. I wasn't affecting our operational security. I wasn't violating any embed rules, and, as it turned out, the food drought didn't last much longer anyway.

Another story the Pentagon was pissed about was the one we broke about chemical drums allegedly being unloaded by Iraqis in chem suits. New York was very excited about it and playing it up big. I told the colonel that I wanted to report it when he gave me the intel and he said it was OK, but we later had to dial it back because there were questions about the accuracy of the information. We did a correction on air and never talked about it again.

This was also the day I read the NCAA's final eight teams over a loudspeaker to the artillery crew and got cheers as I read the names. Most of the men had no access to news from home and we did, so after a couple guys asked me about the tournament, I got an update from New York and then shared it with them. It was a welcome light moment during a very tough stretch.

On March 28 at 1 p.m. local time, I wrote:

> We're on the move again, just a short trip to check out some stuff but who knows. I wash my hair for the first time in eight days, shaved for the first time in five days, shit for the first time in 3 to 4 days, feel 100% better. Hooked up the video phone to a power source in the vehicle for the first time. We need to reconfigure it but hoping it makes a dramatic difference in our ability to file.
>
> We cruise through farmland in shrub. Very rough ride. Marines dismount to check out a Bedouin camp. Find no weapons. I do phoners, then get word to shut down. Centcom [Central Command] was unhappy with our report on Iraqis unloading

barrels in full MOPP gear, probably because [Fox's] Brian Kilmeade [inadvertently] began distorting facts while ad-libbing on air. Oh well. Sucks but don't wanna piss these people off and definitely don't wanna get kicked out. Was looking forward to doing more on-cam today but we've been stuck in this field for hours.

The next day, we got bad news. I'd been racking up thousands of minutes on our Thuraya sat phones since the embed began, checking voicemail, calling friends and family and the foreign desk on a constant basis, and going live with them while we were on the road, since we tried but failed to get our videophone to work while rolling. But that morning we were told we couldn't use them anymore because they had a built-in GPS system and the Marine Commanders learned the Iraqis might be using them to target our location and send artillery in our direction. The Thuraya phones were now strictly off-limits.

From my notes of March 29:

> This will put a serious hurt in my ability to file and my ability to stay in touch. By the way, slept very well last night although it was freezing outside. Woke up to do video phone lives and had power issues. Poor Christian. Working his ass off and struggled for an hour to get the thing working.

This was probably the most frustrating part of our journey. The video phones absolutely sucked, but most days they were our only way to get on TV with any kind of video. It would take us up to an hour of constant re-dials just to get connected to New York, and then if the signal didn't drop out it still looked like shit, really chopping and breaking up into video squares anytime we made the slightest move or pan. For someone used to doing "show and tell" live shots, this was extremely limiting, especially when there was so much to show around us.

> Luckily, we were able to link up with Dusty, who had the dish out and connected so we spent the day doing satellite lives over by some LAVs hanging out, and finally got asked about how we went to the bathroom by [anchor Rick] Folbaum during the 3 AM hour. Hilarious. Got a Marine to demo with a shovel.

This was one of my favorite live shots. I loved keeping it real, and we took the opportunity to show the world exactly how we did our business in the sand. Bet you didn't see that on CNN!

On the 30th, I wrote in my notes: "not an operational pause, but a tactical delay." This was another thing that Clardy pulled me aside to talk about. I guess they didn't like us reporting on pauses because it made the military look bad, like they were taking breaks during a war. But that's basically what it was. A chance to recharge batteries, prepping for the big fight, insuring supply lines are where they need to be.

"Time is on our side," Clardy told us. "We're being smart, making sure all is well for the fourth quarter."

DIRTY TIME

Christian and I really bonded during our time in the desert. When I was worn out, he'd pick me up, and vice versa, and some of my favorite moments were when he'd go on a rant about how dirty he was.

One day, during some much-needed down time, we found time to do some personal cleaning and Christian was in a funny mood, so I grabbed his camera and interviewed him, looking like an absolute mess.

Me to Christian: "Have you ever been this dirty?"

Christian: "I don't think I can ever claim being as filthy and disgusting as I am right now. Here we have a pile of hygienic materials—that's my new shirt, it'll be the first time I'm changing my shirt in about two weeks, and I'll have a new pair of socks on for the first time in about a week and a half."

"How about the underwear?" I ask.

"I'm sticking with the same old gym shorts which are pretty dirty but they're underneath, so—they could be worse so I'm gonna save those for a dirtier day."

"How 'bout the privates, gonna wash those?"

"Oh, we're gonna wash all over!"

Christian had a huge grin and we both laughed, and I asked: "Are you pretty excited about this?"

"The excitement cannot even be explained," he said with great animation, "and I will still be filthy after this, but the funny part is I will feel clean because it's all relative, I will feel clean but even after this hygiene, I will be so dirty that if I were to show up back home, in the condition I'm in *after* I hygiene, people would tell me to get out! But I'll feel clean!"

He was on a roll, so I kept going: "Yesterday you were supposed to hygiene but weren't able to, how disappointed were you?"

"It was a total morale killer," he told me, deadpan. "It took a lot to bounce back from that!"

We had time for a live shot later that day, and I reported on our pause, unscripted and brutally honest.

> No one likes to sit around, and even if we're doing missions in this area, quite often they're not the most exciting missions, and these guys want to go to Baghdad. These guys want to see action. What we've discovered is war doesn't necessarily mean you're fighting every day. War can be boring. War can be slow. War can be standing around waiting for the next thing to happen or the next orders to come down.

Later, in a live shot for *Fox & Friends*, Brian Kilmeade mentioned Greg Kelly, who was embedded with the Army's 3rd ID and revealed that his unit was playing a classic song as they reached the edge of the capital city.

"Wait, hold on a second, did Brian just report the Army was singing a Simon & Garfunkel song as they drove toward Baghdad?" I shook my head and turned and looked at the group of Marines we were hanging with that day, including my man, Cody.

"Do you guys even know any Simon & Garfunkel songs?" The camera pans over to them and back to me. "There's absolutely no way a Marine would be caught singing any Simon & Garfunkel, I'm here to tell you. 'The Sound of Silence'? I betcha they'll come up with some different kinds of music, to be singing as they…" The anchors back in New York are bantering with me, and I laugh and turn back to the men.

"What song, wait, Cody, what song are you gonna sing when you roll into Baghdad?"

Cody has his helmet off, his head shaved, wearing his camos and vest, leaning with one arm against his LAV, and doesn't miss a beat:

"'Kill 'Em All' by Metallica!" He says with a smile.

"There you go, I knew it was gonna be something heavy metal, I knew it!"

The next day we were back on the road and encountered enemy fire, and in my notes I wrote that the Marines "erased the threat. We then go to where the men were firing from and find AK-47s, boxes of mortars, and Iraqi army uniforms scattered amongst some small trees and bushes."

We were tasked with guarding a major intersection where dozens of Marine vehicles were staged, and learned of a major discovery about a mile down the road, so we drove there to find huge missiles on a flatbed trailer, and I shot another unscripted show-and-tell piece:

It's 10 a.m. Tuesday April 1st and this is no April Fool's Joke. [I point to one of the back panels of the vehicle which has "DANGER" spray painted on it in red.] "It says 'DANGER' for a reason on this truck. The combat engineers who came down this road to set up a roadblock and found this truck with a tarp over it, took off the tarp and discovered *two* al-Samood missiles. These things are twenty-four feet long [I'd done a rough measurement myself] and they can carry, I'm told, chemical warheads. The Marines tested these missiles, actually brought their pigeon out here, sort of an early warning. They use it as an early warning device, left the pigeon out here for a while to see if that reacted to it, it did not, the pigeon was fine so they don't believe there are any chemical or biological agents in the missiles, but these are some of the missiles that Iraq was supposed to be destroying [per their agreement with the United Nations] clearly they didn't destroy these. In fact, they were hiding these.

We also got a glimpse at one of the first drones deployed in the war, called a dragon eye. About three feet long, it looked like a small plane with propellers and was equipped with a camera the operator could control and view real-time video from a hand-held unit. They launched it using a huge rubber band, and I actually held one end of it while a Marine stretched it out, holding the unmanned aerial vehicle (UAV), then letting it go. It took off over my head, and we then viewed the images in awe. "Oh my God," I said as I looked in the glasses that acted as a viewfinder, "I can see fields and berms and..." I found it revolutionary, and I guess it was. We hadn't seen this technology before, and it would be years before drones became common toys for civilians back home.

That night, we embarked on another push north, driving all night long into the next morning. When we reached the Tigris, we rolled past a bunch of war-weary Marines camped out along the road near the bridge. They were dirty and looked exhausted, some eating chow, others sharing a smoke or relaxing on piles of their gear. Many waved at the camera as we went by.

As we got closer to Baghdad, the landscape started to change, becoming more urban and more crowded. We encountered real traffic, civilian vehicles crowding the road, and locals in robes and headdresses, some waving white flags. We headed off into the farmland on another recon mission. It was hot and dusty, and I did another standup, popped out of the back hatch. I looked and sounded miserable:

"This is by far the longest, hottest, dirtiest, most miserable day we've had so far in this embed process. We were up at 11:30 p.m. last night, left our assembly area and began driving. We were up all night long. We couldn't sleep because we were inside the vehicle and you can't get comfortable in there."

We arrived at a sprawling Iraqi training center, about sixteen miles outside Baghdad. It was a long two-story building in the middle of a big flat area and reminded me of a horse-race-track pavilion. We followed the Marine scouts as they carefully approached and entered the building with their weapons at the ready, like a SWAT team making a forced entry, except the doors were all open or unlocked. Inside we found a picture of Saddam Hussein hanging on the wall but no signs of life. The Marines then began inspecting the rest of the base and found huge caches of weapons and ammo. I did another standup for a piece we'd edit later that day:

> Behind me are bunker after bunker, most of them filled with ammunition, tank shells, mortars, RPGs, missile launchers, completely surrounding us here. If you look behind us you can see other vehicles with the 3rd Light Armored

Reconnaissance Battalion, and way off in the distance a large building down there that we checked earlier this morning with Marine scouts as we followed them in, and they found a lot of Iraqi uniforms and other types of equipment, it looked like a garage of sorts. Also it looked like they used it as a control tower for a firing range.

One of the things that struck me was how much of the munitions was simply left behind. The Marines weren't equipped to carry it all and didn't always have the time or ability to destroy it all. I have no doubt that some of it (or much of it) was used in the months and years ahead against U.S. forces occupying Iraq, including in the form of improvised explosive devices (IEDs) or roadside bombs. They did take out some armored vehicles abandoned on the sides of the road, lighting them up with C-4 plastic explosives or the twenty-five-millimeter chain guns, and we heard rounds cooking off inside some of them as we drove past.

That night our gunner, Sergeant Gwaltney, spotted another Iraqi armored vehicle hidden in a field not far from us, and it was unclear if it was occupied. Captain Custis gave the orders to light it up, and Gwaltney fired numerous rounds before finally hitting and destroying the vehicle, which we inspected the next morning and determined no soldiers had been inside. (We later gave Gwaltney a hard time because his aim was a bit off.)

We also ran into some Iraqi locals that day who were friendly and welcoming, and a Marine translator was brought in so that the captain and others could have a conversation with them, to try to get intel and also warn the men not to approach or interfere with U.S. forces in the area. They shook hands but then we had to get back in the vehicles in a hurry. The captain learned of a friendly fire incident nearby, and we raced to the scene. A

Cobra attack helicopter had mistaken one of Alpha Company's forward deployed platoons for the enemy and opened fire with its twenty-millimeter Gatling gun, wounding two Marines, one of them pretty badly. They called for a medivac, and while we waited, the pilot of the Cobra that had mistakenly attacked landed and came over to apologize to the men he'd wounded, in one of the most moving scenes of the war I'd witnessed.

The platoon commander, Lieutenant John Bitonti, was pissed. Two of his men were hurt, and their LAV was damaged, riddled by the Gatling gun, some of the tires shredded and some of the gear strapped to the sides damaged or on fire. The safety of the men was his responsibility, and he stayed by the side of the more badly wounded man until the medivac chopper arrived and he was loaded into it on a stretcher. We later learned he survived his wounds.

It was another incredibly long, hot, and dusty day, and nearly a month into the embed, we're growing very, very weary. As we rolled through some random farmland in what looked like the middle of nowhere, searching for the temporary command post (CP), Christian is in another funny mood, so I grab his camera again to record his impressions as we creeped along, hesitantly traveling down a berm barely wide enough for our LAV.

"Words cannot even describe just how dirty I am." Then he uses some kind of valley girl accent and has a conversation with himself:

"Oh yeah when I was in Iraq I got really dirty, I was so dirty. 'Oh really that's cool it was dirty there huh?' Nobody will ever appreciate or understand or know what an absolute tragedy this whole situation is. 'Oh really you guys were dirty there? You guys were dirty? Oh, you didn't shower? Oh that's gross, wow.'"

At this point I pan over to reveal some farmers with a tractor standing in a group checking us out. It appears our driver is lost or isn't sure which way to go next.

"Where the fuck is the CP? Do you know where the CP is? Which way to the CP?" Christian jokingly yells toward the men. Then he turns to me and deadpans: "They don't know where the CP is."

"I don't think the captain knows where the CP is," I reply. The driver starts backing up. "We're about to go in this canal," I say. Christian is losing it.

"Ohhhh my God," he says. I pan down as he rubs his arm above his watch, brushing some of the dirt off. "Yup, it's dirty time!"

The next day we made the very difficult decision to leave the 3rd LAR and join another unit. Saying goodbye was tough. We'd earned these guys' respect and shared an incredible adventure. But we also knew a transfer made a lot of sense. We'd been discussing the possibility for days, once we learned that our guys weren't going into Baghdad and instead were making a wide loop around the city and heading north.

Colonel Clardy didn't really know or couldn't share what their next mission would be but admitted it would likely not be nearly as exciting as what we'd find inside the city limits. The LAR wasn't equipped to fight in an urban setting. It wasn't their mission.

Getting to Baghdad had been Christian's and my goal from Day One, and while we had bonded with our guys and felt a tremendous sense of loyalty to them and had reported some amazing stories thanks to their service and bravery, we felt we could contribute a lot more to the network if we made it to the capital. Public Affairs agreed and facilitated our transfer to the 2nd Battalion, 23rd Marines (2/23), a big group of reservists out of Las Vegas and Salt Lake City nicknamed the Saints & Sinners.

Before we left LAR, we said our goodbyes to all the guys, including Colonel Clardy. I asked him recently if he was sad to see us go that day. He told me:

> Yes. I remember you and I had a conversation at the side of the road. I had no idea what we'd encounter when we went north and you were determined to get to Baghdad but you were part of the battalion. You'd been with us for a while and we considered you one of us, back then and to this day, not just because you were with us but because you acted like one of us. You helped the Marines, talked to the Marines, behaved like you belonged there and they trusted you. It's hard to earn a Marine's trust. You have to earn that. You did, and at that point you became one of ours.

Looking back, I still believe it was the right move considering all that we saw and did over the next couple of weeks, but we also missed out on a huge story. A few days after the 3rd LAR dropped us off on the edge of the city, they rescued a group of American POWs, including Army Specialist Shoshana Johnson, the first Black female soldier ever captured in combat.

Colonel Clardy later told me we absolutely would've been there when the POWs were found and would've gotten the first images and interviews before the POWs were flown out to safety.

I couldn't believe it when I got the call about what we'd missed. We were really bummed, but we couldn't be in two places at once and took comfort in the fact that the LAR didn't do a whole lot between the time they dropped us off and the time they rescued the POWs.

It would've been a stale few days, and we of course would've regretted not going to Baghdad, where we wound up seeing and reporting on *many* cool stories before finally heading home.

BAGHDAD

Meeting up with the 2/23 proved difficult. A Humvee picked us up at our designated rendezvous point, transferring our gear from the LAV to the back of the vehicle, and we made our way toward the 2/23 command post at a former Iraqi Republican Guard base in eastern Baghdad, but we had to stop and wait at the side of a road because the 2/23 was in the middle of a nasty firefight that lasted for hours.

Several of the Marines were wounded in the horrific exchange of fire, and it was near midnight when they finally returned to the compound and we could meet up with them there. We were welcomed by Colonel Rick Cooper, a southern California sheriff when he wasn't serving the Marines, who informed us we'd need to be up again at 5 a.m. because his men would be headed back into town where the firefight took place to try to draw out the enemy and finish them off.

We slept on hard marble floors inside the main building and got up before dawn, got our gear together, and joined the Marines for what turned out to be a long, frightening walk down streets absolutely littered with spent shell casings from the night before.

This was one of our most dangerous missions yet and seemed absolutely insane to Christian and me. We were sitting ducks, walking amongst a battalion of reserve Marines spread out across a few city blocks, actually trying to draw fire from the windows and rooftops of the buildings around us. Colonel Cooper explained if any Iraqis were foolish enough to shoot at his Marines, they'd be revealing their position and the Marines would be able to kill them.

It turned out that this was the only one of the USMC's nine reserve infantry battalions called to serve in the initial invasion of Iraq. Its members had been called up to Camp Pendleton sixteen months earlier, just after 9/11, to be ready to respond to any more terror attacks in the U.S., and after a full year, they expected to return to their day jobs. Instead, they were told they'd be going to war.

They'd been separated from their families for almost a year and a half and dispatched first to a base far from their homes and then to unfamiliar territory in the Middle East. Most never expected they'd actually be fighting overseas. They were teachers, cops, firefighters, federal agents, salesmen, even casino workers.

One guy designed costumes for strippers. Many of them told us they'd signed up as reservists for the benefits, spending one weekend a month at a base, free to live their lives the rest of the time, taking the risk they'd never actually get called up to go to war.

Many took pay cuts when they started collecting their military salary and some lost their jobs at home while they were away. But we found these part-timers to be as capable as any of the guys we'd been with so far, and we never heard any of them complain. They were focused and determined and had amazing stories to tell.

We passed craters in some of the streets, and spent machine gun cartridges and brass shells were everywhere. At one point,

I called in and reported on our mission, and the anchors were incredulous at how dangerous it seemed. It was incredibly unsettling, and I'm not sure I'd been that nervous at any point so far, even during the firefight after we got ambushed. The streets were eerily quiet, and no shot was ever fired that day, but we were on edge the entire time, waiting for hell to rain down on us. We saw residents peeking out windows and some gathered in doorways. The Marines kicked in the door of one of the homes where shots were fired from the night before, and we followed them inside, but they found no one. Whoever had attacked them had shrunk back into the shadows.

We then made our way to a housing complex where Iraqi anti-aircraft guns had been parked between the homes and watched as the Marines explosives team disabled the weapons with C-4. We wound up sleeping in the dirt of an empty lot in the neighborhood, and the next morning saw action when some insurgents or local opportunists tried to drive off in a couple of Iraqi military vehicles that had been parked nearby. The Marines lit up the vehicles with a hail of gunfire, but the carjackers bailed and ran when the shooting started and apparently weren't hit. One of the vehicles was a small box truck used to control surface-to-air missiles capable of taking out coalition jets.

Minutes later we found one of those missiles on the back of an Iraqi truck, which had a cool-looking green license plate with Arabic lettering that looked like "007." I managed to remove the plate and stuck it in my pack as a souvenir to take home. Then I shot a standup, holding a large shell in my hand, walking past a disabled and ancient-looking wheeled vehicle with an anti-aircraft gun in the back:

"The Marines are also busy searching for weapons and ammo and finding plenty of it, including six of these anti-aircraft weapons and ten buildings packed with explosives in this one site alone. They say they also found a school filled with room after room of ammo." -

We then went with the company of Marines to the school and were astonished at what they'd found. Christian followed me with the camera as I walked the halls and revealed what was inside the room.

> We're now walking inside the school which has been secured by Marines with the 2nd Battalion 23rd Marines. This classroom, emptied of desks, now filled with cases and cases of RPG rounds, the rocket propelled grenades with the rounds inside, six of them inside each of those boxes, and over here [we walk into another classroom] another one hundred cases, all full of the RPGs, in fact here's an open case right here, you can see what they look like, these things are lethal. They kill tanks, they kill armored vehicles, and let's walk over this way because there's another classroom over here that has even more ammunition.
>
> [Christian follows me down a hallway to reveal the next stash.]
>
> You can see over here some of it stored in the hallway here. Clearly Saddam Hussein and his men knew the U.S. forces would not bomb schools, so this is where they put most of their stuff and here's another classroom just full of RPGs.

A Marine was standing inside so I did a quick interview with him:

"Sergeant, how dangerous are these rockets?"

"These rockets have been taking out some of our light armored vehicles, our hummers, our AVs, stuff like that. They take potshots at us with them from rooftops and they're very dangerous, very dangerous to mounted and dismounted troops."

"This is the last thing you want to see in the hands of an opposition fighter?" I ask.

"That's right sir, it's the last thing I want to see or any Marine wants to see, these are by far the most dangerous thing to us that they have, they can get them around very easily, one man can carry two or three of them, they can store them in rooms like this..."

After we finish shooting our story, the Marines say it's time to head out. I'm shocked. "What about all the weapons and ammo in there?" I ask the commanding officer. "You're just gonna leave it for locals to take?" I couldn't believe they'd just walk away from all that firepower that could and probably would eventually be used against them.

He explained to me they didn't have the manpower or equipment to pack up and haul it all away while completing the rest of their missions. It would also be incredibly dangerous. Any enemy fighter could fire into the building while they were there, and the resulting explosions would surely kill them all.

The same would be true for any vehicles used to haul the stuff. It also wasn't feasible to simply blow up the school with all the munitions inside because it was in a residential neighborhood and would put citizens and private property at risk. Instead, the Marines trusted some locals to guard the facility and headed back toward base, stopping so their medics could treat some wounded Iraqis.

This was a completely different experience for us. We were now patrolling crowded city streets in Humvees, inside a city still bustling despite the conflict. Most Iraqis would stop and stare at us, and little kids would chase after our vehicles, looking for candy or other gifts. We knew danger lurked around every corner, but we were rarely challenged or shot at.

One morning, after sleeping in the dirt in a neighborhood of unfinished homes, we woke up to learn that the company's NBC pigeon had been killed overnight, so we did a tongue-in-cheek story about it. I interviewed Major Tom West, a Beverly Hills police officer I became good friends with during my time with the 2/23. We fed the story back live using our satellite dish. I had the microphone in one hand and a feather in the other:

> Before the Marines headed into Baghdad, each company was given a pigeon as an early warning sign to alert them if there might be a chemical or biological weapons attack.
>
> Well, the second battalion 23rd Marines pigeon's name was Kent after their former commanding officer. This was his cage but there was an unfortunate accident overnight and Kent is no more. Major Tom West is here to explain what happened to this very important bird.

"Unfortunately, we did suffer a casualty in the company," Kent told me with a straight face. "Our first member of the company to be killed in action was a pigeon. Somehow in the middle of the night, an infiltrator came through our lines and got into the cage and devoured Kent."

"And the infiltrator in this case was a mangy dog?" I asked.

"Probably, that's our best guess, may have been a Special ops type, got in and got out totally undetected."

"Is there an effort underway now to find the killer?"

"When we woke up we did see several dogs in our lines; we flushed them out but ever since then we haven't seen any."

"And what about Kent? What will you do?"

"Well, he'll be posthumously promoted to lance corporal—he was a private first class at the time—and we would bury his remains but there are none to bury."

Later, just a few miles from our location, one of the most memorable moments of the war took place, when Iraqi civilians and U.S. Army soldiers tore down a statue of Saddam Hussein in Baghdad's Firdos Square. As badly as we wanted to go, the Marines said they couldn't take us there, so we fired up the videophone on the hood of a Humvee and got the return feed of Fox's live coverage on the small grainy screen and a bunch of the guys crowded around to watch it unfold. There were lots of smiles.

Later, we moved to a highly secure compound that the 2/23 took over as one of its temporary bases, and after we were given a lay of the land, we shot a lengthy show and tell from the roof of one of the buildings. It was all ad-lib, and I remember it being one of the most difficult standups I did during the embed. There was a lot I wanted to fit in, and I kept stumbling or forgetting the name of a building or failing to mention another, and Christian had to follow along with my description of each of the locations I wanted to talk about. I was known for being very efficient on camera, rarely making mistakes. I'd typically knock out a standup in two or three takes. Sometimes just one was enough, but I must've attempted this monologue ten or fifteen times before I got it right:

> We're on the roof of the Iraqis' Ministry of Intelligence, their equivalent to the CIA. This building behind me here is the Iraqi equivalent of the Pentagon. This facility was seized by Marines with the 2nd Battalion, 23rd Marines after they were in a very fierce firefight. [Here, Christian zooms in on an intersection at least a quarter mile away, beyond the compound walls, then pans to show the damaged houses before coming back to me for the rest of the show and tell.]

> Fox Company was located at that intersection over there, began taking fire from RPGs, AK-47s, and machine guns from buildings across the street, from that compound over there and also from this row of houses over here which as you can see was pretty heavily damaged by airstrikes to support the Marines on the ground. They then came in here to this facility and found all sorts of evidence of what the Iraqis were doing at this facility.

> These buildings over here, we're told, were barracks for the Republican Guard and for Defense Ministry officials, and the rest of these buildings were housing intelligence agents and other government workers, and by the way, up in the distance there you can see the fires are still burning across downtown Baghdad. Some of

them have been burning for several days. Over here to the left, you can see one of the buildings was heavily damaged by a Tomahawk cruise missile. [The front of the building was completely cratered during Operation Shock and Awe on one of the first nights of the war, and it reminded me of what the federal building in Oklahoma City looked like after Timothy McVeigh detonated a truck bomb out front.]

Down here in the center of the courtyard, there is an Iraqi prison of sorts, and to the right of that is what appears to be a subway entrance. That is actually the entrance to a very, very large underground bunker that is home to row after row and stack after stack of documents, thousands and thousands of documents that are believed to be sort of personnel files, files on Iraqi people who the government may have been keeping an eye on, Iraqi dissidents or people who they [the government] thought might be causing some trouble.

Christian followed a team of Marines down into the basement where documents were stored. Some of the files were burned at the edges, suggesting that Iraqis tried to torch them before making a hasty exit. There were boxes and boxes of printed pages and photos of countless Iraqis believed to have been tortured and possibly killed while imprisoned at the compound.

The jails there were heavily used, and equipment that appeared designed for torture was visible in some of the cells. During our time at the facility, locals kept showing up with pictures of family members, asking if they might be inside. When they learned the place was empty, some of them broke down in tears.

We joined the 2/23 on more missions, including clearing another Iraqi military compound with more stockpiles of ammo. This time, the Marines hauled them out to dispose of later.

We also took a trip to the United Nations compound, which had been heavily looted after Saddam lost control of the city. In fact, looters were still there when Marines arrived for the first time.

Vehicles were stripped, offices emptied, and other stuff stolen, but we found an office inside that hadn't been touched since the UN workers left. It was apparently where the weapons inspectors were based.

There were chem suits and a gas mask on the floor and photos of the UN workers on the walls with funny captions written in English. There was also a big map on the wall of the city with arrows added, pointing to sites of interest to the inspectors, primarily government offices including the public health department, a university chemical lab, the vaccine institute, and a drug and medicine facility.

It wasn't clear if the weapons inspectors had been able to visit all the locations, and it definitely looked like they'd left the building in a hurry.

At this point, Christian and I had run out of steam. We had lost considerable weight and had endured incredibly long hours in brutal conditions, and we were both ready to pack it in, especially with the knowledge that far more reporters and photographers were starting to flood into Baghdad, now that most of the danger was over. We found out that Fox had a team ready to relieve us, basically handling mop-up duty. We'd done the heavy lifting and would be welcomed with heavy praise and an offer of significant time off when we got home.

The journey back to Kuwait City was brutal. Traveling with the military isn't like flying commercial. You're often at the mercy of circumstance. Even after reserving seats on a helicopter or transport plane, you could be bounced off if someone higher ranking or with a greater need to travel showed up.

This happened to me numerous times over the years during my trips overseas. We also had to sometimes wait many hours or days for an available lift, with the same possibility of losing seats. On our way back, we sat for hours at a helicopter landing pad before finally catching a lift to another base, where we had to haul our heavy gear to a building that seemed like it was miles away, only to discover they didn't have a record of us needing passage back to Kuwait City.

I remember battling with the guys there to get us seats on the next plane out, which was critical if I was going to make the commercial flight I'd booked home from Kuwait City to New York. We did manage to make it out of there, and I can vividly remember showing up at the Kuwaiti hotel we'd left seven weeks earlier, as some of our colleagues were coming out the front doors of the lobby.

They were happy to see us of course and approached us to give us "welcome back" hugs—and then recoiled when they saw (and maybe smelled) just how dirty and disheveled we were. We all laughed about it and then Christian and I got our rooms and headed upstairs.

I hadn't truly bathed in over a month, so I took a ten-minute hot shower, then got in the tub and soaked for about an hour more, before getting back in the shower for another rinse. It may have been the most rewarding bathing experience of my life.

When I got back to the states, I felt raw, exhausted, and a bit angry. It was actually a really tough adjustment, and I totally understood why many members of the military suffer from post-traumatic stress disorder. They are deployed for many months and even years at a time, in often brutal or horrific conditions. We'd been in the war zone for about nine weeks, and I was a wreck. I found myself getting really annoyed at people for not appreciating what they had, for taking things for granted. The only way you can truly appreciate a cold drink, a warm bed, or a hot shower is to be deprived of them for an extended time. "You people don't have any idea what it's really like out there," I'd think to myself. I also couldn't imagine covering a "normal" story again. Nothing seemed significant enough. I took the next few weeks off, did some traveling, including three trips to Las Vegas, and struggled to re-adjust.

Eventually I went back to work, and my first story was for *Special Report* about a really young political candidate somewhere in upstate New York that the show's producers had heard about and decided would make a good feature. My suit didn't fit very well since I hadn't gained the weight back, and I had a really hard time getting motivated for the interviews and writing the script. "Who cares?" I thought to myself. "This is stupid. It's not *real* news. The real news is happening in Iraq."

It took me a while to get over this anger and resentment, but one thing I've never lost is my deep respect for the men and women who serve our nation. They are our truest heroes, doing tough work in often harsh conditions for low pay and little appreciation, and yet I rarely, if ever, heard any of them complain. The Marines, airmen, soldiers, and sailors I met along the way were sharp, tough, respectful, and committed to their job and their country and they always had my back, so I will always have theirs.

CHAPTER 6

LIBYA

REPORTER'S NOTEBOOK· LIVE SHOT EXCERPT·

"We're in Benghazi, Libya's second-largest city, firmly in opposition control, but just ninety minutes south of us, rebels are fighting for their lives in the town of Ajdabiya. We went there this morning to survey damage from yesterday's airstrikes and almost got hit by another."

People always ask about Iraq and Afghanistan, but rarely about Libya, which was one of the most remarkable and inspiring experiences of my career.

I spent weeks there during the uprising against Muammar Gaddafi, without the benefit of U.S. Marines or U.S. Army soldiers watching my back. Instead, we rolled from the Egyptian border to city after city, from Tobruk to Ajdabiya to Benghazi to Misrata with our own private security guard and a small crew of locals, well-connected guys who knew the terrain and could talk their way past checkpoints, driving us from our hotels to hospitals treating wounded fighters, and to and from the front lines and other dangerous locations, translating for our interviews and protecting us from the more aggressive young thugs who may or may not have been mixed up with terrorists.

Our Libyan driver had a shotgun under his seat and a pistol in his waistband, and fortunately never used either of them while working for us, and I'm not sure it would've helped, considering the kind of arms we saw in the hands of rebels and Gaddafi's troops.

Libya was a straight-up adventure, as exciting as it was dangerous, as exhausting as it was inspiring. We were seven hours ahead of New York, so that gave us lots of time to news-gather before our first live shots were scheduled. We'd be up and out early, by 8 a.m. or 9 a.m. local time, heading out in a two-vehicle caravan with our driver/bodyguard and fixer/translator and our private security guy, moving as close to the front lines as we could get, looking for stories reflecting the mood and actions in the area that day.

We'd stop and go live wherever we were during the afternoon hours, often setting up along the road we were driving on. Sometimes I'd sketch out the live shot in my reporter notebook, other times I'd just wing it. The longer we were there, the more familiar I became with the mood, the terrain, and the developments, and the reporting became easier, and it was a powerful story to tell.

The country was in turmoil. The people were rising up against their leader, fighting for their independence and freedom from authoritarian rule. Gaddafi's army was strong, but its soldiers were outnumbered by the citizens who'd had enough. Some of my most enduring memories are the conversations and interviews I had with shop owners, mechanics, and teachers who were getting quick lessons in hand-to-hand combat and how to handle a weapon before being handed one and heading for the front lines.

"Why are you doing this?" I'd ask, and the answer would almost always be, "Because I love my country and I'm ready to die for it."

These were regular working people with families and homes who didn't want to live under Gaddafi's thumb anymore. They were up-armoring pickup trucks, mounting machine guns in the back, dropping their aprons and calculators for a chance at freedom. They liked to call themselves "revolutionists," not rebels.

They were also suffering from a serious lack of discipline and command structure, a force unlike most I'd covered in the past. They were certainly enthusiastic, eagerly firing their weapons in the air for the camera, but were also disenchanted, frequently asking "Where's the help?" They kept hearing that NATO and Allied Forces would give them air support and possibly arms and troops, and they grew increasingly frustrated when their friends and colleagues were injured and killed and fighting positions weakened by Libyan airstrikes and the assistance wasn't there or wasn't enough.

I did two separate two-week tours of the country, working a rotation with other correspondents covering the war. The days were incredibly long, and our bosses decided it was best to try to keep us fresh, swapping us in and out through Egypt. It was a logistical challenge for them and a hair-raising journey for me, my cameraman, a producer, and a British or South African security guy.

We'd fly into Cairo, stay overnight at a really nice Marriott, then caravan to the border in the early a.m. with an Egyptian driver. It was a six- to eight-hour drive for me and the crew to reach the checkpoint, where we'd unload our gear, show our passports, and find our Libyan drivers, packing our stuff in their vans and trucks for the next stretch of our wild ride. We reversed this commute my first time there, but the second trip ended with us trapped in a small city by the sea, surrounded by Gaddafi's advancing troops, forcing us to take a much more unconventional way out to safety. More on that in a bit.

On my first trip to Libya, I worked with photographer Richard Harlow, a Brit who was a Fox staffer based in our Jerusalem bureau. Richie was a great guy, very tough and focused, an excellent cameraman and editor who would set up and break down our equipment up to a dozen times a day. We'd always make our way back to the hotel before sunset, where Richie would set up the gear again, usually on our balcony, and then edit our package for *Special Report*, which we'd front from our safer location. This meant that our last live shot of the day was at 1 a.m., but some nights one of the prime-time shows would request a live shot, and if we had the strength and stamina, we'd get up and go live again at 3 a.m. or 4 a.m. Our dinners were almost always in the room because we'd be working on packages and scripts and also didn't feel safe on the streets after dark.

When I spoke to Richie recently, he described the trip as "madness" and "one of the best stories I've ever done," and we laughed reminiscing about one day in particular, when he ate something that didn't agree with him and caught a batch of dysentery.

We'd gone toward the town of Brega on the Gulf of Sidra, where rebels were battling for control of the strategic port city against Gaddafi's troops. Richie remembers what happened next this way:

We got on the road with rebel forces advancing on the city, the oil refinery blown up, we were driving west and a convoy of pickup trucks covered with oil and sand stuck to them came whipping past us, one after another with the machine guns mounted in the beds and men with scarves wrapped around their heads and faces, hanging out the sides and the back, fleeing for safer ground with Gaddafi loyalists pushing them out.

Ken [our imported security guy] says, "let's get out of here," they were advancing quickly. I remember us driving back, but my stomach got so bad I knew I couldn't make it and yelled for the driver to stop. I had to run behind a wall before I shit myself. Every ten minutes I had to stop—in a rickety old van, driving back to our hotel, having to stop every ten minutes so I could take another liquid dump. I remember you shouting, "Hurry up! We can't stay here!! Get back in the van!"

Richie says, "I remember the next day you said 'just stay here, we can shoot material without you' because Martin (Francis, the producer) had a camera and you guys went out for half an hour and then had to hustle back to get out of there, pack up, and retreat again. The maddest few days."

I told Richie I'd never forget him in the room trying to edit our story that first night, and him having to stop every few minutes to run to the bathroom again. He was white as a ghost but determined to finish the piece.

"I knew if I sent it to New York, they'd just slap it together," he told me.

It wouldn't be as good. They didn't know the video and wouldn't know where to put the best shots. I couldn't let it go. It was our story. But I remember cutting and shitting, cutting and shitting, cutting and shitting. It was bad. I also remember cutting in the back of a pickup truck, and I'm literally editing in the back as we're going over bumps, the craziest couple weeks ever.

We were on edge the whole time. There was always the threat of an attack, an unexpected advance with very short warning to pack up and go. We lived out of our suitcases because we often did have to move very quickly and couldn't waste time packing our stuff. Richie would also pack the equipment every night and unpack it all the next morning, knowing we might have to leave in a hurry, throwing all our gear in our van at a moment's notice.

One of those rushed exits came on Saturday, March 19, in Benghazi, a major seaport with more than 600,000 residents. Benghazi was a rebel stronghold, considered the center of opposition forces, a place where fighters would retreat to when other cities got overrun or things got too dicey at the front.

Now, the city itself was under attack.

Gaddafi's army had ignored a cease fire agreement and was advancing with tanks and fighter jets, launching attacks from the air and ground, rocking buildings, and sending residents fleeing for safety on the one main highway out of town.

I didn't know any of this yet because I was still in bed, fiercely fighting for a bit more sleep, wrapping my pillow around my head to try to drown out the explosions outside my window. I was exhausted and obviously too tired to know what was best for me in that moment, but then a banging on my door forced me up from under the covers.

I think it was our security guy who woke me yelling something to the effect of, "A plane just got shot down and Richie got the video! You gotta come up to the roof!" I opened the curtains to my wide city view and saw numerous clouds of smoke from explosions and fires.

I ran up to the roof and found Richie there, really excited. Our security guy had alerted him to air traffic over the hotel, believed to be Libyan fighter jets, which was news by itself since a no-fly zone was in effect and we'd seen virtually nothing in the sky for the duration of our trip.

Richie was on the roof shooting video of jets flying overhead for about ten minutes, he says, when he began tracking one traveling from right to left overhead. He was shocked when, as he was filming, he saw a streak of light hit the aircraft, which burst into flames and began plummeting toward the city below. He saw the pilot eject just before the jet crashed in a ball of flames.

"I got it on camera, mate!" He was grinning at me. "I think it's really good stuff, but I need to look at it to make sure."

What's "good" or "great" in TV news usually translates to tragedy. Getting "great stuff" usually means video of some catastrophic event or an interview where the person begins crying or loses composure. In this case, our great video turned out to be more tragic than we thought.

It was one of Gaddafi's jets, a MiG-23BN, but it had been commandeered by the rebels with the Free Libyan Air Force and was then shot down by other rebels who assumed it was one of Gaddafi's fighters.

Unfortunately, the pilot ejected too late and was killed when the chute failed to slow his fall, and he slammed into the yard of an abandoned orphanage, where we found the seat and the pieces of the shattered jet littering the grounds the next day. This wasn't a victory for opposition forces, who initially cheered the downing of the jet. This was a friendly fire fatality, taking out one of the small number of experienced pilots on the rebel side.

Once we got off the roof, we knew we had to get out of town. This wasn't some kind of drill or exercise, this was live fire coming our way, a city under siege, and if rebel forces weren't fierce enough and NATO jets didn't get there soon enough, we could all wind up captured or, more likely, dead.

We grabbed all our gear and hustled it down to the lobby and into our vehicles, and before we headed away from the advancing threat, we took a short drive toward where the blasts were coming from. I remember seeing a tank on a city street rolling in our direction. Richie got a quick shot from inside the vehicle, and we took that as our cue to get the hell out of there.

We drove in heavy traffic, stopping at a gas station when we thought we'd gone far enough to feed our material and do a live shot. We then found a place where we could all crash for the night, but when we heard that NATO and rebel forces had repelled Gaddafi's army and that the city was safe, we drove back to our hotel and brought all our gear back in, going live from there that night and setting out in the morning to find where the jet had crashed.

We loaded up the vehicle with our gear, food, and water and headed out early, expecting a major scene at the crash site. We all saw the video of where the jet had crashed on the horizon, into what looked like a sea of buildings. It appeared to be no more than two miles from our hotel, and we figured there would be crowds there and some kind of cleanup underway.

We also assumed that everyone in that area would know where the jet went down, but finding it was far more difficult than we anticipated. When we got to an area we thought was in the vicinity, our fixer began asking people on the street if they'd seen or heard the crash or knew how to get there. Every single person said no. We kept driving in circles, looking for any signs of what in America would've been a major incident with a huge response from local, state, and federal agents and first responders. But of course, this was Libya, and a war was raging around us, and there would be no National Transportation Safety Board jackets at the scene.

We finally found someone who thought he knew where the MiG went down and after some wrong turns and another bit of help from a local, we found it. The jet had gone down in a large walled-in yard of a large home in what looked like an upscale neighborhood. We were told it was once the home of a prince and later became an orphanage but had since been abandoned. I was astonished at what we saw. I'd covered plenty of plane crashes in the past, but I'd never been this close to the wreckage. In the U.S., any crash scene is quickly secured by local police who search for survivors and wait for federal investigators to arrive on scene to document the damages and collect every piece of the doomed aircraft.

But here we were, standing in the middle of a sea of metal carnage with absolutely no one else in sight. We walked unrestricted through the wreckage, shooting video of the chunks of smashed jet strewn everywhere. Pieces of the wings, tail, engine, cockpit—we even found the ejector seat—but the pilot's body was gone, apparently recovered by locals. We set up our gear and did a couple of live shots detailing what we'd found, along with the information I'd learned, before moving south and west on the road to Tripoli, where the retreating tanks that had fired on the city a day earlier were destroyed by NATO jets.

Here is the transcript from one of my live shots on *Fox & Friends*, at 3:01 p.m. local time (8 a.m. ET), on March 20, 2011:

Brian [Kilmeade], this is the oxygen mask from the doomed pilot of that jet that crashed here on the grounds of a former orphanage in the southern part of the city of Benghazi. We are surrounded by pieces of it that, what we believe to be a Soviet MiG fighter jet, the engine is right behind me, the fuselage, the wings, and there's a tail section in the other direction that has the old royal flag painted on it that is the symbol of the new liberated Libya and that's why we believe along with accounts from locals that this in fact was a plane piloted by a member of the resistance, by a rebel fighter who apparently may have been shot down by his own men who had very poor communications on the ground and thought that it was it a Gaddafi jet in the sky.

We shot video over Benghazi yesterday, you can see the plane hit by anti-aircraft fire and then it hurdles towards this area on fire, the pilot apparently attempted to eject but he attempted far too late. His body was recovered in this area where the plane went down in a ball of flame. The locals tell us that he was a former member of the Gaddafi Air Force who defected to the other side, that he was a family man with four children and he is being remembered this morning as a hero here in Benghazi.

Of course there are jets over our heads, enforcing the no-fly zone, last night after many cruise missile strikes there was anti-aircraft fire from the ground up in Tripoli that was recorded on night vision camera...we know that Gaddafi's military was trying to fight back against these air strikes and against the missile strikes against prime targets, don't know whether any of that anti-aircraft fire was successful but again the situation in Benghazi today much quieter than it's been in days past.

Yesterday morning we woke up to tanks shelling the city...those tanks have since retreated...the opposition fighters remain in control of many checkpoints around the city and are waving victory signs today, telling us they believe the tide is turning in their favor.

Anchor Alisyn Camerota asked me about the mass exodus a day earlier, of citizens fleeing, as she put it "for the Egyptian border," and asked if they were coming back. I responded:

I don't know that all those people who were exiting were heading for the Egyptian border, many of these people overnighted at friends' homes or just the homes of people in other towns to the east of us who offered people places to stay. For the most part the people who were fleeing Benghazi were not fleeing Libya and had every intention of coming back. There may be a trickle back today and then as things get quieter here, we expect to see a lot more people coming back to their homes.

Then Brian Kilmeade asked if I'd met with any of the Libyans being touted as possible new leaders of their country. I told him I hadn't but had met with locals heading up the resistance and others "who feel very strongly about the freedom and democracy that they want in Libya. They all tell us that members of their family or their close friends, everyone's lost someone to Gaddafi's regime, and what I would call, this is a tremendous coming together of a community in support of a new democratic-style government here in Libya. I couldn't tell you specifically about who might take control but I can tell you that the people all seem to be very much united it in support of a new Libya."

Then Steve Doocy mentioned just how rare it was to be standing in the midst of the pieces of a plane that had crashed just a day earlier.

"Rick, thank you very much for getting this exclusive report, because that was the big question yesterday, who exactly was flying that airplane, now we know that it was a rebel with the rebel pilots and it was apparently shot down by his own forces but it is so extraordinary that you're so close to it, I mean you know if that happened here there'd be police tape and you wouldn't be within a couple of miles."

"Oh absolutely!" I told him.

> There would be investigators crawling over this scene, they'd be documenting, photographing, and collecting every single bit of this former, this old Soviet MiG fighter jet, we wouldn't be anywhere near it but because there really is no government in place right now in Benghazi, there was no one to stop us and there's, as far as we know, been no other media to come to this location on the grounds of this former orphanage

which was once the home of a Libyan prince, now just littered, and by the way what we're being told by the locals is they believe this pilot targeted this particular area, this cleared-out area, a home that's no longer occupied, because he knew that no one would be hurt if he crashed here and not in either direction where there are some pretty heavily populated areas.

When we finished the live shot, we began packing up, and (full confession) I grabbed a couple small souvenirs from the ground, including a metal sign plate from the cockpit. Martin grabbed the ejector seat handle. More on that in a bit.

Our fixer heard there was a major scene a few miles down the road, where NATO jets had taken out a bunch of Gaddafi's armor, so we headed that way and found perhaps a hundred people or more celebrating, taking photos, and firing guns in the air in front of a field full of destroyed war machines. Here is what I think was my final live shot from the field that day, completely ad-libbed, at 5 p.m. local time (9 a.m. in New York):

Jamie, we're seeing firsthand results of the NATO fire power. They tore through this field in the town of Jerusha just alongside the highway about twelve miles south of Benghazi and this field is littered with pieces of armor and what you see behind me are what's left of a couple of smoking former Soviet T-72 tanks that belonged to the Libyan military.

This entire area is filled with this kind of scene, tanks that have been disabled by strikes from above, armored personnel carriers, missile launchers, trucks that carry the tanks as well as the boots from soldiers who were here apparently when within the last twenty-four hours those NATO fighter jets came through and tore through these tanks.

Remember the tanks went into Benghazi yesterday morning, we were there when they rolled in, some of them retreated, they may have been staging here but I can tell you that the treads of that vehicle are still smoldering and there is still flame inside that scene right there and this area is now a major tourist attraction.

We have seen a lot of people coming out here with cameras, they're firing weapons in the air and there's a lot of smiles because these are the tanks that were killing their friends and neighbors and family members and these are the tanks that are now completely destroyed by those airstrikes.

Just a short time ago we came from the southern edge of Benghazi, from the actual scene where that fighter jet crashed yesterday, as we have been reporting a jet shot down over Benghazi yesterday, that jet belonged to the rebel forces, we found the tail section with a flag painted, the old royal flag symbolizing the new liberated Libya, on the tail of that jet piloted by opposition forces, apparently shot down by mistake by anti-aircraft fire from those opposition forces, the jet may have been targeting the tanks that were in the southern edge of the city, it crashed on the grounds of a former orphanage, burned there, the wreckage strewn about. We found the ejector seat, apparently the pilot was not able to get out in time, his body was recovered from that scene.

He was the father of four and is being hailed as a hero. Of course there is ongoing, as you mentioned, violence in Misrata, there is also an ongoing effort by NATO and coalition forces to take out Gaddafi's defenses, to take out his tanks like the ones still smoldering behind me and to turn this around, but I can tell you that the people of Benghazi, all the people that we've seen, are celebrating today, they believe that the tide is turning and they will in fact win this civil war.

The anchor then asked whether we'd seen the bodies of dead soldiers or opposition fighters. I responded:

Well, we've heard about the casualties in many of the towns where the fighting has been strongest, including Ajdabiya to our south and Benghazi. We have not seen the bodies. We've heard reports from hospitals and we have seen a couple of bodies in this field that belong to Libyan military members who were killed in this airstrike here on this field but we're hearing the stories from people and from hospital workers about dozens of people who were killed, many of them civilians, dozens more wounded and that's what we're going on at this point. We've had to pull back from some of these areas when the fighting was fiercest and now as we come back in especially here today, we're seeing the aftermath, the results of the fighting, the results of the retaliation by NATO jets.

Finally, she asked if had a sense of the capabilities of the tanks that had been taken out. I said:

Absolutely, I mean we've seen the shelling, the buildings that were shelled in Benghazi by these tanks, and we've felt the concussions from the rounds as they fired and the opposition forces have been telling us repeatedly, they had no answer for Gaddafi's armor. They had more men, they had the spirit and the will to fight, but they were outgunned and out-trained, but what they were calling for all along was some sort of help from above, some sort of international system to take out the armor and this is the result of that and they are celebrating today, Jamie, because this is what they were waiting for. They knew that they couldn't fight the tanks but if they could take out the tanks then they would have a real shot at winning this war and clearly these tanks aren't going anywhere anymore.

When we spoke recently, Richie told me he regretted not being able to join me for that second tour, and he shared a story I don't think I'd heard before. He told me when we were packing in a hurry to get out of Benghazi during the attack, he took the ejector handle our producer Martin had snatched from the wreckage of the downed MiG and stuck it in his kit and never gave it back, primarily because he didn't like Martin very much. He told me, "I still have it to this day and I'm sure he was pissed when he realized he lost it!" Richie said again it was sheer madness "covering whatever happens, never knowing what the next thing would be. It was one of the best stories I've done. Running on adrenaline. And then you're like, did this really happen? This is not normal. Running away from an enemy you can't see."

When I answered the call for the next Libyan adventure, I was paired with the same producer Martin and cameraman Mal James, another brit who spent years working out of our Jerusalem bureau. We made the same journey in from Cairo but traveled much further during our two weeks on the ground. We had more hairy adventures and more close calls, including a trip to Sirte, another seaside town that looked virtually abandoned until we rolled up on a bunch of young guys who eyed us suspiciously. I remember getting the feeling they might be part of a terror group rumored to be growing within the country and being even more nervous than I'd been when tanks were firing on Benghazi. We tried to talk to some of them and got cold stares and stern warnings to leave them alone, so we did.

Someone decided we should head much further west, toward Tripoli, where Gaddafi was hunkered down and where the bulk of his army was based. We wound up driving more than five hundred miles from Benghazi to Misrata, another once-bustling port city that was now a virtual ghost town because of all the attacks and fighting.

In one of my reporter notebooks from the trip, I wrote: "Misrata scarred by weeks of fighting. Many buildings pockmarked with bullet holes. Many windows shattered. Some structures significantly damaged. Power still on, fuel and food available. Good security but Gaddafi's forces booby trapped buildings."

Later I wrote, "battles in the streets left 100s dead and wounded and 100s of buildings heavily damaged or destroyed." Tripoli Street, one of the city's main thoroughfares, was "reduced to rubble after weeks of fighting," I wrote. Two brothers collected spent munitions and built an outdoor museum there, providing evidence "of the brutality Gaddafi brought to this city," with "heavy artillery, tank rounds, rockets, mortars, RPGs, ammo of all calibers, uniforms, even medical kits."

One day Mal and I cut a feature story about how the rebel fighters were eating at the front lines. Some guy with a pizza restaurant in town built a makeshift kitchen closer to the front and was cooking pies and sending them to the rebels in harm's way. He was baking six thousand to eight thousand slices a day with the help of volunteers, none of whom had any pizza-making experience. We interviewed him, got B-roll of the pizzas being prepped and put in the oven, and then followed with the guy delivering them and shots of some of the fighters eating as they hid behind trees and sand dunes. In the script, I called it "the most dangerous pizza delivery job in the world." It was a cute, fun piece and a nice departure from the grim hell of most days.

Here's an example of the ugliness, from my notes: "We got word of casualties on a farm hit by a Libyan military rocket strike, and headed out to find where it happened. When we got there, we learned a mother of eight was killed while watering corn plants. The blast also killed 26 camels, worth more than $1,000 each, we were told. Another day we visited a field hospital in an old tractor garage near the front where doctors were treating wounded fighters. The hospital itself was hit by incoming artillery from Gaddafi's troops. While we were there, we saw a constant flow of incoming ambulances transporting young men with war injuries."

Another day we did a story from a garage where welders and machinists were transforming pickup trucks into armored fighting vehicles, with steel shields to protect the engines, mounting machine guns and other heavy weapons in the beds. Meanwhile, almost every morning when we woke up, we'd see plumes of smoke from the edges of the city where Gaddafi's forces were attacking with rockets and shells.

Being there was a really stupid move on our part, considering we had no chance of defending ourselves if things got out of hand, and in fact, the situation began deteriorating to the point where we felt it was in our best interest to get out.

The trouble was: It simply wasn't safe to go back the way we came.

There were daily battles along the highway and in the towns and cities between us and the Egyptian border. We also didn't feel safe driving toward Tripoli, into the heart of the Libyan military, and we certainly couldn't catch a flight out because there weren't any. The no-fly restrictions were still very much in place.

That left one option: an escape by sea.

We went down to the port (much of it damaged or destroyed during airstrikes and battles), and our fixer began asking around for the possibility of passage on a boat headed anywhere on the Mediterranean. Eventually we found a tuna boat that was planning a run to Malta.

It was a big fishing ship with near-zero creature comforts. Tiny bunks in tiny crew quarters, an unstocked kitchen, and a very low top speed. We were told we could pay for passage (along with a CNN crew and some other Western journalists) and that it would take twenty-four hours to get there.

Of course, we said yes.

What I remember most about that long ride across the sea was how calm and quiet it was. After weeks of incredibly stressful days and nights, trying to get as close to the fighting as possible only to turn around and flee the other way when we got *too* close, with five to ten deadlines every day, shooting stories, viewing footage, writing scripts, setting up and going live, breaking down and moving to another location to set up and do it again, ducking when bullets flew by or bombs landed too close, packing and unpacking almost daily, now here we were, chugging along on calm waters with just the sound of the engines and the waves lapping the sides of the ship.

We took the thin mattresses off the bunks in our room and laid them on the top deck, and we hung out there during much of the day and then slept there at night, under the stars, feeling safe and appreciating life.

Arriving at the port in Malta was a special experience. It's a beautiful island, a place I'd barely even heard of, and it was a welcome return to peace and comfort. We stayed in a nice hotel, took long showers, had a really good meal with some really good wine, got a good night's sleep, and headed for the airport in the morning where I had a comfy seat up front for my return trip to New York. I'd survived another war zone, and it felt really good to be heading home with another solid performance notched in my belt.

CHAPTER 7

THE 2000 ELECTION IN TALLAHASSEE: HANGING CHADS AND A-ROD

In early November 2000, I was dispatched to Tallahassee, Florida, when some butterfly ballots and hanging chads (and some pregnant chads too) turned the presidential election into a chaotic mess.

The race between George W. Bush and Al Gore turned out to be remarkably close on election night. Gore, who was at that time Bill Clinton's Vice President, had won roughly half a million more ballots nationwide, and led 266-to-246 in the electoral college count, but it wasn't over yet.

Florida's twenty-five electoral votes were critical, since a Sunshine State win would provide the margin of victory that Bush needed to inhabit the White House the following January.

About an hour after the polls closed in Florida on November 7, most of the TV networks called the race for Gore, even though the margin of victory was extremely tight, and Bush called his opponent to congratulate him.

But when the panhandle results started trickling in, Bush's tally started climbing, and by the wee hours of the morning, he'd actually taken the lead by close to two thousand votes. The TV networks reversed their calls, and Bush phoned Gore back and rescinded his concession.

The next few weeks saw a nearly unprecedented post-election battle for the Oval Office, and I was at the center of the storm to cover every development.

If George W. Bush could have chosen any state in America to decide whether he'd be the nation's forty-third President, it most likely would have been Florida, where his brother Jeb was governor at the time, and the secretary of state, Katherine Harris, was a big Republican booster and co-chair of Florida's Bush for President election committee.

Jeb gave George a friendly foothold, and Harris would play a key role in some of the decisions that helped to shape the outcome of the recounts and court battles.

The morning after election night, Bush led Gore by 1,784 votes, a margin of victory so close it triggered an automatic machine recount, which meant feeding every single paper ballot into the same machines that had read and spit them out the first time. The results later that week actually made the contest far tighter, trimming Bush's lead to just 327 votes. This prompted a call by Gore's camp for another recount, this time by hand, creating a tidal wave of challenges and sparking dozens of lawsuits, forty-seven of them before it was all over.

I was in Nashville on the night of the election to cover Gore's victory (or concession) speech, and it turned into an extremely late night because of the mess in Florida. I was sent to Tallahassee the next day to help cover the ensuing shitshow, and I'd wind up staying for more than a month, reporting on one of the most challenging stories editorial-wise I'd ever been assigned.

The ballots themselves became the primary focus of many of the court challenges. The so-called butterfly ballots spanned two pages with two columns of names, one on each page, separated by a line of holes down the middle. Critics (primarily in Camp Gore) complained that the names didn't always line up with the proper hole, and that firebrand Patrick Buchanan scored a bunch of votes intended for the Democratic contender.

A bigger issue turned out to be the hole-punch system, which was archaic and flawed. Voters would position a device over the hole belonging to their candidate and knock it through the paper to dislodge the small, square semi-perforated piece there, called a "chad." The ballot would later be fed through a machine that would read and record the hole where the square had been knocked loose.

But the hole-punch system didn't always perform the way it was designed. Sometimes those little pieces of paper would be dislodged only partially, and might be hanging by one, two, or even three corners, so while it *looked* like the voter had intended to hit that hole, it wasn't completely clear. Did the "hanging chad" truly represent the voter's intent? Did the voter really hit that key to knock that chad loose and it just didn't clear the mark? Did the voter only half punch that key because he or she wasn't sure? Did voters change their minds at the last minute? Did the hole have to be clean for the vote to be valid? What was the standard? Were three connected threads too many? Were at least two clean cuts enough, or should only one be the minimum standard? There was no consensus, which became a key issue in the courts.

Tallahassee, Florida's capital, was also home to the state and federal court buildings where the cases would be filed and argued seemingly every day. Just two days after the election, the Bush campaign announced that George H.W. Bush's former Secretary of State, James Baker, and Republican political consultant Roger Stone would handle Bush's legal battles. Gore's campaign snagged Bill Clinton's former Secretary of State, Warren Christopher, plus David Boies, a brilliant and crafty legal mind who handled numerous high-profile cases before and after the election recount, which would eventually be decided by the United States Supreme Court.

The legal teams were incredibly busy, which meant *we* were incredibly busy. On one day alone, four separate court actions—including a lawsuit to get overseas military ballots included in the recount—changed my script four times.

My live intro that evening was this:

> Anyone who thought the State Supreme Court's ruling would clear up this controversial election was sadly mistaken. Florida's state senate is considering legislative action to oppose the court, Miami Dade County has now stopped its recount, Palm Beach County now plans to count at least *some* of the dimpled chads, and the Bush

camp is filing an appeal to the highest court in the land.

How complicated was it? The state legislature, for example, said it found itself in uncharted territory that day, claiming the Florida Supreme Court had "contradicted itself in its ruling by arbitrarily and capriciously, setting another date by which the secretary is to accept amended certifications, making new law instead of interpreting existing law."

Can you imagine trying to dumb that down for a story running a minute and thirty seconds on local news? When this was just one of several developments, including suspension of hand counts but continuing machine returns in one county, ordering hand counts of certain ballots in another, absentee ballots changing results in yet another county, and claims of equal protection violations because the recounts were discriminatory against voters whose ballots were *not* being recounted.

It makes my head hurt just writing that now, so you can imagine what it was like to try to decipher all this and spit it out in any kind of orderly and understandable fashion for viewers.

State law said that hand recounts could be requested if a candidate disputed results in at least three counties. The Gore campaign picked four, which were home to the highest density of Democratic voters, giving him his best chance at gaining enough votes back to win. These recounts were challenged by Bush, of course, since he held the lead, and there were additional disputes over just how those recounts would be carried out and how ballots would be reconsidered, prompting what seemed like endless challenges, rulings, appeals, and fresh arguments from both sides.

The recounts themselves were time consuming, with election officials painstakingly examining each individual punch card, often debating their status in small groups, and when they'd finally finished, it meant a new set of numbers that needed to be added or subtracted from the totals. In one of my reporter notebooks, for example, I found "Leon County, Gore net gain 225, 314 of 2,000 questionable ballots. Palm Beach County, Bush net gain 14, 217 of 637 precincts, 10,000 questionable ballots."

The numbers kept changing, the appeals and new cases kept getting filed, and it went on and on and on, through Thanksgiving, when I wrote "forget about football. The only motion here is the one filed in court."

RESCUING A-ROD

This also wasn't a typical assignment for me because I wasn't reporting for Fox News Channel. They'd sent me down there to be the nighttime Fox News Edge reporter, meaning I'd file pre-edited news packages and live shots for any local Fox affiliate stations across the country interested in the latest developments on "Election 2000" for their 5 p.m., 6 p.m., or 10 p.m. newscasts. Because of the time difference, if a West Coast station wanted a hit for its late news, we wouldn't be done until around 1:15 a.m., which happened almost every night.

The shift was an absolute grind. My producer, crew, and I met at the truck every day by noon so the photographer could set up his equipment for the live shots, and my producer and I could start collecting elements for the early package. This meant scrolling through emails and articles for the best and latest information, making phone calls to anyone connected to the major players involved, and scrolling through video from outside sources and our own, finding B-roll footage and interviews we could edit into our stories.

For example, if a court case was pending and there were clips of the lawyers entering and leaving the courthouse and answering some reporter questions on the way in or out or at a press conference, we'd log the material and choose the best parts to include in the piece. If Bush or Gore spoke, that would obviously need to be included.

Our goal was to sum up the latest developments in a concise edited report running 1:10 to 1:30 in length (70 to 90 seconds total), and I'd be on camera for ten or fifteen seconds to introduce the package and then spend another ten to fifteen seconds tagging out at the end with what we expected would happen next.

This was a drill we were all familiar with. We did it for any number of stories with a nationwide interest. I was a fast and competent writer and always made my deadlines.

But as you can see from above, this wasn't like any other story. It was a nightmare of legalese, long-winded sound bites, boring video, and late-breaking, nearly undecipherable developments.

Every day, I'd start composing my summation of all the developments, mostly which lawyers were arguing in the different courtrooms, as it was happening. I tried my best to keep scripts open-ended, allowing for late-breaking decisions in cases shaping our coverage. I'd try to anticipate what might happen and make sure not to write myself into a corner, but almost every day there would be a wacky new development, a left turn no one saw coming, and it almost always happened between 4:30 p.m. and 4:59 p.m., minutes before we were due to go live.

It was insane how often this happened, when we simply didn't have time to fix the new glitch or edit around the fresh twist or add the new development to the edited piece or remove now-dated information and clean it up, so we'd have to scrap the package we'd spent hours working on and simply go live for the full 1:30-2 minutes the shows were expecting us to fill.

It was frustrating and aggravating and chaotic and stressful and pressure packed. Having to pivot and adjust and make sense of what had just happened and find a way to report on the new developments with minutes or seconds before our critical 5 p.m. live shot.

We'd then have to re-tool our 6 p.m. hits and write all new stories for the late shows. Fortunately, I was quite accomplished in working under pressure, but this was beyond anything I'd experienced, and it made the long and difficult days seem even longer. We were all ready for a drink pretty much every night after our shift came to a merciful end.

At the time, last call in Tallahassee bars was at 1:30 a.m., and since we didn't finish until 1:10 or 1:15 in the morning, we had to make a mad rush to the nearest watering hole to order a couple of rounds before they shut down service for the night.

One of our favorite spots was a wine bar called Café Cabernet. Because of its proximity to the courthouse and excellent drink selection, many of the crews from a variety of networks would meet there after work to unwind. They were all usually hammered by the time we got there so we'd do our best to catch up, ordering doubles two at a time or extra glasses of wine for the short minutes we were able to socialize and have fun before the lights came on.

We also tried different spots, so one night, one of my colleagues suggested the local Hooters, a relatively short drive from the Capitol Complex. I wasn't a big fan of the wings, but we weren't going there to eat so I said, "Sure, why not!"

The producer and photographer didn't want to join us that night, so it was just me and Mike Amor, a very talented satellite engineer who grew up in south Florida. He was driving one of our large SUV crew vehicles and did his best to shave minutes off the late commute, but by the time we got to the Hooters parking lot, we learned the restaurant had closed for the night.

As we were standing there outside the vehicle, maybe fifty yards from the front door, trying to decide if it was worth trying somewhere else, I thought I recognized a face among a group of guys standing nearby.

"Is that A-Rod?" I asked aloud.

"I think so!" Mike said, and then surprisingly called the name of one of the other guys in the group. It turned out Mike and the other dude knew each other from school. The guys all walked over to our black Ford Expedition, and we exchanged hellos and they told us they were stranded.

They'd booked a limo for the night and while they were at Hooters, the guy bailed on them, and they had no ride. "You can ride with us!" Mike offered, and all six of us piled into the truck. Mike was still driving, and I sat in the middle up front with A-Rod riding shotgun and his three buddies in the back, one of whom appeared to weigh nearly three hundred pounds.

Remember, this was November 2000. A-Rod's contract was up in Seattle, and he was all over the sports pages because of rumors he was about to sign the biggest contract in the history of Major League Baseball, somewhere north of $200 million. He was one of the best players in the game, and he was sitting right next to me in the front seat of my buddy's crew vehicle, and we were all headed to find fun spots to party in Tallahassee at 1:30 in the morning.

I started asking A-Rod a bunch of questions, of course, because that's my job and why wouldn't I? Was he going to sign with the Mets, who were rumored to be among his suitors? Might he go to the Texas Rangers? Would he give me the first, exclusive interview when he did his deal? He laughed that one off and said I should reach out to his agent, Scott Boras, whom I didn't know but certainly knew *of* because I followed sports, and Boras was one of the biggest agents in the game.

A-Rod couldn't have been nicer. He was super cool the entire time we hung out, which was close to three hours. We checked out another bar, but it was closed, too, so then we drove to his buddy's townhouse so they could drop some stuff off, then to check on another club that was also closed, then to some frat party where we got beers and walked around for a bit. Eventually we piled back in the Expedition and dropped them off at their place. We said our goodbyes and I gave him my card, and he gave me his agent's contact and that was that.

I didn't get the interview when A-Rod signed his $275 million, ten-year deal with the Rangers and didn't talk to him when he was traded to the Yankees in 2004. But I did wind up crossing paths with him several more times, and he couldn't have been a bigger asshole on all three occasions, each time acting as if he'd never seen me before and had no idea who I was, which I fully admit was possible, but, in my not so humble opinion, unlikely.

The first time I saw A-Rod again was at the Major League Baseball (MLB) All-Star Game in Pittsburgh in 2006. It was almost six years since we'd rescued him and his buddies outside Hooters, and I get that it's a long time, and I also get that he must meet countless people every day, but it seemed to me he was *pretending* not to know who I was because of the random and unusual circumstances of how we met, and it really pissed me off.

During the lead up to every All-Star Game there's a media availability with the players a day or two before the game. The players each sit at their own table or booth and the press moves around the room, from spot to spot, waiting for a chance to throw a question at the players.

My daughter Veronica actually came with me on that trip because I got her an internship that summer. She was fifteen at the time, apparently the youngest intern in Fox News Channel's short history, which proved back then that nepotism was alive and well.

Veronica was following me as I worked the room, getting sound from players, and I'd told her my A-Rod story before, so I said "Hey, let's go say hi to A-Rod and see if he remembers me!"

We walk up to his booth, and it's packed with other reporters, and he's patiently answering questions from them, and I push my way up to the front and finally get his attention. He looks at me, and I say, "Hey A-Rod, how you doing?" He says "Great, what's your question?" showing no recognition whatsoever. "Rick Leventhal, Fox News!" I say, trying to jar his memory. "OK, what's your question?"

"You don't remember me? We gave you a ride from Hooters in Tallahassee after the Miami–Florida State game in 2000?" He looked at me blankly. "Hooters? I must've been drunk. Do you have a question?"

I remember seeing red at this point. It was embarrassing. I could tell he remembered me, but it felt like he didn't want to admit it with reporters and other cameras in his face. It wasn't that I thought I was so memorable, but our meeting had been so random it seemed hard to forget, especially since he absolutely was *not* drunk that night.

He was completely lucid and sober, and I can't imagine he'd been left without a ride after the biggest football game of the year in Tallahassee more than once in his life, not to mention that we rode next to each other in the front seat of an SUV for more than two hours, but whatever. I didn't have a question for him and walked away.

I'd always spoken highly of him after I'd met him, but now my opinion of him completely reversed, and it would be upheld twice more, at two separate events during Super Bowl week in Miami in 2010.

A friend was helping to handle public relations for the opening of the brand new J.W. Marriott hotel in Downtown Miami, off Brickell, and invited me to participate in a celebrity free-throw shooting contest at the indoor basketball court next to the hotel's gym.

It turned out that A-Rod was also a participant. I wondered if he'd acknowledge or remember me, and I wasn't surprised when he acted, again, like he'd never met me before. I didn't try to remind him this time, but at the end of the contest (which neither of us won) he was taking photos and against my better judgement I asked to take one with him (which I regret to this day), and he told me no. I can't remember what his reason was, but at the time I remember thinking, "not only does this guy remember me, he's intentionally being a dick."

I saw him again a night or two later at one the best parties I've ever been to, at one of the coolest apartments I've ever seen, hosted by Wayne Boich, a well-known Miami-based entrepreneur and philanthropist, in his penthouse on Alton Road in South Beach. The place was sick. Two stories with the biggest rooftop and biggest hot tub I'd ever seen. It was like a club.

There were tons of athletes and celebrities there, including former Green Bay Packers linebacker A.J. Hawk, who recognized me because it turned out he was a big Fox fan. I bullshitted with him for about twenty minutes, and we became buds after that. I even flew to Columbus, Ohio, a few years later to act as master of ceremonies at a charity event at A.J.'s house.

When I was leaving the party with my friends, A-Rod got on the elevator with a dude, looked at me, and immediately turned his back, talking to his friend the whole way down and managing to avoid eye contact when he got off.

I get that the guy is *uber* famous, and I'm sure he's constantly asked for photos and autographs. But I wasn't some fanboy. I was a network news reporter who'd randomly given him and his friends a ride when they were stranded late one night in Tallahassee.

To this day, I don't believe he didn't know who I was, and I just don't respect that kind of behavior. I've met many famous people over the past thirty-five years. Very many. Some are dicks. Some are surprisingly down to earth. I appreciate when they aren't completely stuck up their own asses, and this guy definitely was.

ROOM ROULETTE

Because Tallahassee was home to Florida State University, and because it was the height of the college football season, finding hotel rooms was a huge challenge. Weekends when the Seminoles were out of town were not an issue, but for the nights before and after home games, we had to scramble.

Many of the rooms in the nicer hotels were booked a year in advance for big matchups, like when the Hurricanes came to town and A-Rod was there. We had to move at least three times, which was a serious pain in the ass, especially when we had live shots that day and had been up late the night before.

We'd need to pack and get out and still get to work on time, which was often before we could check in to our next home away from home, which meant we'd have our luggage with us all day and would most likely have to wait until the wee hours of the next morning to check in, unless we could race over there in a short window between 7 p.m. and 8 p.m., before we had to get ready for the next round of hits for the late news.

One of my rooms at the Sheraton downtown was a penthouse suite because that was all they had. The Sheraton was one of the tallest buildings in the area at the time, built in a circular shape, and my floor-to-ceiling windows gave me an awesome panoramic view from the living/dining area. The sprawling suite had a big, long dining table and a mini kitchen with an ice maker, so one night when I got off early, I ordered pizzas and hosted a poker game and won a few hundred bucks off my colleagues.

This was the room I hoped to keep for the rest of my stay, but of course it was booked the following weekend, and I had no choice but to find another rental bed.

SHEP'S ARREST

One of the wackiest things that happened during our month-plus in Tallahassee was when one of our anchors, Shepard Smith, got arrested on his remote set on the grounds of the

Capitol Complex, right before he was to anchor *Studio B*, his show at 3 p.m. ET. I'll never forget the moment Don Collopy, one of our engineers, a big, hilariously funny guy, came running into the satellite truck we were using as a workspace.

"Dude! Shep just got arrested!"

"What???" I asked, stunned. "Where?"

"On set! The cops just showed up and took him away!"

I dropped the script I was working on and ran outside to the spot where all the cables ran to, a shaded spot under the overhang of the front deck of what I think was the Senate Office Building on the grounds of the Capitol Complex. Our engineers and techs had commandeered a corner and built a temporary "studio" for Shep's two daily shows, one hour each, every afternoon and evening. The camera and production guys were all standing around looking shocked and confused, and I started asking around to find out what happened.

It turned that out Shep and his favorite producer and pal Erik Liljegren had taken their rental car and grabbed lunch and were hurrying back so that Shep could get in position for his show. When they got to the most convenient parking lot nearby, a woman was standing in an empty space, saving it for a colleague on the way. Shep was a hothead and yelled at her to get out of the way, and when she explained she was holding it for someone else, he got pissed, yelling, "You can't hold parking spaces. Get the fuck out of the way!" or something to that effect.

The woman, Maureen Walsh, a freelance journalist for a local cable outlet, refused to move, and Shep began inching forward to force her out. She held her ground, and he kept getting closer until his front bumper was up against her legs. She claims he hit her hard enough to bruise her legs and showed off the alleged injuries to local authorities. Shep told me that Walsh exaggerated the whole episode, dramatically leaping onto the hood and claiming that he hit her, which seemed a more likely scenario to me.

In any event, he forced his way into the space, grabbed his stuff, and he and Erik hustled to the set. In the meantime, Walsh called police, who showed up, took her statement, then headed to the Capitol Complex to find Shep seated in his director's chair with three cameras pointed at him, mic'd up, IFB (interruptible feedback) piece in his ear, staring at the prompter, about to be counted down to start the show.

The conversation went something like "We're looking for Shepard Smith," and he said, "That's me," and the police said, "We need you to come with us," and he said, "I'm about to anchor the news," and they said, "We don't care, we're gonna need to you to come with us NOW," and he looked into the camera and said to producers watching from the control room: "Well I guess I'm getting arrested." He took his mic off, unplugged his earpiece, and headed off with the cops to be booked and processed.

Shep and I were good friends at the time, and he later told me what a miserable experience it was, with fingerprints taken and a full-on cavity search. I don't recall how long they held him, but I heard later that the control room was in a complete panic, unsure of what to do with just a few minutes until showtime.

He was charged with aggravated battery with a motor vehicle and released on $10,000 bail and was back on the air the next day. His arrest and mug shot made national news. In a statement, Fox simply said: "Shepard Smith was arrested for aggravated battery in Leon County. We're still collecting the relevant facts of the case."

Shep later settled the case out of court and told me he paid the woman somewhere in the mid-five figures to go away.

I COULD'VE BEEN ARRESTED TOO...

After a month of long days and nights of nearly non-stop hanging-chad coverage, I was burned out, homesick, and desperate to get back to New York City. When I got the green light to book a flight, I found one that was leaving in just a couple of hours and required a connection in Atlanta. I packed my stuff and threw it in my rental car and practically burned rubber out of the parking lot on my way to Tallahassee International. I've always loved driving fast, and I've been pulled over a bunch of times, and my Fox News ID card had gotten me out of many, many tickets. Not on this day.

I was desperate to get to the airport on time and encountered some traffic, so I made some crazy moves, including passing cars using a center-turn lane and veering around a semi-truck that had blocked the road to back into some loading dock. At some point a souped-up Camaro or Firebird started following me at high speed and I assumed he was racing with me, and I did my best to lose the guy, but it turned out it was a cop in an unmarked vehicle.

I was maybe five minutes from the terminal when he hit his lights and siren and pulled me over, and when he got up to my window, he was super pissed and asked why I was driving like such an asshole and what my big hurry was. I told him who I was and how long I'd been there and why I was racing to the airport, but he was not impressed, and I'll never forget what he said to me:

"I thought you robbed a bank!"

He wrote me a couple of tickets for excessive speed and reckless driving, and I sheepishly drove the last miles at the posted speed limit and somehow managed to make my flight.

EPILOGUE 1
HANGING WITH THE GOO GOO DOLLS

Two years later, Fox sent me back to Tallahassee to cover the midterm elections and report on which changes had been made since 2000, and to see if there was any kind of repeat of the hanging-chad controversy.

It just so happened that left wing filmmaker Michael Moore was also in town, sponsoring a "Get out the Vote" concert the Friday night before the election at the Leon County Civic Center featuring the Goo Goo Dolls, a rock band from Buffalo, New York. The Goo Goo Dolls were very well known, and the show was packed. One of their albums spent almost a full year on the Billboard 100 charts, and their song "Iris" was number one for eighteen straight weeks.

We didn't know it, but the band was staying in our hotel, and late that night, once we'd packed up our gear after our last live shot, we went to the hotel bar, which was unusually crowded. We assumed it was because the concert had ended and it was one of the closest watering holes to the venue.

My producer, cameraman, and I ended up at the far end of the bar, ordered our drinks, and quickly realized the guys in the band were right next to us. I wasn't a big fan of their music at the time and didn't recognize them, but other people in the bar kept coming up to say hello and I overheard them. Not being shy I started bullshitting with the guys, mostly Johnny Rzeznik the lead singer, and Robby Takac the bass guitarist. Their drummer Michael Malinin was there, too. We proceeded to get hammered together and were having a great time, and eventually, after last call, one of the guys said they had a bunch of wine in their room and went up and got it, and we commandeered a couch area in the lobby near the front door and kept drinking and telling stories.

I remember Johnny was hitting on some girl for much of the time and was trying to make out with her outside the front doors, and since they were all glass, we were watching and laughing because he wasn't having much success, and when she ditched him and he came back in, we started giving him a hard time about it.

He looked at me and goes: "You're a national news correspondent. You must get all kinds of girls!" And I looked at him and said, "Dude, you're a *rock star*! There's *no* comparison!" and we actually debated this for a while.

I saw them a few more times after that, including at the Superdome in New Orleans for the first home game after Hurricane Katrina, where I interviewed them on the field before the game when they were done with their sound check, and saw them again in New York City, when Robby got me backstage passes for a show in Times Square.

It was just another one of those random events I never would've experienced if not for the amazing job I had.

EPILOGUE 2
SEAN HANNITY & THE BAYONET

One of the other wacky incidents that happened in Tallahassee involved Sean Hannity, one of Fox News Channel's most popular prime time hosts. An outspoken conservative and Republican cheerleader who knew the Bush family, Sean flew down to Tallahassee on a private jet a few years after the recount to do a one-on-one interview with Jeb Bush inside the Governor's Mansion.

This was not long after I'd returned to New York from Iraq where I'd been embedded. During my time in the desert, a few different Marines came up to me and gave me Iraqi bayonets they'd found on the ground to bring back as gifts to Fox talent in New York. I actually found another one and kept it for myself. It's clearly old but in great shape, with a long six-inch blade with a curved tip in a metal sleeve, designed to attach to the end of an AK-47.

One of the Marines who gave me one of these knives specifically asked me to give it to Sean along with a note, and I promised I would. When I got back to New York, one of my first stops was the office of Roger Ailes, the former president and CEO of Fox News Channel who created the network with the financing and direction of Rupert Murdoch.

I loved Roger. I considered him a genius, and he was always very, very good to me. He was extremely supportive and complimentary of my work and rewarded me handsomely for my dedication to the channel and the craft, eventually making me the highest-paid correspondent at the network. I gave Roger one of the bayonets the Marines had given me, and then I went to Sean Hannity's office and gave him his, along with the note the Marine had written to pass on. Sean loved it and put the weapon in his briefcase.

Fast forward to Sean arriving at the Governor's Mansion for his interview. There was obviously heavy security there for anyone entering the building, including Sean, who had to put his briefcase on one of those airport-style luggage X-ray machines and then walk through the archway metal detector before retrieving his bag.

The officer manning the machine stopped him.

"Do you have a weapon in your bag?" he asked.

Sean, who does have a permit to carry handguns, was smart enough not to bring one with him.

"No, of course not!" he later told me he told the guy.

They ran his bag through again, and the officer told him he'd need to take a closer look, and he did, and he pulled out the bayonet.

"OH MY GOD!" Sean exclaimed. "I completely forgot that was in there!"

He then told the officer the backstory, and they may have had a laugh about it, and security held the bayonet for him while he interviewed Jeb and gave it back to him on his way out.

CHAPTER 8

HURRICANE HUNTER

I chased and covered dozens of hurricanes over the past three-plus decades, and the story of each storm is different. The experiences could be exciting, even exhilarating, usually exhausting, and frequently completely frustrating.

I was rarely the only reporter sent to cover a storm (it happened just once that I can recall, in Bermuda, detailed below). I'd be a part of "team coverage," and it was the bureau chiefs and upper management who decided whom to put where, often positioning crews over several states with hundreds of miles between them.

If we were "lucky" enough to be assigned to the storm's landfall location as the hurricane approached, we were in for one of the most exciting and frightening rides of our lives.

Countless hours of pounding rain, howling winds, and moments of sheer terror, followed by long and usually hot days of finding the worst damages and stepping carefully through the debris to report on what the fierce winds and violent downpours had done to the residents of that particular community.

More often than not, we wound up at a location outside the impact zone, sometimes virtually untouched by the storm. We'd still have our live responsibilities, going on TV every hour or two to talk about preparations for potential disasters, but we'd be fifty or a hundred miles or more from where the hurricane was actually going to hit, which meant it might be sunny days and clear nights and maybe just some rain in our area, while up or down the coast people were getting slammed and we were missing it.

It was like being sent to cover a murder trial and reporting on it from the wrong courthouse.

We didn't want to be safe and dry. We wanted to be at the edge of danger and soaking wet, but once you committed to a location with a killer storm system barreling toward shore, you usually had to stay there until the worst weather passed, because once conditions started deteriorating, it was simply too unsafe and, in some cases, impossible to drive, because of the conditions you'd encounter along the way.

It was always a big debate where to go, weighing the best guesses of the National Hurricane Center, the National Weather Service, our own Fox Weather Team, history of past storms, our gut instincts, and the positioning of other crews.

If the most likely destination of a particular hurricane was Tybee Island, Georgia, but the network already had three reporters there, we'd have to go somewhere else north or south that was also in the cone of probability, like Savannah or Charleston or Jacksonville Beach. And while what was happening in those cities mattered, including the storm preps and evacuations and cautionary sound bites from officials, it just wasn't as good a story if we wound up safe and dry while another area was getting walloped.

I always pushed for the most likely "ground zero" for the main event. Sometimes I got sent where I wanted, more often I had to go where they told me, and most of the time we'd have to scramble once the worst of the weather passed to make it to the hardest-hit areas so we could at least be front and center for the second part of the story, which was the aftermath and cleanup. It wasn't always about putting the best reporter in the most likely landfall location, since, as with everything else, politics would play a role. If a major storm was headed for Miami, for example, the correspondents in the Miami bureau would be front and center. I could get sent down to work a less desirable shift, like overnights, or report for Fox News Edge, the affiliate news service, doing lives for local stations across the country interested in hurricane updates, or I'd get sent to the next-closest spot in the cone of probability, usually at least forty or fifty miles away.

I remember one time fighting to go to one particular beach town and losing the argument with the Atlanta bureau chief, who left the network not long after that. She wanted us somewhere else, and we begrudgingly went there, and when she realized she'd been wrong' and we'd been right, she told us to go there as the storm was rolling in, and I tried to control my anger as I explained to her that we needed to do that hours earlier when we first pushed to move, and now it was simply too late. It was highly dangerous and just plain stupid to try to drive hundreds of miles in bad weather, and it was irresponsible of her to ask. We couldn't and wouldn't do it. We were stuck where we were until after the storm, when travel was still challenging, hazardous, and slow because of downed power lines, washouts, and the debris littering and blocking many roads.

Following are some of my biggest hurricane experiences and some of the most memorable, compelling, and bizarre moments from those trips.

HUGO, 1989
MY FIRST STORM

There have been many "holy shit" moments in my reporting career, as in "What the fuck am I doing here? Am I gonna die?" type moments. The first of these actual life-threatening experiences was in Charleston, South Carolina, the night of September 22, 1989, when Hurricane Hugo slammed into the Carolina coast.

I was twenty-nine years old, working as a freelance reporter for WPTV-TV Channel 5, the dominant NBC affiliate in West Palm Beach, Florida. My cameraman and I were dispatched a few days before the storm to cover preps on the ground and be in position when the monster made impact. I'd never covered a hurricane before, so I had no idea what was in store for me, but I was about to be tested in ways that would challenge my strength and resolve and prepare me for the countless catastrophic moments I'd face over the next thirty-plus years.

Hugo was a beast—at its peak, a Category 5 on the Saffir-Simpson, one of the most powerful Atlantic hurricanes in decades, and the costliest ever at the time, with an estimated $11 billion in damages (it would later be topped by other storms that I also got pounded by, including Andrew, Katrina, and Sandy).

Hugo's direct effects devastated the homes, cars, and businesses of some two million people. It crushed nearly everything in its path, killing sixty-seven people, thirty-nine of them in the aftermath. The timber industry was among the hardest hit. South Carolina suffered over a billion dollars in lost inventory, with 95 percent of the trees knocked down in Charleston and several thousand more snapped, uprooted, or truncated ten to twenty-five feet above ground. It was heartbreaking to drive through the city and see the beautiful, stately old trees twisted and forced off their roots, crushing homes and vehicles and blocking roads, and to drive on the highways, with the pine forests that lined the roads now looking like fields of sharpened sticks pointing toward the sky, the greenery all but gone. And the destruction didn't end there.

More than three thousand historic structures in Charleston were heavily damaged, some hundreds of years old. Some twenty thousand newer homes and businesses were also battered or obliterated by the high winds, pounding rains, and storm surge. Hundreds of boats that weren't dry docked were tossed everywhere, on lawns and roads, upside down on top of homes, some carried a half mile from shore, most ruined beyond repair. Watercraft were everywhere they didn't belong, and we started getting used to seeing fishing boats and speedboats and sailboats around every corner, upside down on a street or sitting in someone's front yard.

The death toll wasn't as high as it might've been because more than a quarter million people heeded the mandatory evacuation orders, but many of those who stayed behind later told us they regretted it, after suffering through the roughest ride of their lives, and hundreds of them were hurt in Hugo's wake, trying to mend the mutilation.

In the days leading up to the storm, we filed reports on locals preparing for the worst by boarding up their homes and stores, stocking up on supplies, and packing their cars with their most precious belongings before fleeing to higher, safer ground further from the coast. We worked from early morning till late at night, getting very little if any sleep, running on pure adrenaline laced with increasing nervousness at the massive storm system headed right for us.

Watching the satellite images grow larger and seeing the projected path, a direct hit on Charleston, was an absolutely unnerving experience that I would repeat dozens of times in the years ahead.

At one point before landfall, Hugo was a Category 5, the most powerful on the Saffir-Simpson scale. By the time it hit Charleston, Hugo had downgraded slightly to a Category 4, but the beast packed winds of 140 miles per hour when it slammed the coast. My cameraman and I had already retreated to our motel about ten miles from the coast, along with dozens of other members of the media. The NBC affiliate satellite truck we were assigned to broadcast from was parked next to a porte cochere at the front lobby entrance, where we could stand with some protection from the driving rain.

We were sharing the truck and satellite space with reporters from other stations, so we had to wait our turn for our slot in that night's 11 p.m. newscast. We were up third, with a five-minute window from 11:10 to 11:15 ET. Our station had one of the highest-rated local newscasts in the nation, commanding more than 50 percent of the viewers in the market every night, and I'd never been more excited for a live shot, especially considering that the conditions were deteriorating rapidly and we'd be able to "show and tell" just how nasty it was, reporting from the center of the storm with winds howling in the triple digits at our location.

Yet, the connection died, and I never made it on the air that night.

A REASON TO PRAY

It's hard to describe just how gnarly things were, right before the truck lost its satellite signal. The rain was falling in heavy sheets, a rough, pounding downpour driven sideways by the howling winds that were well above one hundred miles per hour at our location. We could hear trees cracking all around us and the loud bangs of transformers exploding on utility poles. It was like a fireworks display on the Fourth of July, with thunderously loud bangs, and sparks cascading in all directions as the lights went out, block by block.

With trees shattering, the wind howling like a freight train, and the thick, sharp, painful rain slapping us in the face and soaking our bodies to the bone, my cameraman struggled mightily to keep his balance, hanging onto his tripod for dear life as other shooters held onto *him* to keep him from getting knocked down.

No one could help *me* stand because I was on camera, doing my best to brace myself against the gusts, one foot firmly planted in front of the other, leaning in, holding a stick microphone, and struggling to hear the producer and programming through the IFB in my ear. I knew this could be a pivotal moment in my young career, and I was ready to rock and roll in Hugo's face.

And then, our shot was gone. The engineer came out of the truck, yelling to us over the thunderous weather that he'd lost the signal and there was no way it was coming back. He had to drop the dish and shut the truck down because things were getting so bad, and we knew we needed to seek shelter. The safest thing we could think to do was to gather our gear and try to make our way back to our room. That relatively short walk to the rear of the building was one of the most frightening experiences of my life.

It was the first time I truly thought I might die, and it was also the first time I prayed to God to spare my life.

Our motel was like one you've probably seen a thousand times, a big square two-story building with interior rooms facing a courtyard and exterior rooms facing the parking lot. The paths to the rooms were exposed to the elements, ringing the inside and outside of the building, with waist-high railings and peripheral staircases, also exposed to the unforgiving elements swirling around us. Our room was around the back, but there was a shortcut through the courtyard.

I got separated from my cameraman at some point as I made my way from the truck in front of the lobby toward the side of the building, now fully terrified as the winds continued to intensify, with stuff flying and breaking in all directions. I kept waiting for a branch or piece of roof or broken glass to hit me or cut me. I was on my own, survival of the fittest in a way I'd never had to endure before.

It was now about 11:30 p.m., just a half hour before the hurricane's fierce winds would reach their peak. When I turned the corner, I was forced to hug the exterior brick wall of the motel, hands spread out, inching along at a snail's pace, trusting that if I pressed up against the solid structure hard enough and made myself flat enough, I wouldn't be blown away.

I was hearing the worst sounds I'd ever heard, ominous life-threatening, life-ending kinds of sounds. Glass breaking, debris flying, the wind howling at insane volume, stuff crashing all around me, the loudest, most evil kind of thundering weather you can imagine. I'd never considered myself religious, even when I was reading the Torah at my Bar Mitzvah. But now, at twenty-nine, in the heart of the most powerful force I'd ever encountered, I understood why and how people found God, or at least a reason to call His name.

At some point as I inched along the side of the building, a group of other journalists, probably the crew scheduled to follow our live shot from the same satellite truck, rushed by in a rugby scrum, shouting as they hustled past me like they were coming from a frat party. On instinct I jumped in behind them through the howling winds and driving rain until we reached the cut-through to the courtyard where conditions weren't quite as bad.

At this point I was able to break away from the group but still found myself inching along, finding the interior staircase and making my way up the steps one at a time, finally reaching our room, where I found my photographer soaked but safe. We were physically unscathed but severely shaken, and conditions outside were only getting worse.

We put towels under the door to try to keep the water from soaking the carpet, waiting anxiously to see if the wind would blow out the rattling windows or rip down the walls. Sleep was impossible, even though we were both completely exhausted.

After a few more hours of howling and shaking, the noise subsided outside as the eye of the storm arrived. It was the calm center of the storm, and conditions improved dramatically. Everything got eerily quiet. Even the rain stopped, so we grabbed our gear and headed outside to survey the damages.

It was still dark, but we could see a graveyard of downed trees and broken glass everywhere, most of it from car windows smashed by flying debris. We made our way toward the front of the building and when we got there, we witnessed an incredible sight.

The motel had one of those enormous signs you could see from the highway, probably a hundred feet tall on two thick steel poles. It failed in the face of Hugo's bullying gusts, plunging right through the roof of the lobby, which we were later told had just undergone a $1 million renovation. I have no idea what it cost to repair what got wrecked.

My cameraman and I collected whatever video we could and then hurried back to the room before the eye fully passed and the storm kicked back up again. After more than forty straight hours on alert and on duty, we both crashed hard, and neither of us thought to set some kind of alarm. This was before cell phones. We didn't even have beepers.

With power and phone lines knocked out, we never got our scheduled early morning wake-up call, and no one from the truck came looking for us, and we slept right through the window for our 6 a.m. live shot and kept snoozing right through the rest of the three-hour morning show. We startled awake around nine, and I'll never forget the sheepish trek to the truck, a true walk of shame, calling the station and finding out they thought we might be dead.

I've always been honest and ready to admit my mistakes, and I told the assignment desk exactly what had happened. Then I had to tell the news director, who wasn't nearly as understanding.

He was really pissed that we'd missed our morning hits. It was a huge story, and even though we'd been there on the ground for days reporting Hugo's every angle, and would stay to report on it for several days more, we weren't on TV the early morning after, which was our job and probably when most people were tuning in to see what happened to Charleston.

It was our job to be up and on camera, and we'd failed our station at a crucial moment. The boss told me he was glad we were okay and that we'd talk about it when I got back.

HERE TODAY, GONE TOMORROW

That meeting happened the next week. I knew I was in trouble, of course, but I also naively expected him to thank me for risking my life, and for all the stellar reports we'd filed for every show from sunrise through the late news each day (except for the hit we couldn't do during the storm, which wasn't our fault, and the shots we slept through the next morning, which was).

He showed me no love in his office that morning. Instead, he gave me a hard, unforgiving stare, reprimanded me, and then said something to the effect of, "If you do anything like that again it'll be the last day you work here."

I bristled at the slight but kept my mouth shut because I didn't want to lose the job, but just a few weeks later the news director at WSVN in Miami decided I was ready for prime time and offered me a higher-paying job in a much bigger market. Telling the guy in West Palm I was leaving for a better gig was one of the sweetest moments of my young career.

ANDREW, 1992
SOUTH FLORIDA

Three years after Hugo, I found myself covering an even bigger storm named Andrew, which I'm convinced would have killed me, my crew, and hundreds or thousands of others had it remained on course and slammed into Fort Lauderdale, where we'd set up our cameras, working and waiting on the beach without a solid plan of escape.

Andrew was a monster Category 5, the most destructive hurricane ever to hit Florida, the strongest to hit the U.S. in decades and the costliest of all time, until Katrina, which I also covered.

By the time he got to south Florida, Andrew had already ripped through the Bahamas and Louisiana, causing major damages, but he hadn't lost any of his punch, projected to make a direct hit near the Miami–Dade/Broward counties line with maximum sustained winds of 165 miles per hour and gusts approaching 200 miles per hour.

It was August 1992. By this time, I was a reporter for Miami TV station WSVN 7's Broward bureau, and as Andrew approached, I was dispatched to wait for him on the strip of beach along State Road A1A in Fort Lauderdale, famous for being home to spring break revelers since the '60s. Every local station had at least one crew there that night doing live shots as the storm approached.

I was excited about the assignment, but nervous too. We'd been watching the footage of the destruction that Andrew had already caused, and the satellite image of the massive storm, an ever-growing giant green blob, was a constant on our screens, a haunting moving image down in the corner, reminding viewers of the hell on the way.

That night on the strip in Fort Lauderdale, I remember being disappointed that we weren't hit harder. It was a driving rain with strong winds, for sure, but nothing like what we were bracing for. The storm had taken a last-minute hook to the left, sparing the most heavily populated areas of the state, slamming instead into a much more rural and sparsely populated section called Homestead.

We were sent there the very next morning to survey the damages, which were beyond anything I could have imagined.

This was 1992. GPS units for cars didn't exist yet. We still used paper maps back then. And as we got closer to the hardest-hit areas, we realized that the wind had knocked down every highway sign, so it was really challenging to figure out where we were, which exit was coming up, and which one was ours. Almost every street sign was knocked down or blown away, too, so finding a specific address was next to impossible. We literally had to count blocks and lots, referring to our maps and asking for directions. Many of the homes were completely gone or left in absolute shambles, knocked off their concrete foundations, roofs ripped away, walls shattered and splintered and scattered across great distances.

It's estimated Andrew decimated well over sixty thousand homes and did significant damage to one hundred twenty thousand more. The death toll was sixty-five, but I believe it would have been *far* higher had Andrew stayed on course. It also helped that more than a million people had evacuated north to safer parts of the state. The damages would have also been much higher had Andrew come ashore in Fort Lauderdale or Miami, but at an estimated $27 billion, it was still the costliest storm on record at the time.

DON'T CALL HIM ANDY

We drove down to Homestead and explored neighborhoods every day, going live from the yards of homes that no longer existed or had roofs and walls ripped off so you could see the furniture inside. One day we went to an area called the Redlands, which had been hit harder than anywhere we'd seen.

I interviewed one longtime resident who told me he kept a big, heavy freezer for extra food on the back porch, and the morning after the storm it was gone. His family searched all over their large property (most of the homes there were built on at least a few acres) and finally found it, completely past the front yard, across the street in the drainage ditch, tossed there like some lightweight trash.

Then I asked about the remains of a roof in the backyard, a big chunk of A-frame with the shingles still attached.

"Is that from your house?" I wondered, since his roof was gone.

"Nope. We think it came from that house over there," pointing toward a structure at least a quarter mile away.

I walked through the yard, which was littered with big heavy C-clamps. Not the little ones you might use for small home projects, but heavy industrial-size ones.

"Are these yours?" I asked.

"Definitely not," he told me. "I've never seen those in my life."

"What about this?" I asked. I'd found a heavy, ten-pin bowling ball.

"Nope," he said. "We don't bowl."

I was stunned, trying to imagine the force of wind that could pick up bowling balls and heavy pieces of metal and a freezer that must've weighed at least a hundred pounds fully loaded, and just carry them and drop them hundreds or thousands of feet away.

SIGHTSEERS AND SCAMMERS

In the days after the storm, traffic began building until it was nearly impossible to get to Homestead by car. Utility crews were trying to restore power, other city, state, and county response teams were clearing debris and searching for victims and survivors, the curious were crowding roads to take pictures and see things for themselves, and there was a massive flood of contractors and con artists going door to door, offering help in everything from clearing debris to repairing roofs to offering help filing insurance claims. It seemed like every guy with a pickup truck and a chain saw was headed south from Miami (and way beyond, including from North Florida and neighboring states) trying to cash in on the destruction.

Remove that tree? I got this, for $1,000. Rebuild your roof? No experience, but no problem: ten grand. There was an epidemic of scammers taking cash and taking off before finishing or even starting the jobs. Hotlines were set up for the victims, who often had no power, no water, holes in their roof but nowhere else to go, and fearing looters would clean out what remained of their valuables if they let their property unguarded. People were getting ripped off left and right, which became another focus of our coverage.

My station had its own helicopter, so it started using it to shuttle crews back and forth. Getting a lift down there was an absolute godsend, saving us hours of travel time each way, and I hitched a ride every chance I got.

The other thing I remember most about Andrew was the stench of rotting meat. We didn't know if it was from dead bodies or rotting food, but in the heat of the Florida sun, any meat or dairy or other products no longer being kept cold smelled really, really bad, permeating the air in the trailer parks and the more densely populated neighborhoods we'd roam for that day's stories. Dead bodies rotted too and would smell even worse, so it was often impossible to know if we were near human death or a defrosted T-bone.

DRIVING INTO DANGER

The crazy thing about covering hurricanes is just how contrary the whole assignment is. National, state, and local officials all go on TV urging caution, warning people in low lying areas and vulnerable coastal communities to evacuate as soon as possible, and we breathlessly repeat it. "Head for higher ground!" "Don't be reckless!" "Protect yourself and your family!" "If the winds don't get you, the surge will!"

And, yet, there we were every time, often the only vehicle driving *toward* the coast while everyone else was headed in the opposite direction, trying to put distance between themselves and the approaching danger.

If we drove in, we were in the photographer's crew car, a big Expedition or Suburban, and sometimes had our own vehicle too, usually a large rented sedan or second SUV. If we flew in, we always rented the biggest SUV available or got stuck with a van because that's all that was left.

Then, before we got where we needed to go, we'd go shopping, making shelf-clearing trips to the local Target, Walmart, Dick's Sporting Goods, sometimes a military surplus store and usually a grocery store, buying cases of water, Gatorade, and Red Bull, along with breakfast bars, cans of tuna, jars of peanut butter, and other non-perishable foods.

We'd buy chips and cookies and other snack food we could munch on during the long days and nights, buying bread and lunch meat and other stuff we could keep fresh in the coolers we added to the back of our SUV, topping everything with ice we often had to search for.

We'd buy plates and cups and trash bags and extra socks and T-shirts and batteries and sometimes hip waders or water-resistant pants and jackets and extra gas cans, anything and everything we didn't have time or room to pack.

All of it would go on the company card, sometimes $800 to $1,200 in a single store, with no worries about getting reimbursed. It was the price of coverage, and the bosses at Fox rarely pushed back. It could comical when they did, like singling out a $7 plastic football from a $1,000 itemized receipt as a non-essential item and forcing me to pay for that myself.

Once we'd fully loaded our vehicle(s) with our new coolers and our luggage, equipment, and other supplies, we'd make our way to the projected impact area, cruising along the coastal highways and bayfront roads, looking for people getting ready to stay (boarding up) or go (loading up) so we could hop out and shoot some quick B-roll and a short interview and then jump back on the road, trying to find and negotiate hotel rooms even as the front desk was calling guests telling them they had to get out *now*.

Most chains wouldn't rent rooms after evacuation orders were issued, in part because of liability concerns, but also because they probably didn't want dead people on their properties. They'd usually keep a skeleton staff on duty, and some of the privately owned hotels would do the same, with either the owner or manager or maintenance guy sticking around to try to protect their investment when things got dicey, and these locations were usually a bit easier to get into.

I got skilled at talking our way past the restrictions and edicts, scoring rooms in countless waterfront locations. I knew exactly what to look for, the kind of structure that would give us the best chance not just for survival, but at keeping our shot up during the storm.

I usually had to do this *after* our original hotel would kick us out, or not let us check-in, because the managers changed their minds or didn't fully understand my request or someone else made the call with seniority over the person I'd made the agreement with. I'd get into heated arguments with desk clerks about them throwing us out into the streets as a beast of a storm was barreling in, after we'd been assured we'd be able to ride it out there.

This happened in Wilmington, North Carolina, when Hurricane Florence had grown into a monster Category 4 with gusts topping 160 miles per hour, on a direct path to battering and flooding the state, with Wrightsville Beach in the center of the crosshairs.

DANNY, 1997
MOBILE BAY, AL

Just months after I was hired full time at Fox News Channel, in July 1997, I was sent down to Mobile, Alabama, with Hurricane Danny gaining strength as it spun over the Gulf of Mexico.

Danny wasn't that powerful a storm and turned out to be the *only* hurricane to make landfall during the Atlantic hurricane season that year. Danny wasn't dramatic and fortunately did far less damage, compared to those that came before and after. What Danny did do is spawn numerous tornadoes that left nine dead and $100 million in property loss (all occurring after it passed over our location) and produced extreme rainfall, more than three feet in spots.

Danny was an incredibly slow-moving storm, generating an insane amount of rain, parking right over us at Mobile Bay, drenching us with torrential downpours that didn't let up for a full twenty-four hours. In other words, Danny turned out to be a miserable pain in the ass, one of my least favorite storms with one bright spot: I collected one of the best sound bites of all time, from a local guy I interviewed during the nonstop monsoon.

"What do you think of this hurricane?" I asked the man.

He looked at me and without missing a beat, said, "Danny is like the drunk uncle who refuses to leave the party."

I used that line for almost every live shot for the rest of that storm.

GEORGES, 1998
MISSISSIPPI GULF COAST

Hurricane Georges may not be one of the most famous storms to rock the world, but he brought considerable misery and pain to millions of people. Georges was one of several powerful and deadly storms spawned during the 1998 Atlantic Hurricane season, causing widespread destruction across numerous island nations blasting its way through the Caribbean as a Category 4, killing more than six hundred people and causing close to $10 billion in damages, much of it on the islands of St. Kitts, Nevis, and Puerto Rico.

We were waiting for him in Biloxi, Mississippi, one of the times we'd guessed right about where to best position ourselves for an approaching storm. Georges had hit the Dominican Republic and Cuba before reaching Key West as a Cat 2, so he was making landfall for the seventh time when it reached us on the Gulf Coast with sustained winds of 105 miles per hour.

Georges brought torrential rains totaling two to three feet in several Southern states, causing extensive flash flooding, and its winds were strong enough to rip roofs off buildings and homes, knocking down power poles and lines leaving hundreds of thousands of homes and businesses in the dark, including our hotel.

We were able to report on the storm's approach and arrival and found damages the next day consistent with a Cat 2, but nothing remarkable. One of the more compelling stories involved a temporary shelter set up in the gymnasium at a nearby community college. During the height of the hurricane, while four hundred people were huddled inside the gym, the winds ripped the roof right off, forcing all the people to jump up and find somewhere else to hide in the building until they could be moved to another more suitable shelter the next morning.

CHARLEY, FRANCES, AND IVAN, 2004 FLORIDA

I found one reporter notebook with not one or two but *three* separate storms hitting Florida, one after another, during the 2004 Atlantic hurricane season. Charley arrived first, on August 13, coming ashore as a CAT 4 in Punta Gorda, about a hundred miles south of Tampa where forecasters had predicted landfall. I don't have any significant notes or memories of Charley, but I remember Frances very well.

Frances came ashore about three weeks later as a CAT 2 on September 5, hitting Hutchinson Island on the Florida's east coast before spawning a bunch of tornadoes as she crawled north.

We covered the storm and aftermath, first from Fort Lauderdale, which was in the cone of uncertainty, and later from further north in Stuart, where it hit. We started in Fort Lauderdale in part because I knew the owner of the Lago Mar resort (not to be confused with Donald Trump's Mar-a-Lago), and he always took great care of me. He let us stay in a beautiful huge oceanfront suite even though the hotel was closed to guests.

By the time it became clear that we were too far south to get a good smack from Frances, it was too late to move. It sucked missing the drama of the storm's arrival, and we were forced to do the kind of shots you've seen a hundred times: "It's not bad here, but forecasters say it could get worse, and just north of us..." We got cleared early that evening so we could pack our stuff and get up super early the next morning to head north and survey the damages. And that's when we saved a guy's life. Maybe. Sort of.

NOT ALL HEROES WEAR CAPES!

We were with an extended team at Lago Mar, so we had several vehicles following each other for the trip up to Stuart, including multiple crews and a satellite truck. Our SUV took the lead, with my producer Gary Gastelu, me, and one of our engineers, Don Collopy, in the vehicle.

We were maybe halfway there when something crazy happened on the highway, which I decided to sum up on a couple of pages of my reporter's notebook right after it happened, probably for a blog I never wrote.

Here it is:

> We left Fort Lauderdale at 6 this morning in a five-vehicle convoy and headed north on I-95 toward Stuart, virtually alone on the usually crowded highway.
>
> We'd just passed a washed-out section of the roadway when our satellite engineer Don Collopy saw a car off the road down a short hill, half buried in a ditch in the woods lining the highway. I don't know if he saw what looked like someone passed out behind the wheel or if he just felt the need to investigate and make sure no one needed rescuing, but he yelled, "Pull over!" and one by one, we all did.

We jumped out and ran down to the vehicle, surrounded by thick trees and branches and sitting in a couple feet of rising water.

It actually took a couple minutes to get close to the car because the brush was so thick, and the water was deep. [Don later reminded me and another colleague, Joel Fagan, that he walked through water almost to his waist to climb on the hood of the car to get a look through the windshield.] We then discovered someone was in fact inside, either dead or asleep behind the wheel.

We started yelling and pounding on the vehicle and window and it took a while to get his attention (he'd apparently passed out), but eventually we determined he wasn't injured.

We got the door open and out stepped the driver, a man by the name of Paul Bulko, who'd already lit a cigarette and stuck it in his mouth. The pack of smokes stayed dry because he had them rolled up in his sleeve. Cool and calm, he told us he'd been in the car for five hours after losing control of the vehicle in the worst part of the storm and driving off the road.

There was water filling the floorboards of his vehicle. I have no idea how high it might've reached and if or when Paul might have been able to get out on his own, or if someone else would've come along and helped him.

We put Paul in one of our vehicles and waited about 20 minutes until we could flag down a passing police car. When we left, the officer was reprimanding Paul for driving thru a hurricane.

He'd told us it was his first, and hoped it was his last.

DRINKING AND DRIVING

Stuart was the epicenter of the storm, which meant there were plenty of compelling stories, along with a severe lack of basic services. One day we did live shots at the only gas station in the region that somehow didn't lose power and was able to pump fuel until its tanks ran dry. Police had to provide security to prevent fights between impatient motorists, since the line of vehicles waiting to top off their tanks stretched more than a mile.

We got hotel rooms in Stuart, but the power was out, so there was no AC and it was super uncomfortable. Some of the guys stayed there anyway, but Don, my producer Gary, and I got cheap hotel rooms near Miami International Airport where they still had power, AC, and hot water. It was a nearly two-hour drive each way from Miami to Stuart, but the three of us felt it was worth it. To help pass the time and make the journey more enjoyable, each evening when our shift was over, we filled one of our coolers with beer and topped it off with some of the ice they were handing out at relief stations along with food and water for local residents in need.

Then we'd head south, with Gary driving while Don and I hammered beers all the way, swapping stories until we got there. We'd get to our rooms and grab a few hours of sleep, then take care of the three S's (shit, shower, and shave), grab some coffees, and hit the highway back north for another day of newsgathering and live shots.

I remember one early evening on our way to a live location, we were speeding down a two-lane highway and all of a sudden reached a stretch of road with objects strewn all over it, and before we realized what they were, we heard and felt them cracking and crunching beneath our tires. It was some kind of mass migration of land crabs, hundreds if not thousands of them trying to cross the road.

We barely slowed down, crushing the sea of crustaceans until we reached the other side of their wide path, continuing on to meet our truck for the last hit of the day.

IVAN THE NOT-SO-TERRIBLE

After we were done with Frances, we made our way down to Key West to wait for Ivan, which began forming in the Atlantic the day Frances hit and at one point reached Category 5 strength, pretty much freaking out everyone in the Sunshine State, now facing the third major hurricane in as many weeks. The Keys appeared especially vulnerable, a string of low-lying islands with few safe places to ride out a storm of that size and strength.

Evacuation orders were issued, homes and businesses quickly boarded their doors and windows, and authorities refused to open shelters anywhere along the island chain, bussing people to the Miami area instead. Even the Boca Chica's Naval Air Station was shuttered, with all personnel flown out on big lumbering C-9 military transport planes, and the rest of the aircraft and equipment stored in hangers or tied down.

I'd spent lots of time in Key West and had been there for a bunch of storms, but I'd never seen this level of preparation, especially on Duval Street, typically filled with drunks and tourists, most of whom couldn't care less about an approaching storm (especially the locals), but because of all the deaths and damages that Ivan was wreaking in the Caribbean and Jamaica and later Cuba, authorities were being overly cautious. I even found a quote in my notebook from Cuba's former Communist dictator Fidel Castro, who told his people: "Whatever the hurricane does, we will all work together to rebuild."

In the tag to a live shot for Greta Van Susteren's show that night, I said: "The people here, Greta, are independent and free spirited, and are enjoying the peace and quiet. Key West has dodged a lot of storms, they haven't seen a CAT 4 here since 1919."

As it turned out, the jaded and carefree locals were right. As Ivan started jogging west into the Gulf, Emergency Management officials started saying they were "cautiously optimistic" but that "we're not out of the woods yet," and then, with Duval Street and the rest of the island almost completely deserted, Ivan went straight into the Gulf, completely sparing the Keys, giving those who evacuated more reasons *not* to do so the next time.

This forced authorities with egg on their face to use some tried and true expressions like "better safe than sorry" and "this is an inexact science" and "it was a good drill" and "the last thing we want is to put people in harm's way."

Ivan wasn't done, of course, roaring into Gulf Shores, Alabama, as a CAT 3, close enough to Florida's panhandle to directly impact that portion of the state, including causing severe damages to the I-10 bridges across Pensacola Bay, with support beams battered by ten- to fifteen-foot waves.

But we missed that part because we were out of position and couldn't fly over or get around the storm in time. I somehow avoided the next one, too, an unprecedented fourth major hurricane to hit one state in six weeks. Hurricane Jeanne was also a CAT 3 that made landfall just two miles from where Frances came ashore twenty-one days earlier. I honestly don't remember if I was asked to go on that one, and if I was, I must've cried uncle to my bureau chief, meaning I'd had enough of getting soaked, and my colleagues would have to handle Jeanne without me.

KATRINA, 2005
MISSISSIPPI GULF COAST

I've covered the impact and aftermath of dozens of storms and natural disasters, but I don't think I've ever seen destruction to the extent I did after Hurricane Katrina hit the Mississippi Gulf Coast in late August 2005.

Katrina first hit South Florida as a tropical storm, coming ashore near Hallandale Beach before crossing the state and re-forming and strengthening in the Gulf of Mexico. When I saw how big and bad Katrina was getting, I asked my bureau chief to send me to cover the story, but she said the assignments were already handed out, and I wasn't on the list.

This really upset me at the time, as I considered myself among the best and most qualified correspondents at the network to handle this type of event. I asked some other bosses about getting added to the coverage team, but it didn't happen for a couple of days, and I was getting antsy as Katrina rapidly grew into a monster Cat 5.

Finally, someone decided I could be useful as a backup to the teams already in position and sent me to Tuscaloosa, Alabama, to wait for and report on the storm when it moved inland.

We did live shots that day, August 29, near the campus of the University of Alabama, while Katrina was destroying miles and miles of coastline a few hundred miles away.

"The storm is headed this way," I said, after reporting that Alabama's governor had declared a state of emergency. "Schools are closed, including the University of Alabama, and authorities are expecting a lot of rain, trees down and widespread power outages, encouraging people to stay home and pay close attention to the weather."

"The county is urging high-profile vehicles like vans, buses, and tractor trailers to stay off the roads and encouraging people to implement their hurricane preparedness plans."

I did the best I could to include the most compelling headlines in my report, and just after our live shot at 6 p.m., we got a phone call from New York asking us to head toward New Orleans. The storm had done significant damage, and the network needed all hands on deck.

"NOW they ask us?" I thought, since it would've been far easier to get there a day or two earlier, but we packed up and got in the car and started rolling south on I-59 for what would normally be about a four-hour drive. It was a straight shot from Tuscaloosa to Crescent City, but not on this night. We were in for one of the longest, strangest, and most ridiculous drives we'd ever made.

PICKUPS AND CHAINSAWS

The weather was still bad, though not horrible, but conditions on the roads were another story. The further south we drove, the worse the damages became. Trees were down everywhere, many of them blocking the Interstate. I'd never seen anything like it. Tall pine after tall pine, splintered at the base and laying across the lanes, partially or fully blocking the road. In some places we could pull onto the shoulders to get around the fallen timber, and in other places we'd use the U-turn cut-throughs where cops would typically hide to catch speeders, and we'd continue south in the northbound lanes until we could cut back over again.

Eventually we wound up behind a caravan of guys in pickup trucks who I think were headed down to make money clearing trees and debris from people's homes and property. They had chainsaws in the back of their vehicles, and when they rolled up on a tree blocking the highway they'd get out and cut a path through them, sawing through the trunks in lane-sized widths and pushing the logs to the side.

I'd never seen anything like this in my life. It was a slow crawl, but at least we were making progress. There's no way we could've gotten to the coast without those guys. I lost count of how many times they had to cut through another tree, but it was a lot. At some point we had to stop for fuel, and this became a whole other adventure because the power was out everywhere, and no gas stations were open. We started going through neighborhoods looking for homes that might be occupied, where residents hadn't evacuated, and when I saw someone outside with a boat on a trailer in the driveway, I said, "Here! Stop here!"

I got out and asked the guy if he could spare any gasoline, and he said sure, giving us the contents of a spare can in the garage. I think it was only five gallons, but it was enough to get us where we needed to go, and I think I gave him $50 in cash.

We got back on the road and continued our long journey south, and at some point we got re-directed to the Mississippi Gulf Coast. There were reports of widespread destruction there, and it was closer for us than New Orleans. When we finally reached Biloxi, it was 2 p.m. the next day. It took us almost twenty hours to get there.

What we saw when we reached the Gulf Coast was shocking. Katrina had spawned a killer storm surge in the Gulf, bringing a wall of water twenty-seven feet high to shore, where it kept pushing inland for miles, flattening nearly every home and business in its wide path. Other reporters kept saying it "looked like a war zone," and I hated that analogy. I *had* been to plenty of war zones, and they didn't look like this. Buildings weren't bombed and left in piles of rubble, they were wiped clean off their cement pads and foundations.

There weren't craters in the ground or burned-out hulks of vehicles hit by enemy fire. The lawns and roads were covered with stuff that belonged somewhere else, and the vehicles were either gone or fully intact but upside down or tossed on top of each other like Tonka toys. Boats, too. One casino ship was sitting right in the middle of Highway 90 along the coast. Other watercraft were scattered everywhere—on the beach, on side streets, on front yards, or propped up on severely damaged structures.

Many trees were down, too, including some that appeared to be hundreds of years old. All that was left of a McDonald's near the beach were the poles that held the sign and some wires sticking out of the concrete pad where the building used to be. The beach and streets and lawns were littered with debris, including sections of brick walls and iron fencing, sinks, refrigerator doors, AC units, box springs and mattresses, bicycles, cinder blocks, roof frames, even a toilet. There was an overturned van and tanker truck in the road, two jet skis sitting on an abandoned trailer, windows blown out on every building still standing.

Everywhere we looked, there was another scene of destruction we could talk about in a live shot, including a Hard Rock Hotel & Casino that had just been built on the Gulf. Its grand opening had been scheduled for that upcoming Wednesday. The first two floors suffered major damages, and the side door was open, so we actually did a walk-and-talk live shot with our wireless camera, taking viewers inside the hotel's restaurant, where the guitars and other memorabilia had already been mounted on the walls and were still there, some of it a bit battered.

This was how I summed it up in one of my live shots that first day:

> Casino row in Biloxi, battered and littered with debris. The Hard Rock is now the "Hard Luck" Casino and Hotel, supposed to open Wednesday at midnight. Now it could be months before this place and this city can recover.
>
> Up and down the Gulf Coast, entire apartment buildings have been leveled, churches smashed

by waves and wind, roads buckled, flooded, or collapsed, and home after home seriously damaged or totaled. We watched stunned residents search for remnants, surveying their losses, and saw grown men reduced to tears, their dreams shattered, their memories washed away, their lives changed forever.

Sixteen thousand casino workers are now out of a job, and many more people are homeless, without phones, power, hot water, and cold drinks. I asked one man if he'd rebuild his home and he said, "the whole city has to rebuild."

There were nine hundred thousand without power statewide. The governor said, "it took years to build the system and one day to wipe it out." Officials estimated that 90 percent of the structures between the beach and railroad tracks in Biloxi, Gulfport, Long Beach, and Pass Christian were totally destroyed. "Not severely damaged," they said, "they're simply NOT THERE."

There were hundreds dead and hundreds more missing. Bodies were found in the streets, and residents who'd evacuated were told not to return home so that they wouldn't get in the way of emergency vehicles and first responders carrying out search and rescue missions.

Boil-water notices were in effect. Ice water and food distribution centers were set up, and long lines appeared almost immediately. The damages were catastrophic and widespread, and we spent the next few weeks doing our best to cover it all, moving from town to town along the coast, highlighting the worst damages and most compelling stories of survival.

Spans on some of the major bridges were broken or washed away, including a big stretch of the Ocean Springs Bridge, adding hours to commute times for folks needing to go from one side to the other.

I talked to one guy who'd ridden out eight hurricanes in his house over the past twenty-two years but lost everything in Katrina. I met another guy who worked as a blackjack dealer on a casino boat. The boat was ripped from its moorings and wound up right next to the man's house, flattened by the storm surge.

The death toll rose with each passing day, as did the damage calculations. Bodies were being stored in refrigerated tractor trailers when the morgues ran out of room. Many of the corpses were too decomposed or damaged to identify. The Red Cross was collecting missing persons reports, getting thousands of calls an hour.

We did flyovers of the devastated landscape in a helicopter and spoke with local, state, and federal officials and politicians, including Governor Haley Barbour and Senator Trent Lott. We followed President George W. Bush as he walked through some flattened neighborhoods, calling the devastation "worse than imaginable," promising that help was on the way.

ROUGHING IT

There were no working toilets along the beach during our coverage of Katrina's aftermath, and early one morning I really needed to take a dump and knew I had to improvise. I grabbed some paper and walked into the parking garage of the casino where we'd parked and set up for live shots and found a box spring in a back corner, just the exposed metal and springs, and used it as a place to plant my rear, with open holes beneath me. I was basically balancing my naked rear on metal wires. It was really uncomfortable, and it was also already really hot and humid, and, unfortunately for me, this particular poop did not want to leave my body. I was badly constipated and sat there straining to try and make it happen for ten minutes, twenty minutes, thirty minutes. I was past the point where I could just get up and take care of business later. I had no choice but to finish the job, and I was pouring sweat.

I think it was at least forty-five minutes before I was able to return to the truck, drenched and exhausted.

STINKY CHICKEN

One day, we went to Gulfport to report on the damages there, which were just as bad as in every other town along that stretch of beach. A large warehouse-type facility there had stored tons of raw chicken, ready for distribution to area stores. But when Katrina swamped the place, it left the chicken strewn everywhere, on the street in front of us and all around us, apparently covering roads and yards in an eight-block radius, and that chicken quickly began rotting in the hot sun. When I tell you it STANK in Gulfport, I mean it really STANK. The smell was so bad, my cameraman and I wore face masks someone miraculously had in their kit, like the N-95s we were encouraged to wear during the coronavirus pandemic. The masks helped, but not much, so we collected video as quickly as possible and got the hell out of there.

HOW TO DRIVE 75 MILES IN 45 MINUTES

There were no good hotel options anywhere near Gulf Shores, Alabama. Everything was closed at the beach, and the few hotels off the highway that stayed open had running water but no power or AC. We got rooms in one of them, and I was so uncomfortable I got out of bed and slept in the car. No way I could do this for any stretch of time, definitely not for the two weeks I was there, so we somehow found rooms just past Mobile, Alabama, seventy-five miles away, on the other side of the I-10 bridge over Mobile Bay.

Every night when we were done with our live shots, we'd get in our rental cars and head east to the hotel. It was a significant distance, especially after our long hard days in the sun, but there was minimal traffic, and I felt like the cops had far better things to do than worry about speeders in the days after they'd been completely upended by the most devastating hurricane to hit that area in modern history. I always drove fast, but on this trip, I drove faster. I'd rented a really nice Lexus SUV at the airport. It was really comfortable with a great stereo system and lots of power, and I made full use of it, drawing the ire of one of our young crew guys Mark Cubrilo. One of his jobs was to fill the tanks of the vehicles at one of the few open gas stations in the area, which fortunately had a set of pumps set aside for police, first responders, and media, so he didn't have to wait in long lines, but it was still a pain for him to go there, and he reminded me that the faster I drove, the worse the gas mileage was, and I was burning through it faster than anyone else.

The other person who got mad at me was one of our photographers, Tommy Chiu, who was following me back to

Mobile one night after our shift ended and trying to keep up at speeds topping one hundred miles per hour when he got pulled over. When I saw him stopping behind me, I pulled over too and doubled back to vouch for him. The cop was pissed, telling us he had no choice but to pull Tommy over because of his excessive speed. I apologized on his behalf, explaining that he was following me, and it was my fault, and it was only because we were so exhausted after so many long days and nights of hurricane coverage. He took pity on us and let Tommy go with a warning. Tommy then warned *me* to slow down, but of course I didn't.

My record speed was 150 miles per hour, which I hit on that seven-and-a-half-mile bridge over the bay.

THE SECRET MISSION OF GENERAL HONORE

One of the things the President did to try to get the situation under control was to hire former Army Lieutenant General Russel Honoré to serve as commander of Joint Task Force Katrina, tasked with coordinating military relief efforts after state and local agencies got heaps of criticism for performing poorly in response to the disaster. He was from the area and tough as nails, earning the nickname The Ragin' Cajun.

Now, on these pages, I will tell a story about him that I have never told publicly before:

One day during our Katrina coverage, I got a call from our D.C. bureau. The producer of *Special Report with Bret Baier* wanted to do a profile on General Honoré and had arranged with his staff for a reporter to spend a day with him, like an embed, traveling with him as he moved across the region handling what needed to be handled.

I was thrilled because I respected Bret's show a lot. I was great friends with Bret and appreciated his no-nonsense style of reporting, which I thought was similar to mine. The show was smart and thorough and strong. It did real news, and I always liked being in its rundown.

I don't remember exactly where we first met up with the general early that morning, but we spent almost sixteen hours with him, flying back and forth across Mississippi and Louisiana in HH-60 Army Blackhawk helicopters, and motoring in Humvees and big transport trucks.

We followed him with a camera as he barked orders at underlings and toured operations centers and distribution points and other areas of interest, whipping underlings into shape along the way. We asked him questions from time to time as we rolled around, gathering excellent material for the profile.

"The storm is the enemy, not the people," Honoré told me and gave me the secret to his management style and how he planned to rectify the relief operations:

"It's like early in a football game when the opposing team is running up the score. You call your team to the sideline. There's still three quarters left! Are you gonna spend your energy talking about what you're doing wrong? Or focus on what needs to get done? The energy should be on the next three quarters."

He was proud of the Army, which was on the ground in New Orleans the day after Katrina hit. After Hurricane Andrew, it took nine days for the Army to reach South Florida, blaming the delayed response on the government taking time to assess damages before sending in the troops.

And he told me that the Public Affairs Officers who handled the bridge between military and media advised him to tone down his cussing because it could "interfere with the message."

We visited the Emergency Operations Center in Jackson, Mississippi, getting status updates from officials there and Governor Barbour, who told Honoré with a smile that he loved him and asked for a hug.

Honoré talked about how the challenge in Mississippi was much different from New Orleans, with the coastline destroyed along with basic services including water, electricity, telephone lines, and cell towers.

"When you can't communicate, you can't coordinate," he said, calling it a "perfect storm." He had all kinds of one-liners, like, "y'all lookin' at the calendar, I'm lookin' at my watch."

"You can't be stuck on stupid," he said. "Let's win this game!"

We took the Blackhawk down to New Orleans and bounced from the USS Iwo Jima to the Superdome to some hotel, then to City Hall and back to the Superdome and then on to Kenner, where the New Orleans Saints training facility in nearby Metairie had been transformed into a relief operations headquarters.

At some point while we were there, Honoré had a whispered conversation with some of his people and then looked at me and said: "We gotta go take care of something. We'll be gone for an hour or two and talk to you when we get back."

I'd built a solid rapport with him and didn't hesitate to voice my objections, despite the former three-star general's intimidating demeanor.

"No way!" I told him. "They told us we could spend the entire day with you and the day isn't over yet. We go where you go! That was the deal. We're coming with you guys."

They whispered among themselves and then said, "OK, you can come with us, but this mission is OFF THE RECORD."

I thought they might be kidding at first but quickly realized they were serious, and I agreed to the conditions because now I was even more curious where they were headed and didn't want to miss it. Now that almost twenty years have passed since

I agreed to keep things under wraps, I feel like the statute of limitations has run out and I can share this story.

As I recall, the General and his staff actually made us leave the camera behind in an office, which my photographer was reluctant to do, but eventually agreed to, and we followed them back to the Blackhawk and flew to the Emergency Operations Center in Baton Rouge. There, they borrowed one of those big Army trucks with the open back, and we all climbed in and drove across town to some apartment complex.

When we got there, I spotted a tree that had fallen in the storm and landed right on the roof of a newer model Volkswagen Beetle, which was one of the only cars still sitting in the parking lot. I said something about how unlucky the owner of the car was, and Honoré said, "that's my daughter's."

It turned out his daughter lived there and had left before the storm. I still wasn't sure why we were there, and watched as one of the general's minions climbed up on a fence and pulled himself up to a second-floor balcony, where he forced the sliding door open, walked in, and opened the front door of the apartment to let us all in.

Then, one of the guys went searching through the place and came back with a cat in his arms.

This was a rescue mission, I realized. His daughter left the cat behind when she took off in a hurry, not thinking she'd be gone for more than a night, but then she couldn't get back, and she needed her dad to go get her cat, and he did.

The general's people grabbed a cat carrier and whatever cat food they could find, and we all left and got back in the truck and drove back to the Emergency Operations Center where they did their best to smuggle the cat in and out, hiding it from view until the general could take it home later that night.

At one point, I swear he looked at me and said with half a smile, "If you report this, I'll kill you."

Before we said goodbye, we sat down for a final, formal interview, where he told me he'd spent thirty-four years in the military, and this was his first time applying military power in a domestic situation. He grew up in Louisiana, in the small town of Lakeland in Pointe Coupee Parish.

"Does it upset you to see what happened here?" I asked him.

"Absolutely," he said, "but it's a force of nature. Who you gonna get mad at?"

"A lot of people look around and see little hope," I said. "What do you see?"

"A *lot* of hope!" He answered with enthusiasm. "War goes away and the city comes back. We did it before and we'll do it again."

RITA, 2005
KEY WEST, HOUSTON, LAKE CHARLES

When I heard that another huge storm was brewing in the Gulf, just three weeks after Katrina, all I could think was, "you gotta be fucking kidding me," but there she was. Her name was Rita, she was on her way to Category 5 status, and she was headed for the Florida Keys, so we went there, too.

I think we did one day of live shots, covering the evacuation of every tourist and all eighty thousand residents of the Keys, including Sugarloaf, Big Pine, Marathon, Islamorada, Plantation, Tavernier, and Key Largo, talking about tolls being suspended and schools being closed and shelters being opened, and all the wind and rain and surge expected, and then—Rita decided she didn't want to visit there after all and made her way into the Gulf, so we made a mad dash for the airport and flew to Houston to get ahead of her.

The next round of live shots was about the more than one million Texas residents being told to evacuate between Galveston and Corpus Christi, in Surfside Beach and Freeport and Lake Jackson, and how Rita could be the strongest hurricane on record to hit that state.

And then I guess Rita decided she wanted gumbo instead, because her path shifted toward Louisiana, so we packed up again and raced for the state line.

FINDING OUR SPOT

One of the biggest challenges in storm coverage is finding an ideal location to report from. It wasn't just about picking a scenic location. Ideally, the photographer would be under an overhang, or in a covered hallway with an open-air end where I could stand and show the elements while he and the camera stayed as dry as possible. It could even be a balcony, where he was in one corner and I stood by the rail. We needed a sturdy structure, of course, but also some kind of elevation. A higher floor was key, but it was better if it was in a building built on stilts, or a dune, or higher ground overlooking a waterway. We needed palm trees or signs or traffic lights in the background, something we could light up that would help to demonstrate just how powerful the winds were.

But it was also imperative that we find a good spot for the satellite truck to park. The best-case scenario was on elevated ground to be safe from floodwaters, on the backside of our hotel or any building facing the direction the winds were coming from. It could be alongside a parking structure or backed into a corner with high walls on both sides. The better the protection the truck had from the winds, the longer the big dish on its roof could stay up pointed toward the sky. As long as he could maintain a signal to our satellite, we could stay on the air and report through the storm. The goal was to be live when things got really bad, but it was very, very difficult to do this because the high winds would invariably interrupt transmission.

Chasing Rita from Texas into Louisiana, we crossed the state line and were headed east on I-10, then jumped on I-210, taking us further south, closer to the Gulf. We were looking for a solid location in Lake Charles to burrow in for the storm, and when we came to the top of the Israel LaFleur Bridge, spanning the Calcasieu Ship Channel and Prien Lake, we saw the tall waterfront tower of the L'Auberge Casino rising above the landscape like an oasis in the desert. It was beautiful and looked perfect for us, and I could swear I heard angels singing. I exclaimed, "Let's go there!" like a little kid pointing at a shiny object, and we exited the highway and found our way to the hotel's front doors, which were locked.

I banged on the doors, and a manager showed up and told us the hotel was closed.

"I'm Rick Leventhal with Fox News," I told him. "We're just looking for a place to ride out the storm and report from and we'll give you lots of on-air credit!"

He laughed, and said, "I love Fox! I just turned CNN away 'cuz I can't stand them. How many rooms do you guys need?"

I can't tell you how many times the Fox vs. CNN thing worked in our favor, but this was one of the better instances.

I told him we'd like at least three, but he said he could only give us one, even though the hotel had hundreds and was virtually empty. I guess they didn't want to have to clean multiple rooms after we left, so me, my photographer "Hollywood" John Kisala, and our producer Maryam Sepehri all shared the room. We offered Maryam one of the two beds, but she chose to sleep on the floor.

When L'Auberge gave us the green light to stay, we first looked for where to put the sat truck and found an absolutely perfect spot out back. There was a parking structure several stories high, connected to the backside of the hotel. There was a corner where the garage and hotel tower met on the far side of the structure, on flat ground, giving the big rig total protection from the winds swirling in. There was also an entrance to one of the stairwells right there, which led up to the roof and a covered area where the photographer could stay dry and shoot out onto the top deck, where I could stand in the elements and show how hard the rains were coming in and how difficult it was to stand in the wind. I also had a much better chance of not being struck by debris, since I was at least five stories up with nothing around me that could break off and fly my way.

The engineer ran transmission and power cables from the truck up the stairs to the roof of the garage. Hollywood was able to keep his camera relatively dry in the stairwell alcove (and I would take refuge in there with him between hits), and we never lost our signal the entire night. The channel kept our shot in a double box on the screen for hours. I think we were the only network able to keep a shot live throughout the storm. I heard later that the CNN crew that tried and failed to stay where we stayed wound up in town and lost their signal early in the storm. I'd go out and stand in the shot once or twice every hour, or more often when there was nowhere else for producers to go or when things got really dicey. It was a brutally long night, and we kept working through *Fox & Friends* that morning before finally getting a break to grab some sleep.

IDA, ROGER, AND THE BACKWARDS CAP, 2009

One of my favorite hurricane stories happened on Dauphin Island, Alabama, during our coverage of Hurricane Ida in 2009. It was the middle of the afternoon as the storm was picking up, which felt rare because hurricanes always seemed to come ashore overnight. We were set up on the back corner of a property at the edge of the Mississippi Sound and Mobile Bay, where the wind was whipping hard across the open water, creating white caps behind us, making a dramatic backdrop.

I was wearing rain pants and a yellow rain jacket and my Fox News baseball cap, but I didn't want it to blow off my head so I turned it around backwards so it was more secure and still hid my hair, which was a soaked mess.

I did what I thought was a stellar live shot with Shepard Smith on his *Studio B* show at 3 p.m. and noticed about halfway through that my producer on that trip, Andrew Fone, took a phone call. When I was off the air, Andrew looked at me with a puzzled and amused expression.

"That was the executive producer in the control room," he told me. "Roger [Ailes] called them during your hit and told them, 'Tell Leventhal if he ever wears his hat backwards again, that'll be the last time he appears on my air,'" or something to that effect.

I was stunned. Ailes was my rabbi, the guy who brought me in and always gave me props for being among his best correspondents. He was gonna fire me for wearing my hat backwards?

I called the executive producer after the show, and she assured me I wasn't being fired, but that Roger Ailes was seriously pissed, and I shouldn't ever do it again. I didn't, until he died, and the next storm I covered, when the wind started whipping, I thought of him as I turned my cap backwards and positioned myself for the next live shot.

THANKS, GOVERNOR!

While we were on Dauphin Island, the power went out. It seemed strange at the time because the weather hadn't gotten all that bad yet. We then learned it was because a sailboat went off course and clipped the main line, and that was that. We'd have to get our power from the sat truck, which had its own generator, but we also realized the island had no high ground, and if there was a significant storm surge, the truck would've been under water, and we would've been done. Fortunately, that didn't happen.

What did happen is that the state troopers closed the bridge and wouldn't let anyone over in either direction, but at some point, we had to go back to the mainland. Earlier in the trip I'd met and interviewed the governor, Bob Riley, and he said if we needed anything, "don't hesitate to call."

I took his offer seriously and rang his office. I can't remember if I spoke directly to him or to one of his people, but I explained that they'd closed the bridge and we needed to leave the island and asked the office to ask the troopers to let us cross, and the troopers said they could open the bridge for twenty minutes. I asked, "Does 7:30 tonight work?" They promised to make it happen, so we packed our stuff and loaded up.

We had two vehicles on this trip. Paul had an SUV, and I had a big Lincoln, and when we got to the roadblock at our end of the highway leading to the span, troopers were there and told us the bridge was closed. Andrew, in his thick British accent, said, "If you call the governor's office, I think you'll find it's open from 7:30 to 7:50."

They came back and begrudgingly moved their cruisers, and we escaped. I took the lead and went racing toward the bridge, with Paul and Andrew trailing far behind me, and as I was headed onto the span, I hit a huge rock that somehow for some reason was sitting in the center lane.

I couldn't swerve to avoid it in time and somehow didn't blow a tire, and I quickly called Andrew and said, "Hey, there's a big rock in the road about a mile ahead of you. I just hit it!" And Andrew said, "How fast were you going?" And I said, "Fast!"

A similar conclave of cruisers was waiting for us on the other side, but they'd already pulled out of the way, and we waved at them as we drove past, headed for Mobile. We spent the night there, hoping to board an early morning flight through Atlanta to connect to our homes in Boston and New York City, but that flight out of Mobile was cancelled, so we drove the 320 miles to Atlanta and flew home from there.

IGOR, 2010
BERMUDA

There's a good reason why you may not remember Hurricane Igor. Even though Igor was a huge and dangerous Category 4 with sustained winds of 155 miles per hour, he never hit the U.S. and never threatened to. Igor just created a bunch of massive waves over the Atlantic Ocean as he churned north, well offshore from the East Coast. Igor's real claim to fame was being the most destructive tropical cyclone on record to hit Canada's Newfoundland Island. But the reason I'm mentioning him here is that Igor was one of the best hurricanes I ever covered, because I somehow convinced my bosses to send me to Bermuda, which *was* in harm's way.

I'd just been in Bermuda on vacation for a long weekend a year or two earlier, and absolutely loved the island and promised my bureau chief that I had good contacts there and could get a deal on an awesome location right on the ocean, an excellent vantage point for the coming storm, which might cause significant damages, so I called the Fox travel office and booked my first class flight (one of the best perks in my contract), and the team from Boston, whom I really liked working with (producer Andrew Fone and cameraman Paul Celeste), met me there.

This was the best of both worlds. I got a free, all-expense-paid trip to a beautiful and lush (and typically very expensive) vacation spot, got paid while I was there, and even earned two comp days because we "worked" through the weekend, without having to suffer through a devastating storm. I used my contacts to rent a large three-bedroom condo with a big terrace and its own private pool, at the same hotel I'd stayed in on vacation, but this time at a significantly reduced rate that I'd be reimbursed for anyway. It had a full kitchen which we stocked, and we bought wine and whiskey and vodka and mixers and had several boozy nights, which usually ended up with my playing pool with my photographer Paul in the game room. It also had a hot tub on the terrace, but I'm pretty sure Andrew was the only one who used it.

At first, we were busy because forecasters were warning that Igor was headed for a "virtual direct hit" on Bermuda. The storm was six hundred miles wide and its eye was twice the size of the island. It was moving slowly, which meant the sixty-four thousand residents could be in for extended battering. One of the fun facts I learned while doing my research for the story was that Bermuda, at just twenty-one square miles, was the third-most-densely populated place on Earth.

Residents might be isolated for days after the storm hit. There could be widespread power outages, shipwrecks, property damage, and beach erosion, but most of the buildings were expected to survive, because they were built to last, made of block and stone with foundations in bedrock and slate tile roofs. But, because the hurricane was so large, the island was expected to get pounded and punished for up to forty straight hours.

We dutifully reported the warnings from the public safety minister that this would be "probably the worst storm we've seen," with a chance for fifty-foot waves, tornadoes, and flooding, none of which materialized.

The island nation's premier gave his own somber address, telling his people: "Today we stand on the eve of the arrival of one of the worst hurricanes to ever threaten our shores. We've rarely faced a storm of this magnitude."

We bought the last portable generator at the only big hardware store in town (and returned it unused the day after Igor brushed past us) and set up for live shots from our terrace.

"Almost every forecast model shows Igor on a collision course with this island," I said on air with conviction and intensity.

"They've dodged a lot of storms but it doesn't look like they'll dodge this one, so locals are boarding up businesses and buying stacks of plywood at Gorham's Home Center which has been busy for days, selling candles, flashlights, torches, batteries, and other essentials."

Gorham's is the place that sold us the generator, and we had to talk them into it, but they were cool, so I gave them the free plug as a small gesture of our gratitude.

I also reported that "a lot of tourists cancelled trips here because of the approaching storm, and many who were here got out early on a cruise ship or on extra flights added yesterday and today." This sucked for the hotels and restaurants, of course, and all of the other businesses relying on tourism, second only to international finance and banking as Bermuda's most essential economic driver.

Then, as often happens, Igor began to weaken, and his course began to shift, and a direct impact became less likely. The dangers started to fade. Lower wind speeds, less rain, smaller surge.

In the end, Igor did bring powerful Category 1 winds to the island, knocking down trees and cutting power to 80 percent of the residents. There was some erosion of Bermuda's famous pink sand beaches from fifteen-foot waves battering the coastline, but property damage was minor.

The next day I reported on "just how *well* this tiny island had weathered Igor's punches," noting that no serious injuries or deaths were reported, and while almost three-fourths of electric customers lost power in the storm, most of them had it restored the next day.

I remember a few years later, when another hurricane was threatening Bermuda, I asked my bureau chief Kendall Gastelu if I could go cover it, and she gave me one of her semi-annoyed looks and found a kinder way to say: "No fucking way buddy!"

IRENE, 2011
FORT MYERS, FL

Hurricane Irene was the first major storm of the 2011 season and is an excellent example of me being sent to the wrong place. Irene made landfall several times in the Bahamas as Cat 3 and then headed back out into open waters. For some reason my bosses sent me and my team to Fort Myers, while the storm went right instead of left and made its way up the East Coast, making landfall in the Outer Banks of North Carolina.

I think we did a handful of live shots for one day on a wide beach with sunshine and sunbathers enjoying the perfect weather. I felt a bit ridiculous standing there talking about a storm hundreds of miles away that would have zero impact on where we were. I didn't overhype it; I didn't try to pretend we were in any danger or that locals were concerned. I told it like it was and subtly made fun of ourselves before tossing back to the anchor.

The tone was basically, "there are no issues here, and it's a bit ridiculous to be talking about the storm from this location, but there are potential threats to other areas in this and other states, so pay attention to the people reporting from *those* places so we can go get a drink."

Which, of course, we did as soon as we were cleared for the day.

We were so far out of position that the network didn't bother trying to send us anywhere else. We got the rest of the day and night off and took a travel day to get home.

IRENE, 2011
ATLANTIC CITY, NJ

I didn't travel far for Hurricane Irene, barely a Category 1 when it hit the Outer Banks of North Carolina in August 2011. I was sent down to Atlantic City when it appeared that Irene might make another landfall on the Jersey Shore. I was a regular visitor to Atlantic City, even though it was a bit dumpy, because I loved playing poker and blackjack and for most of my years in New York, it was the closest place to legally gamble.

I was friends with Don Marrandino at the time, a longtime casino executive who worked at several hotels in Vegas before coming east to handle all of the Harrah's properties. He put us up in some beautiful suites, and we were there for the eventual tropical storm that Irene turned out to be when she reached us.

Irene was significant for several reasons. It was the first time in Atlantic City's history that a mandatory evacuation was ordered, and impressively, authorities said more than 90 percent of residents heeded the orders. But this was a problem because the awful flooding predicted to swamp the low-lying coastal areas never happened.

Homes weren't damaged, roads weren't rivers, everyone could've saved a lot of time, trouble, and money and just stayed home, so the following year, when Superstorm Sandy was on the way and officials began calling for evacs again, far fewer people were willing to pack up and leave. Sandy turned out to be even worse than most could've imagined, and many of the people who chose to ride it out found themselves very much in harm's way.

Irene also wound up being way more expensive than she should've been. The evacuations were ordered just before Labor Day weekend, typically one of the busiest of the year. Every gambling hall was forced to close, costing the casinos millions in lost revenue.

SUPERSTORM SANDY, 2012
POINT PLEASANT AND THE JERSEY SHORE

I couldn't believe it when I heard a hurricane was headed toward the Northeast in late October 2012. It was almost Halloween! I'd never covered a storm this late in the Atlantic hurricane season, which officially runs through November. Most of the storms hit in August or September and that would usually be the end of it.

I was given the choice of covering Sandy either from Long Island or from the Jersey Shore, and I chose New Jersey because it would get hit first, and based on the projections, it looked like the storm would hit the coast somewhere near Point Pleasant, although the entire eastern seaboard was on alert. Sandy had weakened slightly to a Category 2, and then to a Cat 1 before making landfall, but it was the largest Atlantic hurricane ever recorded, diameter-wise, with tropical force winds extending out more than 1,100 miles. Wherever she came ashore, people well to the north and south would get a taste.

We found a hotel that let us stay through the storm on Ocean Avenue, across the street from the beach. We got rooms on the second floor, including one facing the water with a balcony I could stand on and report from outside, while our photographer could keep his gear mostly dry inside the room (rain would invariably blow in when we opened the door for my live shots, but it was better than him being out in the elements with me).

We had no way of knowing just how bad things would get, but this turned out to be one of the scarier and more unsettling storms I experienced.

There was a long, high set of dunes built along the edge of the beach, creating a buffer between the ocean and Ocean Avenue and all the side streets in between. If you parked and walked to the beach, you'd get there by walking between the berms on an elevated path.

We had a clear view of one of those cut-throughs, and that evening when Sandy arrived, we watched as water from the ocean started getting pushed up and through that pathway onto the side street, making its way down the slight hill to the main drag in front of our hotel.

We reported this, showing the breach on camera, and between live shots watched as it got progressively worse. More water came splashing through, and then more, until it became a steady flow, and eventually it was like a raging river.

The Atlantic Ocean and Ocean Avenue became one. At one point, we watched in horror as a dock came busting through the now very wide opening and floated down the street.

The water was now filling the lobby below us. Our satellite truck and my photographer's big SUV were both parked in the lot downstairs on the highest ground available, but it was only a couple feet above sea level, so the water was already surrounding their tires and rising toward the floorboards.

My engineer buddy Don Collopy had left Fox to start his own company and bought Fox's old sat truck and had recently spent close to a million bucks refurbishing it. When he saw the water rising, he re-parked the rig on top of some wood blocks to give it a bit more clearance, but at some point, the water rose to the edge of the truck's back door, and he was freaking out about the potential loss of his investment.

My cameraman was freaking out, too, but it was more about him being scared than about losing his crew car. I think this was his first hurricane. He was a mild-mannered family man and not someone who lived on the edge.

He didn't volunteer for wars or other dangerous assignments. He traveled for politics or events but preferred shooting sit-down interviews or tame B-roll, clocking out at the end of his shift and commuting home. And now he was panicking big time.

"We gotta get out of here!" He screamed at me. "This is SO FUCKED UP! We could all die here!"

I tried to calm him down, but I was also really annoyed: "If you were scared, you shouldn't have volunteered for this gig!" I told him. "The storm is hitting us now. We can't leave. It's too dangerous. We have to ride it out here!"

Hours earlier, before Sandy came ashore, he was already starting to lose his composure and wanted to know what we'd do and where we'd go if things got really bad, so we took a ride away from the coast, looking for higher ground and potential shelters. We found some railroad tracks maybe a mile west and a shack we might be able to huddle in, but it was far from ideal. We decided that area would be the best place to get some elevation and separation from the beach if we needed it and still be able to report on the storm, but I definitely didn't want to go there.

At this point, the guy was a total mess, and, as I recall, he actually took his headset off and walked away and someone else had to run the camera for my next hit.

I could at least partially understand why he was so scared. We all were, watching the waves now crashing against the front doors of our hotel, the water at least two to three feet high, burying the road and everything around us. Sandy had weakened to a tropical storm at this point, but we were really feeling the eighty-mile-per-hour winds and higher gusts, shaking and rocking the building with that all-too-familiar harrowing howl.

We didn't know how high the water might rise or how strong the structure we were in really was. I'd seen too many instances where roofs came off buildings and then the walls would soon blow out and there'd be almost nothing left. Might this happen to us? Would the winds pick up further? Would the sea rise higher and completely compromise what we thought would be a safe haven?

We were definitely at risk, but at this point there really wasn't anything we could do but ride it out. The worst part was that we'd lost power, and my photographer had forgotten to charge his batteries so our camera died near the end of a live shot that evening, and we couldn't even report on what was happening until the next morning, after he was able to charge his batteries in the sat truck.

The weather slowly improved overnight. The water began slowly receding from the first floor, and the vehicles survived the storm with the interiors still dry. When we got outside, I couldn't believe my eyes.

There was at least a foot or two of sand covering Beach Avenue as far as I could see. Before long, the city had front-end loaders scooping it up and dump trucks to haul it off, but we couldn't go anywhere until they cleared the roads, so we wandered the blocks around us, gathering footage of the compromised homes, the breached dunes, the debris in the roads, and the cleanup that was just beginning and spent the day doing live shots off the dramatic ways the landscape around us had changed. We stayed in the area for days, revealing the destruction the storm had caused up and down the shore.

Sandy's damages totaled close to $40 billion in New Jersey alone, with more than two and a half million customers losing power at some point during the storm. Some streets were covered with more than five feet of water, so you can imagine how many homes were compromised, but one of the most enduring images the storm left behind was in Seaside Heights, where an amusement park called Casino Pier was built along the boardwalk, stretching out over the beach into the sea on stilts.

Casino Pier's main attraction, built out at the end over the Atlantic, was a roller coaster called the Star Jet. The pier it sat on collapsed during the storm, and the Star Jet fell into the ocean, but its structure was still mostly intact. The roller coaster looked like it was ready for the next ride, sitting in the relatively shallow water, and after TV news helicopters captured aerial video of that bent and beaten thrill ride, it appeared in almost every Sandy story we did after that.

HISTORIC HARVEY, 2017
EAST TEXAS, WESTERN LOUISIANA

I wasn't sent to cover Hurricane Harvey until after he came ashore as a Cat 4 along the coast of Texas and Louisiana and spurred catastrophic flooding with ridiculous and unprecedented amounts of rain. The huge storm stalled and dumped torrential downpours virtually non-stop for four days, eventually producing more than sixty inches of rain, shattering records and making Harvey "the most significant tropical cyclone rainfall event in U.S. history," according to the National Hurricane Center, which said the scope and amount was the most ever recorded since it started accurately tracking rainfall in the 1880s.

If you've ever been to east Texas, you know how flat it is. It's also widely paved and heavily developed, with poor drainage systems, so the water quickly collected with nowhere to go but up, creating a nightmare scenario for the residents of Houston and a bunch of other towns to the south and east. Harvey caused $125 billion in damages, flooding three hundred thousand homes, requiring first responders to carry out close to twenty thousand rescues of residents trapped in homes and cars, using boats and high-water vehicles to ferry them out.

When Fox realized how bad things were and needed to send reinforcements, my bureau chief dispatched me and one of my favorite producers, Lissa Kaplan, down to New Orleans, where we met up with Boston cameraman Paul Celeste, rented the biggest Suburban on the Hertz lot, and headed toward the impacted areas, stopping for significant supplies along the way. We figured we'd be there a while and stocked up on dry food, snacks, cases of water, and other essentials. We bought extra fuel cans and one of those metal shelves we mounted on the back of the SUV to carry the cans after we filled them up.

We bought coolers and ice and some extra rain gear, and we stopped in Lake Charles and got rooms at the L'Auberge Casino where I'd ridden Rita out, then moved a few days later to the Golden Nugget next door when I realized that my buddy Gerry

Del Prete, an executive with the company, worked there and hooked us up with some high-roller suites at a great rate.

We spent the nights in Lake Charles, and each morning we got up early and drove west on the I-10 into Texas. It was about thirty minutes to the state line, and every day we picked a different city to explore, looking for visuals and compelling stories from residents there. We shot stories in Orange, West Orange, Bridge City, Port Neches, Beaumont, Groves, Pinehurst, Vidor, and beyond.

We met families who had been forced to move out of homes they'd lived in for decades. We met guys who'd driven their monster trucks hundreds of miles to help pluck people from their swamped homes.

We found horses that had broken out from their stables and were now huddled on a front porch of a house surrounded by floodwaters, and we watched as a guy corralled them with a rope and gently led them up the street, through the deep water to dry ground.

We got tours of flooded neighborhoods on boats and trucks and went live at distribution centers providing meals to folks in need.

We'd find the locations and gather the elements and feed stuff in and do multiple live shots, then get in our vehicle when we were cleared each evening and make the hour or so drive back to Lake Charles, where we could get a good dinner and play some cards (Paul liked slots) and have a couple of drinks before bed.

I think we were there for about ten days and were definitely exhausted, but when Fox asked if we could make it to Daytona Beach for Hurricane Irma, we said yes, packing up our SUV and driving more than eight hundred miles east on I-10.

Irma was another monster that briefly attained Cat 5 status, hit the Keys as a Cat 4, hit Marco Island as a Cat 3, and was expected to impact the east coast of Florida as well. Irma wound up whipping us pretty good on the coastal highway outside our hotel, with one particularly dramatic live shot where the wind almost knocked the camera from Paul's shoulder.

FLORENCE, 2018
WRIGHTSVILLE BEACH & WILMINGTON, NC

The director of the National Hurricane Center said that Florence's size was "staggering," and the governor warned residents to "Get ready NOW." We had reservations and reassurances that we'd be able to stay in a beachfront hotel through the storm, but when we got there, the desk clerk told us there'd been a change of plans. They were closing, and we had to go.

I tried reasoning and then arguing with her to no avail, and she encouraged me to speak to the owner, who was there, so I did, patiently explaining we'd done this many times before, would sign any waiver she wanted us to sign, and I'd talk about her place on TV. We would be seen and heard by millions of viewers, I assured her, and this could help significantly boost future business, but it was still a hard no. I suspect she wasn't a Fox fan but can't prove it.

There was nothing I could do to convince the owner, so we headed out in a desperate search for lodging, with a limited window of time, since our first scheduled live shot was just a couple of hours away. We went down the road, checking every hotel we could find on that small stretch of coastline, with zero success. One of our other teams, based in Atlanta, had rented a condo in an apartment complex there and offered to let us stay, but they already had people in every bedroom, and we needed our own space.

❦

PENALTY FOR POOPING

Still homeless, we temporarily gave up on our search for lodging so that photographer Paul Celeste could set up his camera and lights for the first hit of our late shift, available for lives from 1 p.m. to midnight or beyond if needed. I found a spot near the satellite truck (already parked and transmitting for the morning team from Atlanta) next to a row of homes under construction less than a block from the beach.

I noticed workers were moving stacks of lumber and other materials onto big flatbed trucks to haul to a safer location so the stuff wouldn't blow away or damage other homes nearby when the winds picked up. I interviewed the guy supervising the project and afterwards he asked where we were staying, and when I told him we'd been kicked out and didn't have rooms, he offered us one of the model homes he'd just finished across the street.

It was brand new and staged with furniture to help sell it, so we were the first to sleep there. It was an awesome set up until the power went out and the town turned the water off, so our toilets stopped flushing, and within a day or two, all three of us (me, my photographer, and my producer) managed to clog each of our three toilets. We'd filled the tanks with rainwater from outside when the water shut off, but I guess we didn't fill them high enough, and there wasn't a plunger in the house and there weren't any stores open anymore to go buy one.

I sent an apologetic email to the owner after we left, thanking him for the hospitality and assuring him we'd pay whatever it cost to make things right inside.

I think it was at least a week later when the builder was finally able to get back into the steaming hotbox (no power meant no air conditioning, and we couldn't leave windows open because of the rain and winds), and he said the smell was overpowering and charged me something like $2,000 for the cleanup, which was fine because Fox was paying me back.

FRIENDS WITH BADGES

Major breaking news (including hurricanes, of course) always involved local police, who were always on the front lines, handling roadblocks, closures, and re-openings, enforcing evacuation orders, responding to distress calls, handling rescues, and much more. We worked with them constantly and relied on them for interviews, information, security, and access to locations deemed off limits to civilians.

When our first contact with the police in Wrightsville Beach was less than pleasant, the subject came up in a later conversation with a local guy who warned us the cops there were absolute assholes. Don't cross them or you'll regret it. This didn't concern me, since I worked for Fox News Channel, a network which as a rule supported law enforcement, and a lot of cops recognized me and appreciated my work on air. I would often offer respect and praise for officers who accomplished great and important and sometimes heroic deeds on the job, usually under duress in incredibly challenging circumstances. Many of them were military veterans who also appreciated my time embedded with the Marines in Iraq and Afghanistan. I paid my dues and wasn't afraid to get dirty. They liked that and respected me for it. I know this because I heard from them all the time.

I was a friend of the boys in blue and their federal partners with agencies including the FBI, ATF (the Bureau of Alcohol, Tobacco, Firearms and Explosives), and Secret Service. A friend in general to their agencies, and a friend specifically to a long list of guys carrying badges, with their names, cell numbers, and private emails in my phone's address book.

When shit would hit the fan, I'd immediately search to see if I knew anyone in that region, and if not, I'd reach out to others whom I knew nearby to see if they had good contacts there.

Even when I wasn't able to make a connection in advance, the typical reaction from officers or agents when we met was (1) they'd recognize me, (2) tell me they appreciated my reporting and/or my service covering the military overseas, (3) tell me they loved Fox and hated the other networks, and (4) how could they help me?

When we'd approach a roadblock, my Fox ID and/or the officers' recognition nearly always gave us access to where we wanted or needed to go.

But Wrightsville Beach was another story.

There was no warm welcome when we got to the foot of the main bridge giving vehicles access to the beachfront island on the other side. The officers didn't care which network we were with or whether we got good coverage. They needed to know if we had reservations and where we were staying and had strict rules for us to follow once we got there.

We assured them we had rooms at a particular hotel and gave them the information, and they told us not to leave the property once local evacuation orders were issued. We needed to stay off the streets, they warned us, and I assured them we would.

PUSHING LIMITS

Of course, there was no way we would simply sit in our rooms while the storm was pounding the place. No one had ever given me such strict restrictions before. The media were typically exempt from these kinds of rules. We were typically considered first responders, just like the cops and firefighters and high-water rescue teams. We were allowed to be there and encouraged to report on what was happening, to inform everyone else who *couldn't* be there and remind those who *shouldn't* be there why that was.

The first time we got in trouble was when we ventured outside the model home we'd rented to do a live shot on the main beach road which was already starting to flood in the pounding rain.

We were using our LiveU unit, which allowed us to broadcast live using a small box attached to the back of the camera. I used a wireless microphone and IFB and the cameraman could roam cable-free, so we could walk and talk virtually anywhere. It was liberating and gave us opportunities to show and tell even better stories, which we were doing at night during the early hours of the storm, standing at the corner of the absolutely empty main drag and side street lined with parking spots that led right up to the sand.

I was showing viewers the abandoned streets, the rain coming in sheets, and the wind starting to blow trees and street lights and signage poles when the cops rolled up. When I finished, they asked us what we were doing.

I explained we'd just gone live for our millions of viewers, and they told us we needed to stay on our property. I pushed back a bit, incredulous that they were enforcing these some-what ridiculous rules with a hurricane approaching, which no jurisdiction had ever tried to force on us before, but they didn't care and reminded us that's the way they did things there.

Later that night, the flooding in the streets got worse, and the water started pushing up against the garage door with our fully loaded SUV parked inside. By this time, we'd lost power and water in the house, and the walls were starting to rock from the wind blowing in from the ocean less than a block away. There was no compelling reason to stay there and some pretty compelling reasons to move to a safer location, since we had no way of knowing just how high the water might rise and whether the walls of the spec home were strong enough to withstand whatever Florence was about to smack us with.

So, despite the warning not to leave, we grabbed our back-packs and small bags with extra clothes and personal items and some water and food and the most critical gear our shooter would need and, after checking that the beach highway was clear of traffic, we rolled out and drove north about two miles to a Holiday Inn we'd tried to check into earlier that day. While scoping out the facility that day looking for the best potential locations to go live from, we had found the parking garage, which was several stories high, with the typical stone half-walls and openings all the way around with views of the ocean, dunes, beach highway, and homes beyond.

We knew this was a great spot to handle overnight live requests during the storm, since we could park against an interior wall, protected on two or three sides from the strong winds and rain, nap or relax in the car, charge our phones and laptops while gathering what information we could, and hop out when it was time to go live, usually at least once an hour.

So that's what we did, sneaking out of our in-town location, driving up the road in the rain and into the garage, where we found a spot and laid low until our first hit.

Of course, as soon as we went live the first time, the cops watching TV back at their station house saw us and quickly figured out where we were, and no more than fifteen minutes later a patrol car came rolling into the garage and found us sitting in our SUV in a back corner. They pulled in next to us, and I put my window down. I'm pretty sure it was the same guy who'd warned me earlier that night not to venture off our property.

"What are you guys doing here?" He asked.

"We're just using this as a live location," I told him. "We didn't feel safe in that house by the beach."

"You know you can't stay here. You weren't supposed to leave."

Thinking quickly, I said, "We don't feel safe driving back." This was the perfect excuse, and he was momentarily flummoxed. If he forced us out and we got in an accident, he could be held responsible.

He looked at me for a long moment, and I could tell he was pissed. He shook his head, and I think he told us we'd need to go back as soon as conditions allowed, but he also gave me a look like "this isn't over" before slowly pulling away.

KICKED OUT

At some point in the middle of the night, my cameraman Paul decided conditions were decent enough for us to try to drive back to the condo. We didn't have any more live shots scheduled and it looked like the winds weren't going to be as powerful as feared and wouldn't do significant damage to our place, and he didn't want to wait until the roads flooded any further, figuring we were better off being with our stuff and possibly finding a way to drive out to higher ground if flood waters started surging with the tide later in the day. We were also all exhausted and didn't want to sleep in the tight space of the car together. We wanted to get back to our beds, so we made the short drive home with no issues and crashed hard.

The storm rocked the walls in the hours ahead and plenty of rain fell, but Florence was just a Cat 1, not a major threat. When we woke up later that morning we went outside and shot some B-roll and started getting ready for our coverage that day. But a few hours later we discovered the water was rising fast on the main drag as the tide came in. The lower elevated stretches of the two-lane road were completely buried now, appearing to be at least a foot or two deep in spots, so we decided we'd be better off where the other crew had its rented condo, in a building about two miles south, with an elevated outdoor parking lot, well above where the floodwaters were likely to reach.

We packed our stuff and got in the SUV, and Paul started carefully driving south down that flooded road at a snail's pace, creating a wake on either side like he was captaining a small vessel, monitoring the depth on our tires and the front end.

I was shooting video of the now-flooded neighborhood and side streets as we drove past, collecting footage I could post on social media and which we could also edit into our stories later.

Paul's slow crawl soon came to a stop. The water was getting deeper, and he was really concerned that our engine would fail and we'd get stuck right there in the middle of the road.

We decided to find another way, turned around, and headed back to a bridge to the north that took us to another less-flooded road on the west side of the intracoastal waterway where we could make our way down to the *next* bridge that took us back over to the beach, where we were able to make it to the condo building and park at the high end of the parking lot next to the building.

We had an afternoon live shot scheduled, and despite the warnings from the cops, I pushed for us to take our gear back to our end of the flooded street we'd navigated to get there. There was a row of shuttered stores right there with a covered sidewalk we could huddle under to escape the rain that kept falling, and there was a great backdrop of the dune road now completely underwater. So we did a couple of really cool live shots there, and we were getting ready for the next one, when the Wrightsville Beach police returned, this time with a supervisor who was really pissed.

"We told you guys you needed to stay on your property!"

I explained what had happened the night before, how we'd been concerned about getting flooded out at our house so we moved to the garage and then felt safe coming back but then got concerned again when the water started rising so that's why we'd moved down there.

"You're supposed to be where you're staying, and if you've moved to that condo, you need to be up there and not out here on the street. We warned you multiple times. You're done. Pack your stuff and leave town NOW."

I tried to reason with him, explaining how many storms we'd covered and how we'd never been told we couldn't be out on the streets reporting on the current state of affairs. I told him I had lots of respect for police and had many friends in law enforcement and had their backs and assured him we were more than capable of staying safe and assumed all responsibility for anything that happened to us and just need to do our job.

"You lied to my officers last night. We told you to stay where you were and you didn't and now, we're having to chase you off the streets again, and I'm done with you guys. If you don't leave this island right now, I'm going to arrest you."

At this point my producer was freaking out. She wasn't a citizen and was in the U.S. on some kind of work visa and was convinced she'd be deported if we got in any trouble. Making matters worse, she'd left her backpack up in the condo—which I couldn't believe and gave her a really hard time about. It had her wallet and passport and other IDs inside, and not only were we not staying there, we needed to be ready to roll at a moment's notice because of the changing conditions and demands of the assignment and for stuff like what was happening right then and there. She'd never covered a hurricane before, and this was a serious tactical mistake.

"Can I just go up to the condo to get my bag before we leave?" She timidly asked the lieutenant.

"No. You can get the hell out of here or I will lock you all up."

So that's what we did. Paul packed his gear, and we climbed in and drove back over the span, where I couldn't resist having a few words with the cops on the other side about how I felt their colleagues had made a big mistake in the way they handled our situation, and they quickly dismissed us, telling us to get off their bridge.

Despite my anger at being kicked out of town, I do realize I was wrong and I'm responsible for my own actions. The police gave me clear instructions, and I didn't follow them. I get why they were pissed, but I also know from vast personal experience that their rules regarding the media were unfair and unnecessary. They could've and should've adjusted those rules because of the circumstances. We were in fact providing a public service. We weren't in their way and weren't interfering with their operations or hurting anyone, and the time they spent chasing us around would've been far better spent on the residents in need of assistance.

Leaving Wrightsville Beach turned out to be a really great move, not just so we could avoid handcuffs and time in a cell, but because it forced us to find stories elsewhere. And it turned out there was more news than we could ever report, with historic and unprecedented flooding, closed roads, and more than a million residents without power.

POWERLESS AND SWAMPED

Rescue teams were going house to house in numerous subdivisions left swimming in five feet of water, ferrying trapped residents to safety. Officials reported two hundred roads flooded in Hanover County alone, and more than one thousand roads statewide, making travel incredibly slow and challenging, and almost impossible in some parts. The governor called it, "the most destructive flooding in the history of the state."

Dozens of people were evacuated in the town of Leland by first responders with high-water vehicles, the residents leaving homes with only what they could carry, including their clothes and their pets. Eventually, more than three thousand would be rescued, and thousands more were ordered out of low-lying areas with the waters still rising. Hundreds of thousands of customers were without power, and more than twenty thousand were in shelters. More than a hundred vehicles were lined up at one of the few gas stations still open and selling fuel in Wilmington, but drivers had limited options getting around or getting out of town with all of the road closures. At some point Wilmington was completely cut off from the rest of the state because of flooded roads, forcing authorities to bring in relief supplies by air instead of ground transport.

At least three dozen deaths were reported, along with the deaths of nearly two million chickens in the state, after their coops were flooded in the storm.

Another problem I included in my coverage was one I'd never encountered during all my years chasing storms: Sewage plants had flooded, along with hog waste lagoons, and the bacteria contained there was now spreading across the land, going places it was never intended to go, creating a public health crisis and adding immeasurable importance to the advice to "stay out of the water."

DAM SHAME

One of the first nights after the storm, we were having a drink after work at our hotel and started talking to a local resident about the storm's impact, and he told us about a community about half an hour south that was devastated by a series of dam collapses, called Boiling Spring Lakes.

What we found when we arrived the next day was one of the most incredible things I'd ever seen. The homes there were built on waterfront lots surrounding dozens of small lakes connected by streams and controlled by dams, many of which were built beneath roadways connecting the homes to each other.

When the hurricane brought unprecedented rainfall to the area and the streams became rivers, several of the dams collapsed, and so did the streets above them. Washouts were everywhere. Getting from one block to the next could require a detour of several miles. Some residents had no way out at all. When I found the local police captain, he detailed the extent and progression of damages.

First, two upper dams failed, then five more on East Boiling Spring Road, leading to three more washouts on South Shore, and partial washouts elsewhere.

They'd rescued some people, did preliminary repairs to some unpaved roads, and set up food and water drops. He told me they'd opened spillways to lower lake levels in the days before the storm, dropping them three and a half feet, which was no easy task, but once the dams started failing, there was no holding it all back.

Four years later, the lake beds were still empty, except for the weeds and bushes that grew in the dirt, and the docks still extending from former waterfront homes. In 2021, the state finally allocated $14 million for repairs, but it might be years before the town can live up to its name again.

DORIAN, 2019
PUERTO RICO, AND DELRAY BEACH AND JACKSONVILLE BEACH, FL

Dorian was another storm we kept chasing from place to place and failed to fully experience. But what makes it most memorable for me is that it almost completely filled the time frame between my first date with Kelly, in London, and my second date with her on Italy's Amalfi Coast.

I flew to London on a Friday morning and came back to New York that Monday, after the most amazing, incredibly romantic, and life-changing weekend I'd ever experienced. I landed at JFK and learned that a hurricane was headed for Puerto Rico and they needed me to go, so I went home, unpacked, repacked with storm gear, and traveled early the next morning, making sure my passport was in my backpack, where it belonged.

We stayed in a beautiful hotel on the beach and did a couple days of live shots there, enjoying beautiful sunsets as we waited on Dorian to slam the island, but he veered around us instead, so we booked a flight leaving the next afternoon to Miami. We actually did more live shots that Thursday morning on the beach before packing up and heading to the airport, and that evening after we landed and got our rental vehicles, we headed to Delray Beach, where my crew checked in to a hotel, and I drove a few miles back down A1A to spend the night in the condo I had bought in Highland Beach.

We were supposed to be on the night shift that Friday to give us some extra time to rest, and my good buddy Phil Keating, our Miami-based correspondent, was assigned the early morning shift. But overnight, Phil took a spill, smashing his head on his bathroom floor, leaving him a bloody mess.

I was completely passed out and missed a call from the Miami bureau chief and then six more from a producer before I finally heard the phone ringing again and woke up in a fog to learn they needed us on the air *live* at the top of the next hour, which was in about thirty minutes, so I called the crew and woke them up and told them to set up on the beach in front of their hotel. I scrambled to get dressed and grabbed my stuff and raced up there and got in front of the camera with about five minutes to spare.

We did lives from the beach in Delray all that day and night, and then had to drive all the way up to Jacksonville Beach early the next morning, where it now appeared Dorian was headed.

ISAIAS, 2020
FORT LAUDERDALE AND PALM BEACH, FL

We went to Deerfield Beach and then Palm Beach to cover Isaias, but it was a bit of a dud, downgraded to a tropical storm by the time it came ashore. Isaias went on to create all kinds of problems up the eastern seaboard, knocking out power and knocking down trees, inflicting a few billion dollars' worth of damage. I'm mentioning it here for two reasons:

1. Isais was the strangest and most difficult hurricane name I had to say, repeatedly, on television.

2. Isais was the last storm I covered on location in my career at Fox News Channel.

Would I cover another hurricane? Sure, but I'd prefer to do it from behind an anchor desk. I've been rained on enough.

CHAPTER 9

RIOTS IN BALTIMORE

One of my least favorite stories to cover were protests. Not because I'm in any way opposed to people's right to free speech or assembly (part of the First Amendment that allowed me to do my job every day), but because inevitably there are people in the crowd who are there for the wrong reasons, just waiting for an opportunity to unleash violence and mayhem or to commit other crimes against people or property.

In almost every large gathering, there's usually an element of troublemakers who are encouraged or emboldened by the group around them. These are invariably criminals or the less law-abiding among us who take advantage of the cover of the crowd, or of the police being distracted or occupied by the sheer volume or actions of others, and they use that extra layer of insulation to attack officers (and journalists) with objects, start fires, break windows, block traffic, steal property, or cause other disruptions.

I was a punk once too and did things I regret, but over the years I grew up and learned some level of responsibility, and at the same time I lost any tolerance for this kind of nonsensical, disruptive, and criminal behavior.

As a reporter, I had an obligation to cover what was happening around me, and when my job put me in the middle of a protest, it often meant rushing to where shit was hitting the fan. It might be Antifa members wearing helmets and gas masks and protective gear hurling rocks and bottles at police who'd invariably respond with tear gas or pepper spray and sometimes rubber bullets or batons to beat the mob back.

Other times, it might be criminals and opportunists smashing windows and looting stores or vandalizing or setting fire to vehicles. We'd need the images to accurately report on what was happening, but that also put us in harm's way.

Very few people committing these kinds of illegal acts want to be on camera, so they often turned on us, showering me and my crew with rocks and bottles or angry words with threats of violence. Because of my lack of tolerance for this kind of behavior, my gut reaction was to fight back, challenge them, or call them out on their cowardice and criminality and try to shame them into retreat, which rarely worked.

Often, we had our own security team, but their focus was on removing us from dangerous situations or preventing us from getting there in the first place, so there was often an internal battle about going where we wanted to go and then the extra challenge of finding a safe way out.

Considering all of this, you can imagine how I felt about heading down to Baltimore in April 2015 to cover the unrest, violent protests, and rioting that broke out after the death of Freddie Gray, a twenty-five-year-old city resident "known to police" who was badly hurt after he was arrested and transported in the back of a police van.

Gray suffered significant injuries to his neck and spine, apparently because he wasn't belted in, and got violently tossed around during his ride to the station to get processed. Police brass had a difficult time explaining Gray's injuries with any consistency, prompting allegations of misconduct and brutality, and when Gray died a week after his arrest, things got really heated.

Spontaneous demonstrations popped up all over the city, and most eventually turned violent, with hundreds of businesses looted and damaged or destroyed, many burned to the ground. Night after night, the "peaceful" protests turned ugly.

Officers were hit by rocks and bottles. Windows were smashed. Stores were emptied and burned. Hundreds of vehicles were damaged and torched. Even firefighters were attacked when they showed up to put out blazes started by rioters.

It didn't seem to matter how many people were arrested or how many cops were hurt. The violence kept erupting when the sun went down.

The city deployed thousands of extra police officers to the streets, calling in other jurisdictions to help out, including state police and troops from the Maryland National Guard. The mayor declared a state of emergency and imposed a curfew. Public schools and college campuses closed. So did numerous businesses, government offices, and a nearby mall.

The National Aquarium shut down, along with public libraries, and the Baltimore Orioles postponed a baseball game after fans were attacked by protestors, and later the team played a game with *no one* in the stands for the first time in the history of the sport. I was there that day, and it was one of the most surreal experiences of my life.

The first night we arrived in West Baltimore was one of the scariest. It was after Gray's funeral, with the state of emergency in effect and National Guard activated and curfew in place, none of which seemed to matter.

We were dispatched to cover the chaos and went looking for any signs of trouble, and it didn't take long to find them. I spotted a large fire burning in an intersection, so we parked about a block away on a seemingly quiet residential street. It was me, my producer, a freelance cameraman, and a security guy they'd hired for this job who told us his regular gig was working as a bouncer in a local bar.

He was a big dude and a nice guy but definitely not prepared for what was coming. When my camera guy got geared up and was ready to roll, he turned on the LiveU system so we could go live from the scene, I turned on my microphone and wireless IFB so I could hear producers in my ear, and we locked the vehicle and began walking up the middle of the street toward the fire.

I took this route purposely, to stay out in the open and not get caught between vehicles and front doors in less-well-lit areas where we might be more vulnerable to attack. Within seconds, a woman approached, seemingly high on drugs, yelling at us to "get the fuck out of here!" I tried to explain we were journalists and were there to report on what was happening and why, but she didn't seem interested. She just kept yelling at us to leave. I then asked her if she wanted to go on camera and tell us why she was so upset and what she thought viewers should know about what was happening in her city, but this only seemed to make her angrier.

We kept making our way up the street and she kept stalking us and yelling at us, and I think at some point our signal may have gone live, and then bottles started to fly our way. The first one sailed over our heads and smashed near the other curb.

It sounded bigger and heavier than a beer bottle, more like one of those bottles that hold a fifth of hard liquor. Then another bottle came sailing toward us and hit the pavement just in front of us, dangerously close.

Our security guy was freaking out as we made our way to the other side of the street and double timed it to the top of the hill, where I saw a vehicle on fire in the intersection. I also saw a large group of heavily armed and shielded tactical officers positioned in a line across the main road, seemingly unaware or uninterested in the threats to our own safety.

We got maybe thirty seconds of video and decided it would be wise to get out of there, so we did, retreating to our vehicle without incident and making our way to another safer location.

At least twenty cops were hurt in the overnight rioting, some with broken bones, a few of them hospitalized after being hit with bricks and debris. Close to 250 people were busted, almost three dozen of them juveniles. The Baltimore Police Department canceled leave for all city officers, while the mayor and governor condemned the violence and promised a "massive force" would patrol the streets. "We're not gonna stand" for "lawless gangs of thugs prowling streets and destroying property," Governor Larry Hogan said. "We're going to bring every available asset and as much manpower as it takes to get this situation under control. The last thing we want to do is escalate the violence but we're not gonna allow our city to be taken over by thugs." And yet that's exactly what happened.

One of the buildings burned was a senior center being developed to house social services offices and sixty units of affordable housing for the elderly. Being built by the Southern Baptist Church, the project was being designed to include HIV testing, job training, mortgage lending, and counseling. A pastor said the blaze was deliberately set by a man seen running from the scene, and the damages were estimated at $16 million. Another casualty was a neighborhood CVS, looted and destroyed, likely by people who regularly shopped there and wouldn't be able to ever again.

In all, 144 vehicles and fifteen buildings were torched that one night. One responding fire truck had its hose cut and firefighters had to dodge cinderblocks thrown in their direction and called for protection from cops before deploying to more blazes, but despite the widespread violence, arrests, attacks and property damage, Governor Hogan tried to reassure the public that he was "getting the situation under control." Mayor Stephanie Rawlings-Blake added that it was a "dark day for our city but it will not define us."

The next day, the Orioles announced that their upcoming home game against the Chicago White Sox at Camden Yards would be closed to the public, the first game played without fans since baseball became a professional sport, and the team was moving its upcoming home weekend series to Tampa, potentially costing millions in lost revenue.

In a notebook from my coverage in Baltimore I found a rough script for a live shot I did that day:

> Disappointed fans outside and disappointed players inside Orioles Park at Camden Yards... the first time in Major League Baseball's 145-year history a game will be played without any fans. The stadium CLOSED to the public in the "best interests of fan safety and deployment of city resources."
>
> MLB made the decision after talking to Orioles and local officials...playing this game in an empty stadium and moving the weekend series with the Rays to Tampa Bay.

They'll still do stadium player announcements, play the National Anthem and walk-up music and hold a 7th inning stretch, but the gates are locked and concessions closed.

Players I spoke with say they're disappointed but understand. In his press conference a short time ago, O's outfielder Adam Jones talked about the tough time for this city…that they're hurting, that sports can unite a community and to have fans would be awesome but he's not gonna second guess the Commissioner.

The first pitch is at 2:05 PM and we'll be here, along with almost NO ONE ELSE.

I thought my tag was pretty funny, but what I didn't mention was what happened when I approached Jones in the locker room before the game.

Jones was a hometown guy and had been outspoken about the unrest on the streets. I'd hoped to get a quick one-on-one interview with him when officials let us in the locker room for a ten-minute window after batting practice.

I'd been in locker rooms a few times during my career, but I wasn't a sports reporter, so it was only for big events or some random occasions when sports and news intersected. I'd covered a bunch of World Series games, a couple of Super Bowls, some All-Star Games and Stanley Cups, but my interactions with players were limited.

The most contentious moment I could remember was when we did a story on the New Jersey Nets back in 2010, who were threatening to break the NBA record for fewest wins in a season. We sat under the basket for the game, another loss for the Nets, and went to the locker room afterward to get reaction.

I talked to a couple of guys, including Kim Kardashian's ex Kris Humphries, who had a book by my then-colleague Glenn Beck in his locker.

We had a brief chat and then I approached Brook Lopez, one of the team's best players, a seven-foot center who eventually became the franchise's leading scorer. He was sitting in a chair, but he was still incredibly intimidating, and I'll never forget the look on his face when I asked if it was frustrating losing so many games. He gave me a hard stare and paused and said something to the effect of, "What do *you* think?" and I walked away, happy to still be alive.

When we went to the Orioles locker room, I didn't know the rules or etiquette or how things were supposed to work in there. I just knew I wanted to get a few sound bites, and the best guy to get them from (I thought) would be Adam Jones.

He was in the back, sitting at a card table with three other players when I walked up, stick microphone in hand with my photographer behind me.

"Hey Adam, Rick Leventhal from Fox News Channel. Could I ask you a couple quick questions?"

Still staring at his cards and not even glancing in my direction, he said, "Man, you know the rules. You can't talk to us back here."

I was surprised at his reaction and said: "They told us we had ten minutes to talk to players. I don't cover sports! I'm a news reporter from New York."

And then Adam Jones says, "I don't give a FUCK who you are or where you're from. YOU CAN'T TALK TO US WHEN WE'RE SITTING AT THE CARD TABLE."

I didn't back down and said something like, "You don't have to be like that. I'm just trying to get your thoughts on the situation in the city..." and the next thing I knew, the Orioles media guy rushed up after hearing or seeing things getting animated and pulled me away, saying, "Let's give these guys some space. You can talk to him during the press availability in the media room in a bit."

I walked away a bit shaken and confused until the guy explained that was considered a safe area for players. If they were at the card table, you weren't supposed to bother them, and I guess the beat writers all knew it, but I obviously didn't and thought it was pretty stupid.

I was pissed that Jones was such an asshole, but when it came time to try and get him on the record again, I went for it. Sitting on the aisle for the press conference, I kept my hand up when he took his seat and waited through a few other reporters' questions and was surprised when he called on me. I asked for his thoughts on the unrest and the fans being locked out and got the sound bites I needed, but viewers had no idea what had come before.

The O's won eight to two against the White Sox that day. Jones went one for three with an RBI and Chris Davis hit a three-run home run in the first inning. The game lasted just two hours and three minutes but none of that seemed as interesting or important as the fact that the only spectators were the players, the press, and a small number of stadium employees.

It was one of the strangest, eeriest, and most unforgettable contests I'd ever witnessed. I'd been to Camden Yards a few times before and sat way up high in the bleachers for one game when the place was packed. I've been to plenty of other stadiums and there were always thousands of fans in the seats, even for the worst of teams.

On this day, there wasn't *anyone* in the stands. It was so weird to hear the anthem and see the players along the base lines, caps off, hands over hearts, with no one to see it happening live, and to hear their walk-up music as they approached the plate, and see them go through all the motions they always went through before, during, and after every pitch even though no one was there to see it. And the silence when they'd get a hit or a big out was so awkward and unusual, it was a surreal experience, and I was as glad to witness it, though I was sad it was happening that way.

In the end, the empty stands seemed unnecessary. Of course, no one knows what would've happened if they'd let fans in the stands, but it was super quiet in the streets around the stadium. Small crowds gathered at the gates where you could see into the field, but no violence, no incidents, nothing to suggest it might've been dangerous for people to be there. I felt at the time (and still do) that it would've been better to give a bunch of tickets away and turn it into a celebration of the city and an inspiration to find a way out of the mess and turmoil swirling there.

We did one more live shot post-game, from outside the gates where a small crowd of fans had gathered earlier to watch. Here was my script, as written on the pages of my notebook:

> This was a remarkably strange event...the first time in the 145-year history of Major League Baseball a game was played without fans.
>
> The official attendance was zero. Maybe 20 to 30 people were gathered outside this fence to cheer on the home team, but this was as close as anyone besides players, coaches and press could get to today's action.
>
> That's what the stadium looked like during the game. [During the live shot, I had the cameraman zoom in to show the empty stadium.]

Major League Baseball made the decision to close the game to the public after conferring with the Orioles and city leaders, deciding on Tuesday it was in the best interest of safety and the deployment of city resources.

It was the morning after the worst riots here in nearly 50 years, but things were much calmer last night and again today so it seems strange the fans were locked out.

Before the game I talked to a couple of players including Orioles closer Zach Britton, who said they'd just pretend the seats were full, and we heard from O's outfielder Adam Jones, who said he was disappointed because sports unite people, and this city is hurting, and he had this message for the kids. [Here, we played a sound bite from Jones encouraging young people to protest peacefully and help the city heal.]

The game itself took just two hours and three minutes...the Orioles beat the White Sox 8–2...a great day for the team, balancing their record at 10 and 10, even if no one was here to see it.

The next day we went to the Mondawmin Mall, which had been closed days earlier after a standoff between rioters and police. A number of stores had been looted and damaged, and the mall was trashed, with piles of broken glass and debris at every entrance.

One store owner told us the mall looked like a disaster zone or war zone, and he was frustrated and angry that he was temporarily out of business.

***

The Washington Post reported that a prisoner who'd shared the van with Freddie Gray could hear him "banging against the walls of the vehicle" and "intentionally trying to injure himself." The *Post* reported that the prisoner, currently in jail, was separated from Gray by a metal partition and couldn't see him. His statement was apparently contained in an application for a search warrant, and the *Post* was given the document with the condition that the prisoner not be named.

Gray was found unconscious in the wagon when it arrived at the police station. Gray's family questioned the reporting, wondering how he could've done so much damage to his own spine, but in the end, it may have been one of the reasons why the six officers charged with various offenses in connection with his death (including second-degree murder) were all acquitted or had the charges dropped.

The riots lasted six nights. The curfew was lifted May 3, and the National Guard was sent home the next day. We went home too, and I think that was the last story I covered in the city of Baltimore.

CHAPTER 10

DANNEMORA PRISON BREAK

The brazen and incredibly clever escape by two convicted killers from the maximum-security Clinton Correctional Facility in Dannemora, New York, on June 6, 2015, was like a movie come to life, so of course it was actually made into a TV movie and then a seven-part miniseries for Showtime, directed by Ben Stiller.

The prison break was a shockingly remarkable effort by two dangerous convicted killers named Richard Matt and David Sweat, and it consumed my life for weeks, with coverage of the breakout, the manhunt, Matt's death, and Sweat's subsequent capture, finishing with Sweat's appearance in court.

I believe I was first to report Matt's end after a state trooper tipped me off he'd been gunned down in the woods by a border agent, after the drunk and disheveled felon pointed a shotgun at the officer. Sweat was wounded and apprehended two days later by a state trooper who spotted him just a mile and a half

308

from the Canadian border and shot him a couple of times after he went running through a field toward what he hoped would be freedom in the Great White North.

We were in the courthouse for his first appearance, with prime seats in the jury box (designated for press since there was no jury for the hearing), where we watched him shuffle in with handcuffs and leg irons.

I still have pictures of Sweat at the defendant's table, bandaged up and appearing to be in significant pain, listening as the judge read the charges against him.

I drove up to Dannemora not long after the news broke of the escape in the early morning hours of Saturday June 6, and spent the bulk of the next three weeks covering the hunt for the convicts (and breaking developments with alleged accomplices), until the pair's journey through the wicked woods reached its violent conclusion.

I left just once, for a weekend back in the city, and was worried the whole time that the pair would be caught or killed while I was gone. When you invest that kind of time in a story, you want to be there for the conclusion.

I got burned once, when I was covering the hunt for the Tsarnaev brothers who bombed the Boston Marathon in 2013. I'd been on the story for just three (very long) days but had a pre-planned trip to Los Angeles and didn't want to miss the weekend in California. I asked my bureau chief if she was still cool with me going, and she said yes, since there were others on the ground to fill in for me, but I was nervous about missing the end of the hunt. Sure enough, right before I left, the FBI released a surveillance photo of the brothers, and by the time I'd landed, one was dead, and the next night the other was in custody. I was really bummed and felt really guilty.

One of the biggest challenges of the job was juggling any kind of personal life with the crazy hours and travel and taxing schedule of a well-traveled network correspondent. Being a successful television reporter requires tremendous sacrifice, working long hours, nights and weekends and holidays. You can't work your way up the ladder if you're not willing to work.

You have to take the shifts they offer, and you have to be willing to drop everything when news breaks or they'll stop calling you. So I learned to say yes, and most of my social plans were tentative, with an asterisk attached. My availability was typically subject to the amount of shit hitting the fan at any given time. If the shit hit close, or there was enough of it anywhere in the world, my phone would ring, and I'd most likely be packing a bag or running to the office.

Dannemora was one of those stories that required sacrifice. It was a long drive from New York City in an area of the state with very little going on. Small town, cheap hotels, basic restaurants, and not a lot of them to choose from. It was the kind of place where TGI Friday's was a big night out.

The story itself was incredibly taxing. Long days of live shots, swatting mosquitos, and sweating in the heat and humidity. Lots of driving from location to location, trying to keep up with searchers fanned out over a very wide area, following leads and hunches. There were frequent storms with heavy rains.

The terrain was ridiculously rough, and we often had to venture out in it. There was a lot of running around to keep up with the hunt, but I was also always aggressive in finding new locations to report from.

I think many photographers and engineers really disliked working with me, even if they respected me, because I never wanted two live shots to look the same. It was important to me to mix things up and stay a step ahead of my competitors, which meant setting up for hits, then breaking down and moving and setting up and breaking down again, often multiple times a day.

On this story it was usually about tracking the searchers who were tracking the suspects, trying to find the next hot spot where authorities would be gathering to venture out into the woods on new missions.

Whenever I'd head out on a story, I tried to grab a fresh reporter notebook. You've probably seen them: about three inches wide and eight inches long, with a spiral at the top, and white lined pages. They fit in the inside pocket of my suits, but I typically carried them in my right-back pants pocket.

On my way to the story or event, especially in breaking news, I'd start writing down the key people, places, and timeline I'd need to refer to during my reporting. I found this incredibly helpful, not just to reinforce in my mind the principals' names and other information (which happens when you write things down), but also as a quick reference during interviews or lives shots. All I'd have to do is look down at the top page with my notes to remind myself of the key players or stats.

The front page of my Dannemora Prison Break notebook read like this (I often put key names or words in ALL CAPS to emphasize them and make them easier for me to see):

> DAVID SWEAT, 35. 5'11", 165. Life term without parole. Cop Killer (sheriff's deputy, 2002). Allegedly began relationship with [prison employee Joyce] Mitchell until inmate ratted them out. He was moved out of shop.

RICHARD MATT, 48. 6' 210 lbs. Black hair, hazel eyes. Tattoos. 25 years to life in 1997 for kidnap, torture, and hacksaw dismemberment of former boss. Investigators believe he was having sex with Mitchell, convinced her they were in love.

CLINTON CORRECTIONAL FACILITY

Upstate Dannemora, NY, "Little Siberia," cold climate & isolation. Largest max in NY, 3rd oldest. 1974, two inmates escaped, one captured 2 years later, other six years.

JOYCE "TILLIE" MITCHELL held on $220k bond. Charges: promoting prison contraband and criminal facilitation.

Prison worker, supervised both men in sewing shop.

May have had sexual relationship with both men, accused of supplying them with tools—hacksaw blades, chisels, a punch, and screw driver.

Allegedly wanted them to kill her husband. Speculation they would've killed her instead.

May have planned to drive them to VERMONT. Also boxing gloves, lighted glasses.

SHERIFF DAVID FAURO

Says Mitchell Plan B, not Plan A. "She would've been baggage to them."

TRAIL IS COLD [This is circled on the pad.]

GOV ANDREW CUOMO "launching formal investigation by state inspector general into all factors involved."

This was all on the first page. The second page (actually the back of page 1, since I always flipped the notebook and filled both sides) reads like this:

FBI, US MARSHALS, US CUSTOMS AND BORDER AGENTS

Motion detectors and cameras in woods

K-9 & AVIATION UNITS

800+ officers: state, local police, federal involved in search, checking cars, trunks, homes, sheds, hunting cabins. Dept of corrections officers and Forest Rangers too. 13 square miles, 8300 acres. 1000+ leads. ERIC FREIN-on run 7 weeks. [I included this for perspective since I'd covered the Frein story extensively and reported on his capture.]

Convicts used power tools to cut thru back of adjacent cells, broke thru brick wall, cut into steam pipe and slithered thru it, finally emerged thru manhole outside of prison. Planning at least 5 weeks.

Would use contractor's tools at night, then return them to toolboxes so no one would notice.

RICHARD MATT also an artist

2600 other inmates on 24-hour lockdown since
escape—no communication with outside world—
no visitors or phone calls. Known as most violent
facility in NY, housing most violent criminals.

ANDREW WYLIE, Clinton County DA

(End page 2).

The rest of my notebook follows our journey back and forth across the search area, including the notes of our interviews with local authorities, press conferences, and significant updates from sources and other news agencies (which we'd confirm or attribute to them). The pages include live-shot scripts and details I would include in my stories, like Matt's tattoos, among them "Mexico Forever," a heart on his chest and left shoulder, and a Marine Corps insignia on his right shoulder. Sweat had tats on his left bicep and right fingers.

We learned just how ingenious and involved their breakout was: The two cut through the steel wall in the back of their cell, crawled down a catwalk, broke through a brick wall, cut into a steam pipe, crawled a distance, and then cut *out* of the steam pipe before slicing through a lock and chain on a manhole cover outside the prison walls to emerge onto a street visible from the prison walls and guard tower, using tools smuggled into the facility by Joyce Mitchell as well as tools found inside the walls left by construction workers doing repairs.

It was the first escape from the maximum-security section of the prison since it opened in 1845.

The men apparently planned to meet Mitchell in the neighborhood where they emerged from the manhole, but she allegedly got cold feet and didn't show up, so they were forced to make their way on foot and managed to put enough distance between themselves and the prison that their trail was already cold by the time authorities began their search later that day.

At first, our stories focused on the incredible challenges and stunning success the two had in cutting their way out of Clinton Correctional. We covered the search too, of course, but there wasn't much to report on in the early days because there were no significant leads or developments. But there were plenty of tips that investigators would scramble to check out every day and night.

One of the first apparent leads came just three days after the escape, a reported sighting thirty miles southeast of Willsboro, twenty miles south of the Canadian border, a heavily wooded area with lakes, streams, and mountains. Authorities came up empty handed. There were many more sightings after this, and all but one or two of them turned out to be false alarms. Along the way, officials released details that might help to identify and catch the suspects.

Early on, Clinton County Sheriff David Fauro told us that there wasn't much physical evidence to track. He said that law enforcement "across the state and country" were ready to respond, and felt it was only "fifty-fifty they were still in the area." He said there were lessons learned in the Frein case involving scents, military technology, and infrared tracking where they were very confident that Frein was in the area, but he wasn't hearing that "with these guys. Initial scent, then nothing."

He described the escapees as "maniacal, manipulative, and extremely intelligent. They would've probably killed her [Mitchell] and wouldn't tell her their actual plans." He also told us the rain was making it more difficult for searchers. It was wet, muddy, and cold at night, and the terrain was incredibly rough, "rugged and unforgiving."

Many of the searchers were unfamiliar with the territory, which only made things tougher, and the infrared and thermal sensor worked by picking up body heat, which could be shielded in the rain. Drooping leaves didn't help, and mud can also mask heat.

Authorities told us that the search areas continued to shift and expand, with personnel redeployed based on information gathered during the investigation.

Roadblocks were set up to close roads and usually reopened hours later. Teams of officers and agents would swarm scenes, responding to calls and tips or just working their grid. School buses full of cadets would roll out to wooded areas and fields in search of clues and evidence that the dangerous criminals might've left behind.

Sometimes dogs would pick up what they thought was the men's scent, and a wave of uniforms would roll in, only to roll out soon after we arrived to try to capture images of the scene. Other times we'd be stopped by officers before we could get close, or they'd already be gone by the time we got there.

Day after day I reported on roadblocks being established or removed, how the weather was affecting the search, updates from authorities on the latest sightings, the likelihood they were still in a particular area, and how close authorities thought they might be to catching the pair.

We were getting fresh information about the extent of Joyce Mitchell's alleged involvement, and the impact of the escape on the prisoners still behind Dannemora's walls. We also kept a running tally of how many agents and officers were involved and how much ground they covered.

After eleven days, I shared that there'd been "virtually no physical evidence reported to be recovered in over a week. The trail has gone cold, according to the sheriff, and there is an increasing sense these two guys may be long gone."

The next day, authorities held a news conference, and I reported some major updates:

> The number of officers and agents involved in the search for the escaped killers has shrunk somewhat, from eight hundred to six hundred, as roadblocks and perimeters have dissolved in the area closest to the prison. New York State Police say they are expanding and shifting the search area based on tips and leads. They've already scoured more than 10,200 acres. They're doing more patrols now and have teams ready to deploy if there's a sighting or other evidence and say they can't rule out the possibility Matt and Sweat are still in the area.

> Police confirmed U.S. Marshals are working the border with Mexico, passing out fliers in case the men made it that far south, and Customs agents are watching the Canadian border too, but still no concrete sightings in twelve days.

> The D.A., Andrew Wylie, confirmed Joyce Mitchell, now charged with helping the men escape, told them there *was* a plot between Matt and Sweat to kill her husband Lyle after they escaped.

He says she was aware of the plot but wouldn't say if it was her idea.

He also wouldn't say whether Lyle had been warned about the plot, but he was questioned by police at a barracks about an hour north of here, near his home, with his attorney present. A source tells me he is not being arrested, and the Clinton County Sheriff says Joyce Mitchell is so far handling her incarceration pretty well. She's composed but also being watched 24-7.

Despite a lack of sightings or evidence, law enforcement is saying very confidently the men *will be caught.*

My notebook contains several versions of the script above since I often did multiple live shots within hours of each other with little new information to change or update the story. If, and when, I did get something new, I put that at the top. Otherwise, I tried to mix it up as best I could, including something I didn't have time for the previous hour or changing the order of the tidbits I had to share.

For me, it was all about taking the information I had and using the best pieces of it in every report, shaping it in a slightly different way each time to keep it interesting and informative. I tried to take advantage of the extra airtime by highlighting and focusing on different aspects of the story, while reinforcing the key points and mixing up the order of elements so that every report sounded different, and people who watched all day would glean something new from each of my appearances on their TV.

Thirteen days after the breakout, we had a new angle:

> When Richard Matt and David Sweat escaped from this maximum-security prison thirteen days ago, it was locked down. Inmates lost virtually all privileges—including no visitors and no phone calls.
>
> Today, Clinton Correctional Facility is lifting the lockdown and returning to normal operations, but authorities have announced no new progress in the search for the two killers on the run.

Later in the report I added:

> Her [Mitchell's] husband Lyle was questioned by police for hours yesterday and we spoke with Lyle's attorney today, who says his client is in shock, never saw this coming, was still in love and is overwhelmed by the whole situation. He also worked in the prison with his wife and knew the men. Meanwhile the couple have kids who are also in shock. Lyle apparently had no idea Joyce was cheating and conspiring against him and may not bail her out because of what he knows now.

I added in my tag that "the concept of divorce is looming."

One of the items I didn't have time for in my story that day was that the convict Matt painted pictures for Joyce Mitchell that hung in the couple's home, and that Sweat had actually approached Lyle in the prison eighteen months earlier to deny having an affair with his wife after the prison removed Sweat from the tailor shop where he worked and investigated allegations of a romantic involvement.

At a news conference with the New York State Police, the Clinton County sheriff, New York State Corrections officials, and federal agents, we learned that officials had "fully transitioned" from grid searches to potential means of egress, including trails and railroad beds. Searchers were using all-terrain vehicles to get through some of the more rugged areas and had cleared more than six hundred miles of trails along with hundreds of seasonal camps, abandoned buildings, and other structures and hundreds of occupied homes. Close to 170 troopers had been deployed in the area on roving patrols around the clock, and authorities said they were "chasing new leads as fast as they come in," "grinding through" them "one by one."

They renewed their plea for help from the public, including any security or trail camera footage, and warned the search could take months.

The U.S. Marshals Service revealed that some of the same agents who worked on the search for Eric Frein had been on scene since the beginning, swapping out with the New York/ New Jersey regional task force, clearing buildings, tracking trails, trying to cover all the bases. "These guys are motivated," the Marshals Service told us, with some working thirty-two straight hours without breaks. Forest rangers had joined search teams too, especially valuable because they knew the woods better than most.

On Saturday, June 20, there were reports of a possible sighting three hundred miles away, in the southwest portion of New York State near the Pennsylvania border. My team and I thought the alleged sighting was bullshit since it was in the absolute wrong direction from where the pair were most likely headed, toward the Canadian border, but since it was the news of the day and police had actually responded, we covered it from our live location outside the prison walls, and since it was a weekend when fewer reporters were available, we did live shots almost every hour.

The anchors tossed to me this way for one of my first hit that day:

> Fox News Alert: New developments in the massive manhunt for two escaped prisoners in upstate New York. Police say they have a new lead that the convicted killers might be in Allegheny County, New York, after they were possibly seen near the Pennsylvania border a week ago. David Sweat and Richard Matt used power tools to cut their way out of a maximum-security prison earlier this month. Rick Leventhal is live at the Clinton Correctional Facility in Dannemora, New York, with the very latest. Rick?

I reported:

> Police have been waiting for a break and this could be it, although it is still on an unconfirmed sighting apparently by a citizen in that area. As you mentioned, Allegheny County is southwest

of here, in the southern part of New York State, very close to the Pennsylvania border, very close to I-86, Interstate 86. According to *The New York Times*, it was a woman who was driving through the area and saw two men come out of the woods near some railroad tracks. She says one of the men dove back into the woods and the other one pulled the hooded sweatshirt over his head. We have not confirmed those details with the New York state police, but we can tell you state police converged on the area with canine and aviation units, they sealed off roads, they set up roadblocks, and they are now working that perimeter and working this search. We heard on scanner traffic that they asked for more officers with shotguns on the railroad tracks.

New York State police tell us they have followed up on 1,500 leads, many similar to these over the past couple of weeks and so far, there's been very little hard evidence to suggest where these two men might be. That's one reason why the U.S. Marshals Service put both men on its "15 most wanted list" which is reserved for the worst of the worst. They added a $25,000 bounty to each man's head so there's now $75,000 for each of them for information leading to their arrest or capture but again we have this new report of a possible sighting in this area in the southern part of New York State near the Pennsylvania border of two men in the woods near railroad tracks and police are following up on those leads right now.

Of course, this tip, along with almost all others proved to be false. Somebody may have seen two guys, but it wasn't the guys who broke out of Dannemora. And on it went.

As it turned out, the two convicts had been hiding out that weekend in a hunting cabin in the woods near the small town of Owls Head, roughly twenty-five miles due west of the prison in Dannemora. That following Monday, June 22, they got flushed out by a guy checking on his place. We didn't learn about it until hours later but still managed to be first on the scene to report the sighting.

The response that day and the days that followed was a dramatic and thorough show of force. Hundreds of cops, federal agents, and corrections officers in cars and all-terrain vehicles, some with dogs, others on foot and in choppers overhead, scanning the terrain for signs of movement or heat signatures.

On the ground, the searchers moved in teams through the thick woods of the Adirondacks while others set up roadblocks on the long winding roads and at key intersections. There was incredible tension in the air and a real sense that they were finally closing in on the killers.

Law enforcement officers and agents were everywhere, checking car trunks and searching every structure they came across, with a heightened sense of urgency. There was no doubt they were as close as they'd been so far, after the boots, bloody socks, fingerprints, and prison-issued underwear were found and a lab confirmed a DNA match to both men. I covered the progress of the searches hour by hour over the next few days, including this bit:

> I spoke to the Franklin County sheriff this afternoon. He told me he doesn't think the men could travel more than two to three miles a day because of the rough terrain and all the eyeballs out here. He thinks they're still close and will be caught in the next twenty-four to forty-eight hours.

The sheriff was partially right, but optimistic by a couple of days.

Authorities continued to shift their resources and roadblocks around the region, and we did our best to keep up.

On Wednesday the 24th, my last shot of the night was on Greta Van Susteren's early evening show for a live shot and lengthy Q&A. I loved doing these mostly unscripted hits and especially loved the unscripted questions. So often, producers want reporters to submit the questions in advance, and it all feels a bit stilted. Being off the cuff allows more latitude and real reporting and adds a sense of urgency and unpredictability. I also respected Greta a great deal. She's super smart, and her legal background would make for compelling and lively conversations.

She tossed to me at the scene of a police roadblock on the outskirts of the most recent and very intense reaction to a tip call, and here was my report, word for word (please excuse the grammatical mistakes, as this was live and unscripted):

> And, Greta, we saw a rapid response this afternoon like we haven't seen before, with waves of

officers and fast-moving caravans racing to a scene. There appeared to be more than a hundred officers converging on a wooded area along route 27 in Mountain View after yet another reported sighting of those two escaped killers David Sweat and Richard Matt, who've been on the run now for eighteen days.

We made it to the edge of the search perimeter before the state police pushed us back. We saw tactical vehicles, troopers armed with shotguns and automatic weapons, and at least two helicopters hovering overhead. The search lasted for close to an hour but eventually they began clearing the scene.

We're told it was sparked by someone who thought he saw something in the woods but it didn't pan out, just another of the more than two thousand leads that didn't pan out, but of course there was one lead that has proven legit. That was on Saturday when a man went to check on his hunting cabin, saw a jar of peanut butter and a jug of water inside, yelled out, and someone he says bolted out the back door.

Police converged on that cabin and reportedly found evidence including bloody socks, prison-issued underwear, and fingerprints and we have confirmed with multiple sources that there was a DNA match for the escaped killers, so police know they were within a couple of miles of here on Saturday and they've been aggressively searching this part of Franklin County to try and flush them out. But a tip last night the pair might've been up on Titus Mountain didn't pan out and a tip today that they might've been close by also didn't pan out, Greta, so they continue to aggressively be searching down and hunting down these leads but so far these guys remain on the loose.

There was yet another reported sighting late that night in the woods above our live location, sparking yet another frenetic search that lasted several hours but ended with a whimper, and the next day we set up near Titus Mountain where a perimeter had been established for another sweep that also ended with zero positive results. One of the things I reported on that day was just how difficult it was for the guys doing the searching:

> Remarkably challenging terrain, very rugged, woods are very thick, lots of water too. Lakes, ponds, streams, creeks, rivers, and SWAMP. Thick underbrush and lots of bugs.

We updated with this:

> The New York state police tell us the search area here in Franklin County now covers seventy-five miles. They believe, but can't be certain, the escaped killers David Sweat and Richard Matt are within the perimeter. The other headline is they may be armed.

Police wouldn't confirm reports of a missing shotgun, but say many of the hunting cabins in these woods have guns inside and authorities are operating under the assumption Matt and sweat are carrying weapons.

Police have responded to numerous sightings in the Owls Head area over the past couple days, including a swarm of cops in Mountain View yesterday afternoon, but none of the 2,200 tips called in has panned out except the hunting cabin where the men's DNA was found.

A state police major wouldn't confirm bloody socks were among the items found in a cabin, or if one of the men might be injured, but says in the end it won't matter.

He reiterated the challenges of the rough terrain and weather here and says active searches continue with large groups of heavily armed officers. A law enforcement source confirms to Fox that authorities believe Joyce Mitchell used hamburger meat to smuggle hacksaw blades to the inmates to help them escape. The source also says the correction officer placed on leave, Gene Palmer, gave the meat to the inmates but didn't know tools were inside.

One other note: These escapees had earned privileges and were housed in an honor block at Clinton Correctional. A source close to the investigation tells Fox that honor block has been dismantled and the gallery where Matt and Sweat were housed is secure and currently vacant.

The next day we covered the arrest of corrections officer Gene Palmer (mentioned in the previous report), who claimed he had no idea he was smuggling tools to the men. After speaking with his lawyer and covering his appearance in court, I totally believed him, but he wound up getting fired and convicted, in part because he also did other favors for the pair that wound up contributing to their escape. He was the one guy I felt really bad for during coverage of the story because I think he got a raw deal.

This was one of my reports on Palmer's arrest:

> Gene Palmer is a 27-year veteran officer at Clinton Correctional. He worked on the honor block where Matt and Sweat were housed and dealt with them on a daily basis.
>
> He admitted to investigators he gave the men needle-nosed players and a flat-head screwdriver and access to the catwalk behind their cells to alter electrical boxes to allow the men to cook in their cells. They later used that catwalk to escape.
>
> He also gave them paint and accepted paintings which he allegedly later tried to burn and bury to hide the evidence.
>
> Finally, he admits to handing Matt the hamburger meat stuffed with hacksaw blades inside Styrofoam containers in a cloth bag, but says it was given to him by Joyce Mitchell, also charged as an accessory. Mitchell apparently

put the blades in the burgers, and Palmer didn't know they were there.

Palmer is out on $25,000 bail and there's another hearing on his case this afternoon.

After that hearing, I reported that Palmer's "attorney announced he would no longer be representing Gene Palmer. A new lawyer will be at his side for his next appearance Monday. Outside the courthouse, the DA said he believes Palmer was misled or duped by the crafty convicts, who this evening remain at least one step ahead of the manhunt."

Palmer's first attorney, who "unexpectedly stepped down," said he did so because he's "just a small-town lawyer with minimal staff" and was overwhelmed by the case and the attention.

Palmer faced two felony counts of tampering with evidence and another felony count of introducing dangerous contraband into the prison (the screwdriver and pliers) which could've gotten him years in prison if convicted.

In the end, Palmer pleaded guilty to promoting prison contraband and was sentenced to six months in jail and a fine of just over $5,000. After four months, he was released for good behavior.

While I felt sorry for Palmer, I had far less sympathy for Mitchell. Her husband worked in the same prison, and they'd commute there and back together. She allegedly cheated on him with both of the scumbag repeat offenders in a closet for months and months and then conspired to help them break out with an apparent promise by the inmates to take her with them to Mexico and live some kind of fantasy life on the beach.

During one of her court appearances, I sat in the front row next to her husband Lyle. I introduced myself and tried to talk to him, but he clearly didn't want anything to do with me. He wouldn't acknowledge me or answer any of my questions. He just sat there stone-faced, eyes forward, ignoring me, so after a few attempts, I left him alone.

In the end, Mitchell pleaded guilty to a few charges and got two and a third to seven years in prison plus more than $85,000 in fines and restitution to the state. She served about half her sentence before making parole and got out in early 2020.

Sweat pleaded guilty to promoting prison contraband and two felony counts of first-degree escape and had several more years added to his life sentence (which makes little sense, I know). One can only assume he won't be breaking out again and will die behind bars.

Recently I spoke with Ron Ralston, a former Fox News Channel producer whom I worked with for most of my time up in Dannemora (and on countless other stories). He's in Utah now, running video operations for Brigham Young University. I asked him what stood out about the Dannemora assignment, and he told me this:

> It was so Hollywood, so much like the show *Prison Break* or any one of numerous jail escape movies. People couldn't believe they were able to do that! I also remember the constant changing of locations.

On the day Matt was shot we were up at the Canadian border after a tip from a cop they were looking in that area, and we drove to a neighborhood on the water just across from Canada and were getting ready for a live shot when a trooper called. [I hadn't remembered this until Ron brought it up.]

We didn't wait for the cameraman to break down his gear. I remember we ran and jumped in your Mercedes and we went flying to the scene, doing like ninety-five miles per hour on windy country roads and at one point you did a live phoner with Neil Cavuto. [When we can't be in front of a camera, sometimes producers will have us call in instead so we can still get the news on the air.]

You were cool as a cucumber while speeding and talking to Cavuto at the same time, relaying facts and details like a pro with the audience having *no idea* you were driving like a madman at the time. Then when we got to the scene where another crew had set up and were waiting for us, we jumped out and mic'd up and got right on the air within minutes.

Every day we were scrambling to get to the right spot. Where are we going today? Where do we think they might be looking? I remember one time we hung out at a church all day, then went to another spot in the pouring rain and found a bunch of cops and asked them, "Hey, what's going on?" And they said, "Nothing," and we were like, "Yeah right." It was like that almost daily.

I felt like we were part of the cat-and-mouse game. Every day we were part of the chase, part of the search, chasing the chasers, trying to make sure we were well positioned.

Our biggest challenges were the weather and terrain, and we never had enough resources. Just like always, we were forced to do more with fewer people [compared to CNN and other networks who always seemed to have more hands on deck], and yet we consistently kicked butt.

Some of it was dumb luck. I remember one day we were with the D.C. cameraman Rick [he'd driven up from Washington to help out with coverage] and we're driving in his black Suburban crew car with tinted windows and D.C. tags and the cops thought we were federal agents and waved us through a check point and we got right up where the guys were and got exclusive footage!

We had some other big achievements and notable experiences, like sitting in the jury box for Sweat's first appearance and breaking news on multiple occasions, including when Matt was killed.

This was literally the story that kept on giving, like Joyce Mitchell for example. You had these wacko small-town characters who lived in this shitty little area, everyone worked for the prison and depended on it. One reason the men got out so easily is it was so laid back there. Remember someone told us the guards would use a rope to drop a pail over the wall from their watchtower to get their lunch from a delivery guy?

There were homes right across the street from the prison walls. No one ever dreamed anyone would escape.

I also remember it was a bare bones town and I'll never get over how incredibly thick the woods are up there. You couldn't just walk through the woods. One day I completely destroyed an outfit chasing after searchers with a small camera and then I was like, where do I get clothes? I asked a local and he recommended the Family Dollar store so that's where we went!

Before I hung up, Ron told me: "There is a small handful of people that I treasure I had the experience of working with and you're one of those people. You taught me a lot and you were really fun to work with!"

I thanked him and went back to working on this chapter.

CHAPTER 11

THE MINNEAPOLIS BRIDGE COLLAPSE, NTSB TRAINING, AND THE ONLY TIME I BURNED A SOURCE

Late in 2009, I got an email from someone with the National Transportation Safety Board (NTSB) introducing himself and inviting me to join a conference the NTSB held annually in suburban Virginia, just outside Washington D.C. I considered it a great privilege and honor since I was the only journalist asked to come, based (I believe) on affection within the agency for Fox News Channel and my coverage of so many of the events they'd be discussing at the conference.

The event was a chance for first responders to get together and share the challenges they faced in handling major incidents.

Invitees included police chiefs, commissioners, and high-ranking detectives from various departments, fire and EMS chiefs and executives from Chicago and Los Angeles among others, airport officials from multiple states, Port Authority Police, New York and New Jersey state police (including more than a few friends of mine), federal agents and FEMA investigators, the American Red Cross, scuba-diving team leaders, and more.

Anyone who played a significant role in a long list of transportation-related disasters was on the guest list and would speak to the minute by minute "tick tock" of what transpired. The incident itself, the response by numerous local, state, and federal agencies, the confusion all those agencies caused and their ultimate coordination, and, inevitably, how they handled the press, which was where I brought value to the table.

They'd all dealt with the media swarms that descended on their scenes and shared stories of how they engaged all the reporters, but I could offer them a different perspective and perhaps some ways of making things go more smoothly the next time. This was the goal of the conference: to figure out what worked and what didn't and learn from mistakes that were made.

The three-day conference included speakers on numerous plane crashes including a bad landing at Teterboro, New Jersey, that ended with a jet blasting through an airport fence, crossing a highway, and smashing into a building. Also up for discussion were TWA Flight 800, the crash of Egypt Air Flight 990, the Buffalo crash of Flight 3407, and the so-called Miracle on the Hudson, all of which I'd covered extensively.

There were talks on a gas pipeline explosion in Bergenfield, New Jersey, presentations by a member of the FBI's evidence response team, and the NTSB breaking down how it conducts investigations. It was all incredibly helpful and informative for me as a reporter, but there were also some big reveals about stuff that happened off camera, behind the scenes.

By far the most shocking and mind-blowing revelations came on Day Two of the conference, when members of the Minneapolis Police Department spoke at great length about the August 2007 collapse of the I-35W bridge and the turf war that led to horrific and, I believe, never-before-revealed efforts by the Hennepin County sheriff to maintain control of the crime scene. You can read about it for the first time here.

I was playing softball in Central Park the night of August 1, 2007, when the I-35W Mississippi River Bridge had a catastrophic failure. The bridge was nearly 2,000 feet long, 113 feet wide (carrying eight lanes of traffic), at a height of 115 feet. It was completed in 1967, made with steel, multi-girders and concrete slabs with arched trusses.

The bridge had been cited multiple times during annual inspections for structural issues, rating "structurally deficient" as early as 1990 and again in 2005, when the span was flagged for replacement by the Department of Transportation.

More issues with cracking and fatigue were discovered in 2006, and it was rated as one of the worst bridges in America. This didn't stop state transportation workers from moving heavy equipment and truckloads of sand, gravel, and concrete onto the span for maintenance, including joint work, lighting, guard rails, and resurfacing.

Just after 6 p.m. on that hot August night, with rush hour traffic moving slowly over the reduced lanes, the center span suddenly collapsed, sending a long stretch of the structure down to the river, followed by 111 vehicles, their occupants, and eighteen construction workers, who fell onto the riverbanks, into a rail yard, or down to the river itself. Thirteen people were killed and dozens more hurt, including at least twenty-two children.

Back in Manhattan, a short time after the collapse, one of my teammates on the softball field got an alert on her phone, and mine began ringing soon after. "Can you go to Minnesota tonight?" my bureau chief asked. "Sure, I just need to run home and pack a bag. What time's the flight?"

It was already pushing 8 p.m. It was too late to catch a commercial flight from New York to Minneapolis that night, so Fox had to book a private jet which ferried me, some anchors, and camera crews to Minneapolis. We didn't leave Newark till close to 3 a.m. and landed as the sun was coming up. We rented a vehicle and headed straight to the bridge and began our coverage almost immediately.

At the conference, I learned some remarkable facts about the sequence of events in the minutes, hours, and days after the span fell, and about the bridge itself, from then-Deputy Chief Rob Allen and Inspector Mike Martin.

Chief Allen's presentation was a nuts-and-bolts breakdown of the incident and response.

He told us the bridge was built over a river just eleven feet deep at the time of the collapse. It was ninety-two degrees in Minneapolis that night, and even hotter on the days that followed. When it happened, the Minneapolis PD assumed jurisdiction and set up three AO's (areas of operation): on the South Bank, at Center Falls, and on the North Bank.

Allen told us: "The North Bank had a very hard fall. A wheelchair athlete almost hit a construction worker coming out of a porta-potty and crawled up to safety. A swat team repelled down to retrieve the wheelchair."

Responders had to climb over a six-foot wall to reach victims. One of the first things they did was investigate whether terrorism might be involved and also monitored to see if there was a potential radioactive material release, deploying University of Minnesota lab techs. The response was complicated by the fact that Minneapolis PD "don't have life rafts in their cars and water rescues were necessary. The incident commander told us a 'party barge' had just passed under the bridge so it was sheer luck there weren't as many as ninety more fatalities."

Some of the responding officers were able to assist in rescue operations, including water rescues. One came from home and used a yellow rope to reach someone trapped in a car.

Another step, Chief Allen said, was to close a lock upstream and open another downstream to lower the water level, but divers were still faced with poor visibility, plus rebar and concrete in the water, which made their job extremely difficult and hazardous.

There were "lots of construction vehicles on the span" and a school bus carrying sixty-three children back from a field trip to a water park. The bus fortunately got caught up against a guardrail and didn't fall off the edge, but the driver's door was stuck shut so a volunteer with the kids kicked out the rear emergency door and was able to help the kids to safety.

Chief Allen told us if the bridge had collapsed "three seconds later, it would've been in flames, two seconds earlier it would've flipped on its nose, and eight seconds earlier it would've been on center span in the middle of the river." Instead, all of the kids were able to walk off to a Red Cross center with immediate medical care.

One of the first priorities was establishing a unified command post. Command began on the truck of one of the first arriving police cars "with a non-erasable marker" until a mobile command post arrived, and eventually the operations required more than an acre to provide enough room. There were ongoing jurisdictional issues between the Minneapolis PD, which controlled the land, and the Hennepin County Sheriff's Office, which owned the water, creating conflicts that allegedly led to a remarkable and horrific series of acts under the river's surface, detailed for the first time ever below.

Chief Allen told us that investigators were given priority over all other branches because their job was critically important. He also told us his biggest challenge was bringing "control to chaos."

"I never yelled," he said. "I always maintained a level voice. I didn't want to get anyone excited," so he used calm and a sense of humor. He held regular briefings and tried to ensure that he had the right people in the right places. "Over one hundred public safety agencies were involved right away," he said, "including police, fire, sheriff's office, state patrol, EMS, and feds, including the United States Secret Service.

Over twenty-eight public safety watercraft were part of the initial response, and more than five hundred officers were assigned to manage the perimeter. Other concerns included preserving evidence, ensuring the safety of the divers, and establishing a credentialing system to discourage sightseers posing as journalists. They brought a printing company to the command post to create the credentials.

The scene was still dangerous, he told us. The "metal was shifting, you could hear creaks and groans. We had to create red zones determined to be unsafe, and yellow zones deemed hazardous." He said, "thinking like a cop, even the bridge engineers could be suspects," so they were allowed in with police escorts.

At one point during the recovery operations, it reached 102 degrees, creating tremendous food and hydration problems for the investigators and first responders. Cell service was spotty, too.

A local Target store sent a tractor-trailer full of water, ice, Gatorade, and food just forty-eight minutes after the collapse, thanks to a pre-existing agreement based on what authorities thought they'd need in the event of a major disaster, which this most certainly was.

Authorities improvised a warehouse at the scene and assigned a quartermaster operations supervisor to provide meals and hydration, with help from the Red Cross. The chief told us one volunteer made everyone wash their hands before eating.

They used Polaris four-wheelers to patrol the perimeter while they began planning for the next twenty-four hours, including making arrangements for family members of the possible victims.

"Don't talk to the press when you're tired!" he said, calling us their "best friend and worst enemy." They had to deal with crowds of sightseers, fortune hunters, and self-responding civil engineers, and of course "dignitaries," meaning elected officials who invariably show up wanting briefings so they can then go in front of the cameras to tell everyone what they've just learned and remind everyone how important they are.

Allen's lessons: "Leaders must bring order to chaos; staff is looking to you to set the example; clearly articulate the commander's intent; tell people what you need done and let them decide how to do it; take care of your stuff and take care of yourself (food, water, mental health)."

Pre-existing relationships with other jurisdictions are important, he said, along with private and corporate support. Organization matters, including the use of whiteboards to set up shifts and security assignments. Also on his list: plotting maps, printers, interoperable communications between responders, timely briefings with members of the unified command several times a day, and separate briefings for all investigative agencies. He told us he had a scribe to keep operational notes of every decision point along the way, but also realized he had no pre-existing protocol for tracking finances and spending for FEMA reimbursement. A lesson learned.

They had cameras in the Emergency Operations Center so they could watch the rescue and recovery efforts as they played out live, with three incident commands: fire, police, and the sheriff's department.

Allen told us his "collapse structure team" was on scene in just eight minutes, and the efforts of first responders "reinforced my faith in humanity."

Then Inspector Mike Martin took the podium to brief us on the investigation and the shocking complications that later developed.

Incredibly, Martin had driven home over the bridge just twenty minutes before it failed and got a text message reading "35W collapse into river."

"We're heat seekers," he told us. "We run to bullets." And run back he did, to establish investigations and try to answer the most pressing questions, including "Why did the bridge fall?" and "Could there be a secondary collapse?"

His team did sweeps with bomb techs and explosives-trained K-9s, and other officers performed "tactical mingling" in the crowds that had formed, to see if anyone looked suspicious with "too keen an interest" who might be a suspect if this were the work of terrorists. They interviewed construction workers and surveyed local homes and businesses for surveillance video.

They determined there were 120 construction workers on the bridge at the time of the collapse, with sixty on the south side and sixty on the north. The span fell during a shift change, so all but one of the workers was in his car, coming or going. That lone worker on foot was one of the fatalities, but his colleagues thought others died too, because they couldn't see them.

Teams of investigators were sent to interview the men, while other teams were sent to every hospital to find out who the injured were with, which vehicle were they in, and so on. Thirteen hospitals took in patients, with eighty-eight brought by ambulance and the rest "self-transported."

The Minneapolis Police Department fielded 1,200 missing persons calls in the first twenty-four hours, but the number was narrowed to eight missing just a day later. Video was retrieved just ninety minutes after the collapse, courtesy of the Army Corps of Engineers.

There were more than a hundred vehicles to match to the people who would've or should've been in them. If no one claimed a car or truck, it was presumed the owner might be among the dead. And Martin gave one incredible example: One guy was thrown into the water, swam to shore, went to the airport, caught a flight home to South Carolina, then called the rental agency in Minnesota to tell them the car might be in the river. Investigators also found cars in the water that were unconnected to the collapse, along with two snowmobiles; they'd been there awhile.

It was crucially important to preserve evidence, so the authorities were diligent about controlling access to the scene. One cop was caught with a souvenir, "a knuckle bolt from an expansion joint on the bridge." Martin didn't say if or how the officer was disciplined.

They were corralling "self-responding engineers and pro-fiteers" along with plaintiff's attorneys demanding access to the site. They set up a Family Assistance Center (FAC) at a nearby Holiday Inn, which became the first source of information for families and protected them from the media, also "protecting the dignity of victims," he told us. The FAC was run by Minneapolis PD but for some reason, "others wanted control," including the Sheriff's Office and Red Cross.

Then things turned graphic. Martin described one of the worst fatalities. The driver of a tractor-trailer truck with a load of bread lost his life when the cab was chopped in half. He lost his legs and burned to death when the truck caught fire.

"The scene smelled like burnt toast and burnt flesh," he told us. The pieces of the man's body were recovered on two separate days.

When the subject turned to "River Command," the story got really ugly, and I don't think that what I'm about to share has ever been made public before.

As I said earlier, Inspector Martin explained that the local sheriff had jurisdiction over the rivers. The sheriff's name was Rich Stanek, and Martin couldn't stand him. He called him "a politician" because he had to run for office every four years, and he also called him an "arrogant prick." Martin says Stanek set up a "dog and pony show," holding his own briefings to get his face on the news every day and night. I remembered he was on Fox News Channel a *lot*, and I met and interviewed him more than once. I thought he was a good guy and good on TV, but I didn't know then what I was about to learn.

Martin says the sheriff did have a team of twenty great divers who used side-scan sonar to find the scores of vehicles underwater. They were trying to search the metal hulks and recover bodies, but faced numerous challenges, including rough currents, poor visibility, debris, and E. coli in the water, which got most of them sick.

U.S. Navy divers were brought in six or seven days after the collapse. They were SEALS, considered the best of the best. They were highly trained salvage divers, and this task was "what they do." They were an unparalleled group, and the city wanted them to take over the recovery operation.

But Martin says the sheriff had "ego issues" and refused to relinquish control. This was *his* show, and he wanted to remain the star, call the shots, and get on TV every night. If he gave up the river, the Navy and others would share and even steal the spotlight. As Martin put it, "Catastrophic events bring out the best and worst in people."

Ten years later, in an interview with a local paper, Stanek took credit for the Navy divers, claiming that bringing them in was one of his top priorities, but that's not what Martin told the group of dozens of law enforcement professionals gathered in that auditorium to share lessons learned at catastrophic events.

Martin says that not only did Stanek not want the Navy there, but he also ordered his men to saw one of the victim's bodies into pieces rather than give up his power, and this, Martin says, was the final straw.

Martin claims the body of a child was trapped in a vehicle underwater, and divers couldn't extricate it from the car and didn't have the proper equipment or ability to cut through the metal while the vehicle was still underwater to get the child out whole.

If they'd used the cranes that were brought in to lift the car from the river, it would've immediately become the jurisdiction of the Minneapolis PD, and the sheriff would've no longer been in charge.

Instead, Martin says, the sheriff was willing to desecrate the body, telling his team to *cut off the head* of the child and carry it and the rest of the body from the car in pieces.

According to Martin, the sheriff's divers "actually removed the head of that child."

When others in charge found out, Martin says a huge blowup ensued, and the sheriff eventually acquiesced, in the face of tremendous pressure, finally allowing the Navy to assume the lead on water recoveries.

Navy divers didn't cut any bodies.

The Navy's Mobile Diving and Salvage Unit used cranes to lift the vehicles out, covering them with blue tarps so loved ones wouldn't see their dead family members on the news.

The vehicles were then moved by truck to a recovery area, led by a police escort with lights and sirens and flanked by school buses also covered with tarps to help shield the recovered vehicles from view. The eighth and final body was lifted out on August 20, nineteen days after plunging 113 feet into the river.

Martin shared his lessons learned:

"True leaders are decisive and willing to take a calculated risk."

"Prepare relentlessly for worst case scenarios and train your staff for the same."

"Be flexible and ready to adjust to circumstances."

He asked the group if they'd be willing to let staff expose themselves to hazards in the river. Because all his guys got sick. There was also the economic factor of the closed waterway, calculated at $1.8 million lost daily in boat and barge traffic. Then he asked if anyone would be willing or able to make the decision to dismember a body to recover partial remains.

Briefing families was the most difficult task, he said. "Could you stand in front of a hundred people and be brutally honest? Would you take that risk, even if it was the right thing to do, if it could harm your career?"

The authorities did bring families to the site on the Monday after the collapse in two buses with police escorts, on the span still standing. They were actually worried some of the grieving relatives might jump off to join the ones they lost, so they positioned officers every five feet along the rail, facing the families. He told us the Red Cross bought roses and wanted to join the families on the buses, and when police told them no, the Red Cross wouldn't pay for the flowers.

Inspector Martin finished with some final thoughts on the sheriff: "He made consistent bad judgement calls. He was a politician and was endangering divers. He had the wrong priorities. We had to force a meeting and a 'come to Jesus' crossroads."

He said it got really, really ugly before the sheriff gave in.

"It was the only glitch in the entire operation," Martin told us.

Months after the bridge collapse, Stanek would receive criticism for spending $30,000 on a "training video" that focused on his department's response to the tragedy. Many saw it as a not-so-thinly-veiled campaign commercial to build support for another run for office.

Local TV station KMSP reported that the company that produced the video also handled advertising and marketing for Stanek's 2006 campaign, and Minneapolis Police Chief Tim Dolan reportedly said of the video in an email: "His theft of credit is not going to sit well with my staff and our hard-working partners."

Ironically, Stanek says the video was produced for a national training conference for first responders, but I can assure you it wasn't played at the conference I attended two years later. Instead, Inspector Martin was there to detail how Stanek should be the *last* guy taking credit for a job well done at that scene.

BURNING A SOURCE

During and after the conference I became friendly with one of the NTSB's public affairs guys, Erik Grosof, who was my point of contact for the event. He had to convince others at the agency to allow us to take part, and I was truly grateful. We had meals and beers together that week and stayed in touch afterward. He was a good guy to know in the event of any major incidents, someone I could call to get more than the minimum being handed out to the general press corps, and three months later, I had the opportunity to do just that.

I was in my office at Fox News Channel headquarters in New York the morning of Thursday, February 18, when we got word of breaking news in Austin, Texas. A small plane had crashed into a seven-story office building downtown. There were almost certainly multiple deaths and injuries, and it looked like it could be an act of terrorism.

My bureau chief called and asked me to head down to Studio N ASAP to report what I could as soon as I was ready. Studio N was one of my favorite spots in the building to report from. It was a glass-encased box in the middle of the basement newsroom with a roomy plexiglass desk, three cameras with prompters, a floor director, and a printer where writers and producers could send me scripts, and I could print stuff when I needed it. There was a landline phone, and a laptop and monitors to watch our channel and live satellite and tape feeds.

I could cover pretty much anything from the chair behind that desk, and it wasn't unusual for me to do multiple hits there every week, often in situations like this. I'd sometimes run in there with only the most basic bits of information, and report something like:

> There's been a shooting in Times Square. We don't know how many shots were fired or if anyone was hurt or killed and we don't have any information on the suspect. We've only been told it's an adult male. We don't know if he's dead or alive or if he's in custody but we *do* know the NYPD is on scene. It happened roughly twenty minutes ago near the corner of 42nd Street and Broadway. We're waiting on an update from a police spokesperson and as soon as we get more information, we'll bring it to you.

I'd make calls and send texts to every law enforcement contact I had and hope one of them would answer or get back to me, and when they did, I'd take whatever scraps they gave me and flag the producer and tell them, "I've got an update!" and wait for the producer to put me back on the air, usually without a script, but if I had time, I'd bang something out quick on the computer and put it up on prompter.

After the plane hit the tower, I ran to the green room for some quick make-up and then on to the studio, where I got mic'd up and put the IFB earpiece in so I could hear the control room and programming, and then I waited for them to toss to me. I also put a call in to Erik Grosof, and he told me he'd get right back to me.

I did a live shot covering the basics of what we knew at the time, that it appeared to be a small plane, no word on the pilot, no firm number on injuries or deaths, first responders on scene, fire in the building. We had live pictures from an affiliate in Texas, and the images were pretty dramatic.

When I was off the air and in the newsroom, Erik called me back, and I headed up the escalator to the lobby where it was a bit quieter and the service was better, but the connection still wasn't great on my cell phone.

Erik gave me incredible information that I never could've predicted or expected. Authorities figured out quickly that the pilot was a man named Andrew Joseph Stack.

He'd set his own house on fire that morning, then drove to a hanger he'd rented about twenty-five miles outside Austin where he kept his plane, a Piper Cherokee, and he flew the plane into the building.

Authorities were convinced he did this purposely because the building housed IRS offices, and Stack had a beef with the IRS.

He'd posted a six-page statement/suicide letter on a website connected to his ex-wife, blaming the IRS for many of his problems, including being audited at the time of the crash.

Grosof told me pretty much all of this. I think it was less than an hour after the crash, and *no one* was reporting anything beyond the basics: plane crashed into building, unknown fatalities and injuries, terrorism suspected but not confirmed, no other information about the pilot or a possible motive.

Meanwhile, I had the whole story from an incredibly reliable source who told me there was virtually no question this was the guy, and this was why he did it. I read some of the key points back to him, thanked him profusely, and hung up.

I raced back down to the newsroom and up to the assignment desk, where I told the main guy there I had exclusive details on the crash and needed to get back on TV right away. He called the control room while I ran back to Studio N, got mic'd up again, and waited for them to toss to me.

Within minutes I was back on the air and broke the news, close to two hours before any of the other networks could confirm any of it and go with it themselves. I reported the pilot's name, that he set his house ablaze, and flew the plane into the building because of his tax issues and the fact that the building housed the IRS offices and close to two hundred federal employees. I also, in my unscripted excitement, named Erik as the guy who gave me the information, since he worked for the NTSB, and I assumed he was, or would, be giving this information to everyone else when they called.

When my live shot ended, I walked out of that glass cubicle feeling very, very good about myself. I'd just broken a huge story wide open, beating every competitor thanks to one of my amazing sources. I couldn't wait for the accolades from my bosses. Then my phone rang. It was Erik.

"What's up man? Did you see my hit?" I asked him gleefully.

He sounded like he'd just been carjacked. "Dude, what did you just do??? You're gonna get me FIRED!"

"What?" I was stunned. I was careful to couch things, and I was sure I hadn't misreported any of it.

"I TOLD YOU IT WAS OFF THE RECORD!" He screamed at me. "YOU SAID MY NAME! IT WAS OFF THE RECORD! I'M GONNA GET FIRED FOR THIS!"

My heart was in my stomach, and I felt like I'd just failed a final exam. "Erik, you never said it was off the record!" I told him, because the truth is, I never heard him say that. It's possible he did and I missed it because of the spotty cell connection or because of my hearing, which wasn't great thanks to years of rock concerts, loud music on headphones, and the gunfire and explosions I'd been exposed to on numerous battlefields. If I'd heard him say it, I would've asked him what I *could* say on TV and would've gone through it with him step by step. I'd never burned a source before in my nearly twenty-five years of reporting. It was a point of pride for me, and a standard no decent journalist should violate. If people felt they couldn't trust you, they wouldn't tell you anything. But if they did trust you, you got the good stuff. I'd paid my dues and built a solid reputation, and it was very important to me. This was bad.

He sounded like he might be crying. "Erik, I'm SO sorry. I swear I didn't hear you say that. I never meant to get you in trouble."

"You gotta go back on the air and retract it!" He told me.

"Was the information accurate?" I asked? "Yes, but you said I told you and it was off the record! It hasn't been cleared for release yet and I'm probably gonna get canned!"

I apologized once more, profusely. And then Erik told me before he hung up, "Don't EVER call me again."

I knew I couldn't retract the story because it *was* the story, and it was already out there. What I could do was go back on TV and try to couch a few things, without quoting Erik.

Which I did: "Authorities believe," "we're being told," "they suspect," "unconfirmed," and so on. I think the anchor might have been a bit confused as to why I had backed off from some key points. I didn't change the facts, I just sounded slightly less sure of a few things, in an effort to appease and protect the guy I'd just burned.

Not long after, authorities held a news conference and confirmed everything I'd reported that Erik had given me. They also said Stack was killed in the crash along with an IRS manager working in the building. Thirteen others were hurt, two severely. I listened closely to see if I'd gotten any facts wrong. I hadn't. I was first, and I wasn't wrong on any of it, but I'd burned a really good bridge and felt awful about it.

It wasn't who I was. I didn't do stuff like that. But I did that day. Erik didn't get fired, but I don't know if he was disciplined in any way. In the long run, it didn't hurt me, except that I never talked to Erik again, and I was never invited back to the NTSB Training Course.

In fact, I heard after what happened, that the NTSB decided to not invite any media again. I was the first (and possibly the last) reporter to take part in the conference. I also made sure from that day forward to confirm what any source told me, and what was reportable and what wasn't, a refresher course I didn't think I needed, but a lesson well learned.

CHAPTER 12

THE DECAPITATION OF DANIEL PEARL

In late January 2002, I flew to Islamabad to prep for another trip to Afghanistan. This time we planned to drive in with two pickup trucks full of gear and a bunch of local Pakistani guys as our security team.

We traveled down to Quetta, along the southwestern border where we planned to head toward Karachi and continue our coverage of the hunt for Osama Bin Laden, this time without the restrictions the military had put on our movements when we were embedded with them the previous couple of months.

This would be a much more dangerous journey since we wouldn't have the protection of the U.S. Marines. I was more than a bit nervous, but also excited at the prospect of doing more original reporting on the ground there.

We spent thousands of dollars on food and supplies, including sleeping bags and tents, ready to rough it wherever we happened to wind up. Our trucks were fully loaded, and we were within minutes of heading for the border when we got word from New York that our assignment was changing.

A reporter for *The Wall Street Journal* named Daniel Pearl had been kidnapped by terrorists he was trying to interview in Karachi, and my bosses wanted me to head down there immediately.

Pearl, thirty-eight, was based in Mumbair and had been covering the war in the region for several months. He was in Karachi pursuing a story about the shoe bomber Richard Reid, but failed to follow basic security protocols, heading off alone at night for a meeting he was told would be with Sheikh Mubarak Ali Gilani, suspected of being associated with the radical Islamic group Jamaat al Fuqra.

Pearl's kidnapping was a really big story for Western news agencies and especially for Fox, since our parent company owned the *Journal*. Pearl was one of ours.

It was about a ten-hour drive from Quetta to Karachi, Pakistan's largest city (and the twelfth largest in the world) with close to thirteen million residents at the time. The city wasn't just bustling, it was like Manhattan on steroids, with ridiculously heavy traffic, packed sidewalks, lots of noise and grime, and a big crime problem.

We were told carjackings and smash-and-grab robberies were common. Many people got around on motorcycles and scooters, and they'd often be used to commit crimes because it was easy to escape on a bike, eluding police by weaving through traffic on the jammed roads.

We had a couple of local drivers and bodyguards, one of whom carried a pistol and a shotgun under his robe, so I felt relatively safe, but as a Jewish New York journalist, I couldn't help but see similarities between myself and Pearl, and it was more than unsettling to think of the possibility that I might wind up in a similar predicament. I was constantly on edge, looking over my shoulder every time we left the hotel, often greeted with curious and hostile stares.

We got a bunch of rooms at a Marriott downtown and set up our gear (including a satellite dish on the roof) for what we expected could be a long stay. Our crew created a standup location on one of the hotel balconies, and we turned that room into a workspace where we could log in to our computers and track the latest developments in the story when we weren't out on the streets conducting interviews and shooting B-roll, visiting Pearl's last known locations before he was snatched.

I found the second reporter notebook I used during coverage of Pearl's kidnapping, which has a live-shot script written out on the first page:

> A dead witness, a possible India link to the case and still no sign of WSJ reporter Danny Pearl. The kidnappers' deadline has come and gone with no new emails and no word on whether Pearl is alive or dead.

> He was last seen nine days ago, just blocks away from us here in Karachi, reportedly dropped off by a taxi driver behind the Metropole Hotel where he planned to meet a source.

> Pearl was working on a story about alleged shoe bomber Richard Reed, and one of the men Pearl talked to before he disappeared is now consider-ed a prime suspect. Mubarak Gilani is a leader of the radical Islamic cult Jamaat al Fuqra.

> Police picked him up Wednesday and have been questioning him ever since, and raided

properties linked to his group across the country, seizing computers and other records. The FBI is involved as well, and President Bush is following the case very closely.

[Here, we included a sound bite from the President, and my track continued after.]

On Sunday, Pearl's abductors sent out an email with pictures of Pearl and a list of demands, including freeing all Pakistanis held in Afghanistan and improving conditions for Taliban and Al-Qaeda detainees at Gitmo. Wednesday, they gave Pearl 24 hours to live. Thursday, they extended the deadline one more day and included this message:

"You cannot fool us and find us. We are inside seas, oceans, hills, graveyards, everywhere. We have given our demands and if you will not meet them, then we will act and the Americans will get what they deserve."

Pakistani police say their investigation has been hampered because a key witness is believed to have been killed. They also say there is an Indian link...that Gilani's cell phone records show the prime suspect had been in contact with three Indian government officials, people who hold important positions inside the Indian government.

A spokesman in New Delhi calls the charges "ridiculous." In the meantime, Mariane Pearl waits here in Karachi, six months pregnant with the couple's first child, not knowing if Danny is still alive. In Karachi, Rick Leventhal, Fox News.

Soon after Pearl's kidnapping, a militant group calling itself the National Movement for the Restoration of Pakistani Sovereignty sent an email to officials in the U.S. claiming that Pearl was a spy. The group included a list of demands, including freeing all Pakistanis detained by America on terror charges, plus the delivery of a U.S. shipment of F-16 fighter jets to the Pakistani government that had been put on hold. The email also had a threat:

"We give you one more day. If America will not meet our demands, we will kill Daniel. Then this cycle will continue and no American journalist could enter Pakistan."

There was also a series of phony demands sent by others, including a phone call to the U.S. consulate in Karachi, allegedly from the kidnappers, demanding $2 million ransom and the release of the former Taliban ambassador to Pakistan.

We covered these potential updates in the story but qualified them as unconfirmed. Most days there would be silence from his captors and little news to share. Authorities were searching for Pearl and the men who took him with no success, so we watched the wires and tried to advance the story as best we could.

I saw Pearl's wife in the coffee shop in the lobby of our hotel a few times. I think she was meeting with officials who were staying there. I said hello and asked if she wanted to do an interview as she waited for any positive news, but she politely declined. My notes said she was "composed" and "demonstrated patience and courage." A *Journal* spokesperson later told me the government was providing her with medical care and other assistance and that she was staying with a friend and was "holding up pretty well."

The FBI was involved in the case, working with local police and the Inter-Services Intelligence (ISI), the Pakistani intelligence service, but I'd heard from sources that there were concerns about leaks within that agency, which complicated matters, and that one of the prime suspects may have been an informant or double agent. The ISI couldn't be trusted, I was told. One day we got word of a commando raid carried out the night before as part of the search for Pearl, but it was unconfirmed, and if it happened, they didn't find him.

Then, on the second Friday after his disappearance, Fox News received an email from a group claiming to be the kidnappers. The email claimed Pearl had been killed and his body dumped in a Karachi graveyard. We shared the potential lead with authorities but didn't report it because of skepticism regarding its legitimacy. Karachi had about three hundred graveyards, and, out of an abundance of caution, police told us they spent all night and much of the next morning searching all of the cemeteries, finding nothing.

After the searches ended that Saturday, I spent close to an hour with Karachi's inspector general, the city's chief of police, who told me in our exclusive interview his department had formed "various teams of specialists, working vigorously around the clock, reviewing progress three to four times a day," with "technical assistance from the FBI, proceeding forward in the most scientific way we can."

He said they'd taken numerous people into custody including several overnight but had no substantial updates on the search for Pearl or his captors. He told me a recent email and phone call to the U.S. embassy demanding ransom was probably bogus, and he also did some blaming of the victim, pointing out that "Pearl was keen to interview Gilani. The organization didn't go looking for him, he looked for them."

We were told the terror group "offered to have him email questions and they would write back" and that "it would have been more prudent for him to take more care." He added that "there are more than three thousand journalists operating in this country and we have not experienced any such incident in the past."

Near the end of our sit-down, he said that Karachi "is not a lawless city. Life is normal. One has to be a little more discreet," he said, and added that in the eyes of law enforcement it was "technically not a kidnapping but an illegal detention." He also said authorities were aggressively working the case under the assumption that Pearl was still alive, and the managing editor at the *Journal* said the staff of the paper believed it, too.

Meanwhile, Mariane Pearl sent a letter to an Urdu-language newspaper in Pakistan, asking the kidnappers to free her husband "as people inspired by Islam's ethics. I ask them to be people who have the courage to actually take the first step to end this cycle of suffering," she wrote. "Let real justice win." Her letter also asked, "What will they get by torturing an innocent man, a sympathizer of all neglected people? I appeal to these people to release him."

That night, police raided a house in Islamabad and detained a teenage boy who they say confessed to making the ransom call to the U.S. embassy a day earlier, demanding the $2 million ransom and prisoner release. Authorities told us the call was a hoax and the boy had no connection to the kidnappers. They also busted two others believed to be involved in sending the email to Fox falsely claiming Pearl's body was dumped in a cemetery.

Eleven days in, we were told that Pakistani police had formed a new squad led by their top anti-terrorism expert who'd been trained in the states, and they were turning their attention to areas outside of Karachi where desert tribes were known for harboring criminals and offering protection. The new squad was also intended to fix the poor coordination being reported between the various agencies investigating the case. Pakistani Police told us they were focused on Islamic extremists and were looking for a couple of "primary suspects" including a follower of Gilani who helped to arrange Pearl's interview that led to his abduction.

One night a body was found, and there were rumors it might be the missing journalist.

One of our camera crews and a producer went flying out the door to race to the scene near the main jail, but the victim had already been moved to the hospital. Our producer somehow got in and saw the body, describing it as an Arabic-looking man in jeans and Western clothes with short hair and a mustache. He said it wasn't Pearl and that was confirmed by Karachi's police chief, deputy chief, and a representative from the U.S. consulate who'd met Pearl several times. They were all at the hospital and confirmed it wasn't him.

On the twelfth day, I reported that a top U.S. Treasury official had arrived in country to push for Pearl's release, meeting with Pakistan's President Pervez Musharraf, urging his government to do all it could. The country's interior minister said they were pulling out all the stops, that efforts to find him were "massive in scale" and had "spread to all parts of Pakistan," claiming they were "getting closer" to the men involved.

The night before there'd been another commando raid on a house where they suspected Pearl might be held, only to be frustrated yet again. It had been five days since anyone had heard from the kidnappers, who'd sent images of Pearl in chains to prove he was in their custody. Gilani was still being held and continued to maintain his innocence.

In an interview with French television, Pearl's wife made another plea for his release, offering to take his place:

"If anyone's going to give his life to save him, it's me. Please make contact with me. I'm ready!" She also told the kidnappers that "using Daniel as a symbol is completely wrong."

The next day I interviewed one of the last people to see Pearl before he was abducted. Jameel Yusuf, chief of the Citizens-Police Liaison Committee, who Danny interviewed for about an hour in the late afternoon of January 23. During the interview, Yusuf says Pearl got a couple phone calls about a later meeting, which turned out to be a trap. Yusuf had a lot of experience with previous kidnappings in Pakistan, saying he helped the police to solve most of them.

He said that most victims "usually don't know their kidnappers, but in this case, he walked into their hands, forcing himself" on them, ignoring advice from others not to go on such a dangerous mission. Yusuf seemed to think there was a good chance Pearl would eventually be released, based on the tone of the email sent to authorities which was "not very aggressive."

"They're not fearsome, they're not terrorizing," he said of the kidnappers, and said he was also encouraged because Pearl had a "friendly rapport" with them. He also said "the pressure is definitely on" authorities to solve the case. "Everybody is concerned. We've never had such a high-profile kidnapping in this country, ever."

My report that night also included an open letter from the WSJ's managing editor at the time, Paul Steiger, written to Danny's captors, hoping to start some kind of dialogue:

We could resolve this situation if we communicate more privately and more often. I suggest we use an email account of one of Danny's close friends, such as either of the two best men at his wedding, or a private phone line of one of these friends, or even a letter mailed to such a person. This line of communication would show me that Danny is with you and would allow us one to one contact. We are eager to hear from you soon.

My next script offered some hopeful news from Pakistani authorities who said they "still believe Danny Pearl is alive and say they are now very close to solving his kidnapping. A top police official says they [the police] know who has Daniel, and predicts they may solve this case 'sooner than you think.'"

The police were apparently more confident because of the arrest of two men, following two separate raids on apartments in Karachi. The men were believed to be responsible for sending the original two emails about Pearl's kidnapping. Not the fake emails, but the legit ones that included photos of Pearl being held.

A source told me the men were considered to be "low on the totem pole," and while there were no signs of Pearl at either location, the men did tell police they worked for Ahmed Omar Saeed Sheikh, who'd been linked to an Afghan plane hijacking in 1999. That hijacking was connected to a radical group known as Harkat-ul-Mujahideen, the same group that authorities believed all along was behind Pearl's kidnapping. Connecting the dots to the possible mastermind meant they could refocus their efforts on all known members of the organization. Police would be tightening the net in their search with massive raids predicted, putting additional pressure on the kidnappers.

But their optimism was destroyed by the revelation that Pearl had been murdered nine days after his capture, confirmed with one of the most horrible and disturbing videos I've ever seen, which haunts me to this day.

The three-and-a-half-minute digital videotape was delivered to authorities in Karachi a few days after Pearl's murder. It included several different scenes edited together, making it impossible to say exactly how, when, or where Pearl was killed. It began with Pearl reciting his biography and background, including his heritage.

He says, clearly under duress, "My name is Daniel Pearl. I'm a Jewish American from Encino, California, USA. I come from, uh, on my father's side the family is Zionist. My father's Jewish, my mother's Jewish, I'm Jewish. My family follows Judaism. We've made numerous family visits to Israel."

Pearl, apparently reading someone else's script, then says, "Americans can't walk around free as long as our [US] government's policies continue. Americans will bear the consequences of our government's unconditional support for Israel." Pearl's family insisted he was "a proud American and he abhorred extremist ideologies."

They also said he gave signals indicating he didn't agree with what he was saying on camera. Soon after he finishes, there's a close-up of a wound in Pearl's chest where he was apparently stabbed, which investigators said was likely what killed him, meaning Pearl was already dead for the following, incredibly gruesome scenes showing his throat being cut and his head severed from his body.

I was hesitant to view the video when we got a link in our computers. I don't think I'd ever watched an actual beheading before, and I knew we couldn't (and wouldn't) ever show it on television. I felt closely connected to Pearl and his story after immersing myself in it for weeks, and felt it was almost disrespectful to view his death, but at the same time I believed my role as a journalist should take precedence.

If I watched it, I could report on it accurately without relying on the interpretation of others. I could convey the horrors without having to subject others to it. I steeled myself, clicked the link, loaded the video, and pressed play. It was by far the worst thing I've ever seen. It turned my stomach and made me realize just how vulnerable all of us journalists were.

This man was a reporter like me. He wasn't a combatant or a criminal or a threat to the kidnappers. In fact, he was trying to learn more about the radical groups who were striking out against America so he could present their side to readers. He was doing his job, or trying to, and they used him to advance their sick agenda. Watching his death was a stark reminder of the savage brutality that exists in the dark corners of the world.

We reported on Pearl's death, and the video, and stuck around for the pursuit of his killers. Eventually we learned that the man suspected of planning and carrying out the kidnapping was in custody, with a huge twist.

Ahmed Omar Saeed Sheikh had surrendered to a former ISI officer who didn't tell Karachi police for a week. Sheikh was well known to authorities for the kidnapping of tourists in India years earlier, and when he was brought to court in Karachi for his first appearance before a judge, I was there, sitting a few rows from the front.

It was a pulse-racing experience, watching this suspected kidnapper and murderer being led into the courtroom. He looked nothing like I expected. He didn't have a long beard and he wasn't haggard or disheveled or dirty with long hair and wild eyes.

He was tall, handsome, and well dressed, born in Great Britain to a somewhat wealthy family, looking very civilized and intelligent. He definitely did not look like a terrorist, at least not like the stereotype and not like any I'd seen before.

And he looked right at me as he walked past. I watched the proceedings in near disbelief, that this was the guy who did it, and he would actually pay for his crimes. To the judge, he said, "Yes, I did this," when asked about his involvement, saying it was in protest of Pakistan's support of America's "War on Terror."

Nearly two weeks later he was back in court, and once again I covered the proceedings.

I wrote in my notebook:

> The Bush administration is strongly considering bringing criminal charges in the kidnapping and murder of Wall Street Journal reporter Danny Pearl, possibly convening a grand jury in the DC area to hear evidence and bring an indictment to try and ensure Sheikh Omar and his accomplices are punished for their alleged crimes.

> Omar, considered the mastermind of the abduction, was brought to a Karachi courtroom with two other suspects, their heads covered in white sheets, surrounded by heavily armed police, but they were not charged with kidnapping and murder as expected...Instead, the judge sent them back to jail for 14 more days to give the prosecution more time to interrogate the men and search for the murder weapon and Pearl's body.

It turns out U.S. authorities have been pursuing Omar for months, secretly indicting him last November for his role in kidnapping four British and American tourists back in 1994. They were pushing the Pakistani government to catch and extradite Omar to the U.S. at the same time Omar was allegedly orchestrating Pearl's abduction.

The U.S. Ambassador to Pakistan calls Omar "a nasty character" and plans to raise the extraction issue with Pakistan President Pervez Musharraf during a meeting here tomorrow.

It was later revealed that Omar was believed to have helped funnel money from Osama Bin Laden to the lead hijacker in the 9/11 attacks and may have met with Bin Laden *after* 9/11. Yet, Pakistan chose not to turn Omar over to American authorities, charging him and three others with murder. All were convicted.

Omar was sentenced to death but appealed, and nearly twenty years later, in April 2020, his murder conviction was overturned, and his sentence reduced to time served.

That decision has been tied up by fresh appeals filed by U.S. officials on behalf of the Pearl family, and at last report, Omar was still being held in a detention facility, but allowed visitation by his family.

One reason for the Pakistani court's about-face was a confession obtained from Khalid Sheikh Mohammed, the notorious terrorist being held by the U.S. at Guantanamo Bay. Mohammed said he was the one who decapitated Pearl, and the FBI said it was probably true, after the agency used "vein matching" technology to compare a bulging vein on his hand to one seen on TV.

Pearl's decomposed body and severed head were found months later in a shallow grave outside Karachi and were eventually returned to the states where he was interred by his family at a California cemetery.

I went home a few days after Omar's second court appearance with a heavy heart and great sadness. Catching the men responsible didn't erase the horrors and savagery of Pearl's murder, and it was clear to me that the level of hatred and animosity in the region toward America was only increasing. It appeared the worst was yet to come.

CHAPTER 13

THE DAY DALE EARNHARDT DIED

*"Driving a stock car is like dancing
with a chainsaw."*

—CALE YARBOROUGH

I covered dozens of major sporting events during my career, including several Super Bowls, numerous World Series and MLB All-Star games, NBA Championships and Division series, and a couple of Stanley Cups. But I was dispatched just once to the Daytona 500, the first year Fox paid for the rights to broadcast the race, and I was at the speedway that Sunday in February 2001 when Dale Earnhardt died.

We were there for several days leading up to the race, covering preliminaries, doing features on drivers and the new HANS safety gear and interviewing race fans who set up camp inside the oval with million-dollar motorhomes equipped with easy chairs, barbecues, and coolers full of beer. It was a really fun assignment and a great departure from the wars and hurricanes and terror attacks I was so often buried in.

Our credentials got us access to pit row with an incredible vantage point of the track, the drivers, and the action. Since I hadn't covered NASCAR before, I didn't know the protocol leading up to the start of the race so we just kind of winged it, walking around gathering footage, looking to talk to drivers or their crews, and before the race began, we made our way to the concrete wall separating pit row from the track.

I didn't know many of the drivers, but I obviously knew who Dale Earnhardt and Dale Jr. were, and I told my crew we should try to grab them on camera before they climbed into their cars.

I saw the two of them and we moved down the wall to get close, and my cameraman was rolling as we watched both their wives join Dale and his son, and the four of them put their arms around each other in a prayer circle.

We kept a respectful distance, and I waited for an opportunity to ask them some questions, but it never came. They spoke amongst themselves, kissed their wives, then climbed into their cars and got strapped in, helmets on, ready to race.

We focused on Dale the entire time, recording all of it, not realizing those were his last moments with his feet on the ground and his last time climbing into a race car.

I found the reporter's notebook I used that trip. The first pages include scripts and notes from the 125-mile qualifying races to determine Sunday's starting positions.

I referenced another pre-race prayer, this one also with Dale Earnhardt, along with Bill Elliott and Jeff Gordon. The next page has a rough script for a piece I planned to cut later in the day, beginning with the ritual we'd just witnessed.

"The quiet before the storm on Pit Row," I wrote. "Pre-race prayers, last-minute strategy sessions, and final preps for the all-important 125-mile qualifiers, deciding who starts where in Sunday's Daytona 500."

I wrote a tease, calling it "The Super Bowl of Stock Car Racing." Then I found notes from an interview with Brian France, the former CEO and chairman of NASCAR, about the use of the HANS safety harness designed to stabilize the drivers' helmets, securing them to the seat's headrest in a way that would protect the driver's neck in the event of a crash.

I was putting the HANS piece together that afternoon and found several drivers who'd be wearing it. It was still optional, and Dale Earnhardt said no. He and some of the other drivers didn't like the HANS because they said it limited their ability to turn their head side to side and see other drivers around them. Dale was old school, of course.

My notes quoted France saying, "Safety is always our number one priority" and "It's their choice...a couple different schools of thought," and then I wrote in parentheses "(Mandatory? Long way off)." Driver Steve Park called them "too cumbersome." Only seven of the forty-three drivers wore them that Sunday. When I asked one of the crew guys why more drivers weren't strapping on the HANS, he said, "Habits are hard to break."

Then I found the opening and closing standups that I'd recorded for the piece just a few days before Earnhardt's fatal crash. My intro said: "Every time drivers roll onto tracks like these, they're risking death in pursuit of the checkered flag.

There is a device that might help reduce the chance of fatalities, but most of the road warriors out here choose not to use it."

Then, after the package, my standup close said, "NASCAR is *not* ready to require drivers to use the HANS, and while many say they're considering it, it might take another tragedy, or a life being saved, before more drivers start strapping them on."

Sunday, race day, I jotted down some key facts and stats at the top of a page:

> 43rd annual Dayton 500 at Daytona International Speedway
>
> 200 lap race—2.5 mile oval
>
> Record purse $11,049,049
>
> Bill Elliott, Pole Sitter, leads 43 car field in a Dodge

An hour into the race, there were two caution flags, thirteen leaders, and forty-two lead changes. Later, I noted it was "smooth sailing till lap 175...18 cars collide. The field shrank considerably."

Throughout the race, Earnhardt, in his #3 Chevy Monte Carlo, was among the group at the front, leading seventeen laps and running strong. Meanwhile, his teammates Michael Waltrip and Dale Jr. were running first and second, swapping the lead back and forth over the final few laps.

As the race neared its end, Earnhardt was positioned right behind them, blocking attempts by Sterling Marlin to pass him and challenge for the win. On that fateful final lap, Marlin was just behind Earnhardt with Ken Schrader and Rusty Wallace battling to get by.

As they approached the final turn, turn four, Earnhardt made contact with Marlin and lost control, crossing in front of Schrader, banging into his car, then smashed head-on into the wall at an estimated speed of 160 miles per hour.

The car was badly damaged, rolling down the steeply banked track to the infield along with Schrader's. When Schrader was able to extricate himself from his cage, he checked on Earnhardt and later said he knew right away he was gone.

"Here's the deal," Schrader confessed in 2011. "When I went up to the car I knew. I knew he was dead, yeah.... I didn't want to be the one who said, 'Dale is dead.'"

But no one else at the time knew just how serious it was, including us. It was a crazy quick series of events. Dale hit the wall and seconds later, Waltrip crossed the finish line to both a checkered flag and yellow flag warning drivers of the crash.

Most of the focus was on the race being over and Waltrip winning for the first time. It wasn't clear right away just how bad Earnhardt's wreck was. It certainly looked bad, but there was no way of knowing for sure until we got word from officials, and that took a very long time.

In fact, just after the race ended, I wrote a quick standup in my notebook. "A wild race, a wild finish and Michael Waltrip gets the checkered flag, his first win in 463 races, collecting a record purse of just over $11 million. At Daytona, Rick Leventhal, Fox News."

We made our way to the winner's circle, still unsure about the severity of Earnhardt's injuries. We watched on monitors as Daytona's safety team got Earnhardt out of his car soon after the crash. He was then transported by ambulance to Halifax Medical Center a couple miles away, with Dale Jr. following the ambulance to the hospital in another car, but his dad was beyond saving.

Doctors tried but failed to revive him, and Dale Earnhardt was officially pronounced dead at 5:16 p.m.

We didn't know it yet, but I had an early indication at the winner's circle, where things were far more somber than you'd typically see on TV. A dark cloud hung over the speedway, and I was watching Michael Waltrip closely when someone came up and spoke to him.

His face was grim, and I think he might've cried. I knew it was bad, and there were rumors starting to float around that Earnhardt didn't survive the crash.

Then, ninety minutes after the race ended, we were called to the track's press conference room to hear NASCAR president Mike Helton confirm the worst.

"This is undoubtedly one of the toughest announcements that I've ever personally had to make, but after the accident in turn four at the end of the Daytona 500, we've lost Dale Earnhardt."

Helton said first responders gave CPR at the scene but "quickly identified this was a very bad situation," and once Earnhardt reached the trauma center, they attempted full resuscitation for twenty minutes, but he was unconscious and unresponsive. He wasn't breathing and had no pulse.

Helton refused to take questions, saying "this is a very difficult time." He concluded by saying "NASCAR has lost its greatest driver ever, and I've personally lost the greatest friend."

Earnhardt, a seven-time Winston Cup Champion, was just forty-nine years old. His cause of death was officially listed as "blunt force trauma" to the head.

He suffered numerous other critical injuries in the crash, including a fatal basilar skull fracture when he hit the wall on the final turn of his twenty-third consecutive start at Daytona.

He would've turned fifty that April. In the autopsy, the coroner said, "His car stopped on impact, his body held in place by restraints, but his head whipped forward with catastrophic energy."

In my notes I found quotes from drivers including John Andretti, who said, "I feel like somebody kicked me in the chest. I'm stunned and I'm really sad. That's about all I can say."

Kyle Petty called Earnhardt "the nicest, most competitive driver," and Waltrip, in his first public comments, said, "My heart is hurting right now. I would rather be any place right this moment than here. It's so painful."

I was shocked when I learned that Waltrip had never won a NASCAR Cup Series race throughout his first fifteen full-time seasons, and when he crossed the finish line first that day, it snapped his losing streak in the first race of his sixteenth year in his debut with a new team, Dale Earnhardt, Inc. Dale was his boss, his mentor, and his friend.

On that final lap, heading into the final turn, it was Waltrip out front with Dale Jr. pushing from right behind and Dale Sr. right behind them.

In an interview with *Forbes* in 2021, twenty years after the crash, Waltrip said of Earnhardt: "We were friends for years. When I was racing and losing, he'd always tell me, 'You'd win if I put you in my car.' So I said, 'Put me in one.' It took the right circumstance and timing to make that happen, but when it did, that's exactly what he did."

Then he was asked the obvious question: How it felt to win the race and then learn his friend and mentor Dale was dead.

He said:

There's really no way to tell what it was like. Nothing can compare. You think you've had the best day ever, then you start getting hints that something isn't exactly right. It's thirty or forty minutes later and you still haven't seen your buddy, the guy who was a big reason why you won. You start to ask questions and wonder. And then, eventually the news came to me that Dale had died. I don't know how else to sum it up. It went from the best day to the worst day. Today people say, "What a bitter-sweet race." But I don't remember the sweet part. When you sum it all up, it was just a hard day.

"President George W. Bush called Teresa Earnhardt last night, according to NASCAR officials," I reported the day after the crash.

"The flag flies at half-staff at Daytona International Speedway. The racing community mourning the loss of a legend. Dale Earnhardt, one of the winningest drivers in NASCAR history, died instantly when he hit the wall on the last lap of Sunday's Daytona 500."

After sound bites from Dale Jr., Johnny Weatherford, and Mike Helton, I said: "More than a hundred mourners paid their respects outside Earnhardt's North Carolina shop. Race fans also built a makeshift shrine on the fence near turn four. Earnhardt, known as 'the intimidator,' chose not to wear the HANS safety device designed to prevent this type of death, but the track doctor says he isn't sure it would've made a difference."

I also reported Dale Jarrett's crew chief saying Jarrett won't get in the car again without the HANS safety device.

Chris Myers, one of the broadcasters for Fox on race day, said: "This isn't like Michael Jordan retiring from the NBA. It's like him expiring in game seven of the NBA finals. It's like Tiger Woods suffering a heart attack as he charges up the eighteenth on Sunday at Augusta." He said Earnhardt was like John Wayne on a three-thousand-pound steel horse, "feared and fearless."

Earnhardt was actually the fourth NASCAR driver in eight months to die in a race, after Adam Petty, Kenny Irwin Jr., and Tony Roper, all from basilar skull fractures.

The day after the crash, more than forty drivers ordered HANS safety equipment, and NASCAR soon implemented a slew of safety upgrades, including new barriers on oval track walls, tougher rules for seats and belts, and mandated head and neck restraints for all drivers.

Remarkably, no other drivers have lost their lives during any of NASCAR's three major series races since Earnhardt's fatal wreck.

CHAPTER 14
(THE BEST CHAPTER)

KELLY, COVID, AND CALIFORNIA

People often ask how I met my wife, Kelly. It's a great story because of all the things that had to happen to make it possible, fulfilling what I believe was our destiny to be together.

Kelly had been living in Newport Beach, California, for almost ten years, and in San Francisco for a few years before that, and she grew up in Scottsdale and Phoenix, Arizona. She was from the desert and the West Coast, and I've always been an East Coast guy. I'd never been to Newport and only visited San Francisco and the Phoenix area once in my life.

From those basic geographical parameters, it would seem pretty unlikely our paths would ever cross.

But in late June 2019, Kelly flew to New York City to spend time with friends attending Pride Week events.

Kelly had just finished filming her fourth season of *The Real Housewives of Orange County*. She was one of the most famous and controversial cast members on the Bravo show, which was the first of the franchise that grew to include numerous other cities including Beverly Hills, Potomac, Atlanta, Dallas, Miami, Salt Lake City, and, of course, New York. I'd never watched the show.

While in Manhattan, Kelly accepted an invitation to join her friend Ramona Singer from *The Real Housewives of New York* to spend a few days at Ramona's home in the Hamptons.

It was the week of Independence Day, and I was just twenty miles away at my beach house in Westhampton, getting ready to host a big pool party that Saturday, July 6. I'd been throwing bashes at the house every summer since 1999, soon after my wife and I split, and started renting the place year-round, but this would be the first party I'd thrown in three years.

The house was my great escape from the city. I could make it there from my apartment in Manhattan in just over an hour if I left later at night after rush hour and drove really fast, and once I got there, I could truly relax.

It's a small, one-story ranch with only about 1,600 square feet under roof, but it has five bedrooms, so I could share it with lots of friends, or my daughters and their friends when they'd come visit. It has a huge pool and a sprawling series of decks and a big yard that doubles as a wiffleball field when my buddies would come for the weekend.

It's super quiet and peaceful there, and at night you can see every star in the sky.

The place was modest by Hamptons standards, but comfortable, and it felt like home.

One of the friends I'd invited to my summer party that Saturday was former New York Rangers hockey legend Ron Duguay, who was as famous for his refusal to wear a helmet over his long blonde hair and for his affinity for supermodels as he was for his skills on the ice.

He came up to New York and stayed with a buddy of his in Southampton, and the night before my party, they went out to some bar and ran into Kelly and Ramona and her other friends.

The next day, Ron told Ramona about the party, and she asked him for my address and rounded up the girls. Kelly later told me she was reluctant to go because she had several other parties she hoped to attend that day further east (in the opposite direction), but she hopped in Ramona's car and headed west on Route 27 toward my house.

When the ladies pulled up and parked on the street, I was playing yard games with Ron and his buddy, Chef Andrew Molen. There were about seventy people at the house by then. It was a beautiful day, and we were a few drinks in.

I looked over toward my driveway and saw Kelly walking onto my yard.

I was thunderstruck. She was tall and absolutely gorgeous, with a killer body and an incredible smile, wearing a white Panama hat, big Louis Vuitton sunglasses, platform shoes, and a white sundress with a black bikini bathing suit top underneath.

I walked up to her and said, "Hi! I'm Rick! This is my house! Welcome!" She smiled and introduced herself, and I asked, "Can I get you a drink?" and she said yes, so I walked her to the tiki bar by the pool and ordered us margaritas from the bartender I'd hired for the party.

We stood there next to the bar for ten or fifteen minutes getting to know each other. I asked her about her show and her daughter and her life in California, and she asked about my job and my life, and I bragged about having built the bar and she asked me lots of questions about it, which was my first hint she might be interested in me.

At some point she told me she was recently single, and I told her I was, too, and I remember then saying something humble like, "I'd love to take you out sometime, but I don't know if you'd want to—you're way out of my league!" She said she'd like to. For some reason I didn't get her phone number. Maybe I didn't want to come on too strong. I did get my phone out and suggested we both start following each other on Instagram.

Meanwhile, my daughters were both freaking out because they were huge *Housewives* fans and recognized Kelly and Ramona right away. Veronica came up while I was talking to Kelly and was bugging me to get pictures with her and Ramona, so at some point I made it happen. I also took a selfie with Kelly and Ramona, and then, after only being there about thirty minutes, she said they were heading back east to go to all the other parties on her list.

She kept liking my Instagram posts, and after about three weeks, I finally asked for her phone number. She gave it to me, I called her, and we talked for hours.

Before long we were talking multiple times a day, sometimes ten calls or more, which quickly shifted to Facetiming. We got to know each other really well, and I couldn't wait to see her again, but she was hard to pin down. I offered to come see her in California, but she had shared custody of her daughter Jolie (who was thirteen at the time) and the weeks Jolie was at her dad's, Kelly was travelling.

In mid-August, just over a month after we'd met, Kelly went to Greece to attend the wedding of her British friends Sanjay and Doug, and one night she was on the phone with another of her friends who worked for *People* magazine, and I guess she was a bit tipsy, and she told the guy she was dating me.

The next time we spoke on the phone, she told me what she'd told him, and I was stunned.

"Dating?" I asked. "We haven't even gone on a date yet!"

She laughed about it and sure enough, within hours there was a post about us on *People*'s website, revealing I was her new man. I told Kelly, "If there are stories out there about us dating, then I absolutely need to take you out!"

She said, "Come to London next weekend!" She was headed there from Greece and said if I didn't make it, it might be at least another six weeks before I could see her again because her social calendar was absolutely packed.

I started looking at flights right away and found one on Virgin Atlantic that was leaving super early that Friday morning, August 23, and would get me to London by dinnertime. I cashed in about 250,000 Amex points to grab an "Upper Class" ticket, packed my stuff Thursday night, and got up at 4 a.m. to catch my car service to JFK Airport.

We made it there in no time and when I got to the counter to check in, the agent asked for my passport, and I looked in my bag and it wasn't there.

I started to panic. I always put it in a particular zipped pocket of my backpack and thought for sure it was in there, but it wasn't, so I frantically started checking every other pocket of all my bags and pants and coat and—no passport.

I called the driver who'd just dropped me off and asked him to check the back seat, convinced at this point it must've fallen out of my pants pocket, and while I was waiting for him to search for it, I made my way back to the terminal entrance to check the sidewalk and street. The driver called back to tell me it definitely wasn't in the car, and my search outside turned up nothing. I asked the skycaps if anyone had found a passport and they said no, and I called the front desk of my building and asked the doorman to use the spare key to check in my apartment. He went upstairs to look and called me back and said it wasn't there, so I called the driver back and asked him to look again, and he did and assured me my passport was not in his vehicle.

I was ready to cry. How was this possible? I was an experienced traveler! I was freaking out. At some point I even called Kelly to let her know what was going on and she sounded really bummed.

She later told me, "I was disappointed and sad. I thought, 'Does this guy not want to see me? Is he making excuses?' and my friend Taylor said, 'He must have another girlfriend or something. He's a correspondent for Fox and travels all the time? There's no way he'd forget his passport like that.'"

When I had no options left, I decided the passport *had* to be in my apartment, so I called the doorman back and got really specific.

"Please check the counter on the living room side of the kitchen., there's a small shelf there in front of the support column and I think I might have left it on that shelf, next to the note reminding me of all the things not to forget!"

I'd asked him to look there earlier but might not have been clear enough.

He went back upstairs and called me right away.

"Found it!" he said. It was right where I'd told him to look. I asked him to hold it at the front desk, and I immediately booked an Uber for a pickup at my apartment to JFK, and when a driver accepted the ride, I called him and asked him to get my passport from the doorman and get to the Virgin Terminal at JFK as fast as he could.

When the driver rolled up the ramp, I ran to his vehicle, handed him a bunch of cash as a tip, grabbed the passport, and ran back to the check-in counter. The flight was on time and would be taking off in just under an hour, but I was TSA Precheck with a Global ID flying first class, so getting to the gate was a breeze, and I was probably the happiest, most stressed-out person on the plane when I got to my seat.

Our weekend in London was magical.

The best part was how well Kelly and I got along. It just felt right being with her, and we wound up having an amazing three nights and two days there. We took a double decker tour bus around the city, visited the Tower of London, walked through Buckingham Palace, went shopping, and had more fun lunches and dinners with her girlfriends.

Leaving her that Monday morning was tough, but she was headed back to California, and I wound up spending just one night at home before packing and leaving for Puerto Rico to cover Hurricane Dorian. The crew and I spent three days there before the storm swept past us, and we bounced to south Florida where it was headed, then drove up the coast trying to be where Dorian might make landfall.

We wound up in Jacksonville Beach, which is right next to Ponte Vedra Beach, where Ron Duguay lives! I hung out with him quite a bit over the next few days, and he was very impressed I'd made it to London and sealed the deal with Kelly.

Our second trip together was even better than the first, when I booked a series of cars and flights to take me from covering a hurricane in Jacksonville to catch a flight in Orlando to Newark to Germany to Italy and down to the Amalfi Coast, where I joined Kelly on her friend's yacht for a week of amazing adventures, getting to know each other even better, in one of the most beautiful places on earth.

We then made our way to Amsterdam for a couple nights before flying to Teterboro, New Jersey. That gave me one more night with Kelly, our first together at my apartment in Manhattan before she went home to Newport Beach.

It was one hell of a second date, and the whirlwind of our life together hasn't slowed down since.

Kelly and I got engaged that November. The next January, she threw me a sixtieth birthday party at the W Hotel in South Beach, one of the best bashes either of us had ever attended. It was right before the world was about to undergo a dramatic transformation.

COVERING COVID IN NYC

The coronavirus had reached America just as I was heading home from Miami. In fact, I was told my birthday party was one of the last, if not the last, event ever held at the W's Wall Lounge. It closed for COVID and still hadn't reopened during the writing of this chapter more than two years later.

I don't think anyone could've predicted just how dramatically our world was about to change because of the virus, but I was never scared of the coronavirus, and the shutdowns pissed me (and Kelly) off. I knew the virus could be dangerous to the elderly and infirm, and was contributing to many deaths, but from the beginning, it was clear that the vast majority of those who caught it survived.

What I was more concerned with was the direction of mass media coverage, scaring the world with on-screen tickers counting the cases and total deaths. There was so much *not* being reported. The flu killed, too, tens of thousands of people a year, many of them children. Did the authorities ever force masks on people during flu season? Did they shut down commerce and restrict travel? Why not, if it could have saved lives? Why now?

I couldn't say these things on TV. I wasn't an opinion guy. I didn't have a talk show. I was assigned to cover the news and report the facts, so that's what I did.

But Kelly and I talked about it daily. She was passionately opposed to the shutdowns and restrictions placed on Americans and was equally unafraid of the virus. For this and many other reasons she was the perfect person to ride out the pandemic with. It was a truly strange and unusual time, and Kelly I bonded in powerful ways.

In Manhattan, streets normally packed with traffic stood empty. Sidewalks usually bustling with pedestrians were nearly bare, inhabited by a small but growing number of homeless people who became more aggressive as time went on.

Most of New York City felt like 6 a.m. on a Sunday morning, twenty-four hours a day. It was incredibly quiet and often almost completely deserted, especially Downtown.

It reminded me of the old film *The Omega Man* with Charlton Heston, or its remake *I Am Legend* with Will Smith, when they had the city virtually to themselves, except for some mutants hiding in the shadows.

I'm not overdramatizing when I say some of the people wandering the streets actually looked like zombies.

It was surreal seeing the city shuttered. The only other time I'd experienced anything close to it was almost twenty years earlier, in the weeks and months after 9/11, but the desertion was limited to lower Manhattan, not affecting the entire island and beyond.

And while this might sound even worse, Kelly and I had an amazing time during the pandemic. We had *fun*. I was on a late schedule at this point, reporting for prime time shows, and most nights I only had one hit during the 11 p.m. hour, usually two to three minutes, wrapping the day's Covid developments, starting and finishing with stuff in New York and filling the body of my stories with virus news-of-the-day from across the country.

I worked from home since no one was going to the offices in Midtown. I did research on my laptop and wrote in my reporter's notebooks, and I didn't need to start collecting editorial and working on my script until three or four in the afternoon.

This left Kelly and me plenty of time to take really long walks every day, through the empty neighborhoods and parks, sometimes right down the middle of Broadway, exploring Gramercy and the East and West Villages and Meatpacking and Tribeca and Chelsea, doing fifteen thousand to twenty thousand steps before I had to start my shift.

I opened a CitiBike account, and when the weather started improving, we'd ride instead of walk, from near my apartment in Murray Hill (32nd Street & 2nd Avenue) down the path along the East River to the South Street Seaport and the financial district, on to Battery Park and then up the West Side along the Hudson, taking detours and side streets whenever we felt the urge.

When CitiBike added electric scooters to its fleet, we'd share one, with the streets and avenues virtually to ourselves. A few times we strapped on some old rollerblades and covered about eleven miles each outing, criss-crossing the Downtown area and back. Neither of us fell once.

It was like the city became our playground, and while it was a depressing place in so many ways, being able to share it with the love of my life 24-7 was an incredibly special and rewarding experience.

In October 2020, we got married in Napa.

CALIFORNIA BOUND

I'd been based in New York my entire career with Fox News Channel. I was the man there, first out the door for breaking news, first to get asked to cover the really big stories and events, a strong, dependable, trusted, respected, and valuable member of the network. Fox had just completely remodeled and upgraded the twentieth and twenty-first floors at the Fox News headquarters at 1211 6th Avenue, and I finally had my own office, spacious and bright with three windows and a partial view of Times Square.

I had no plans to leave the city until I retired. I had my summer home in Westhampton and bought a spacious three-bedroom condo with a forty-five-foot terrace in Highland Beach, Florida, between Delray and Boca Raton, where I planned to spend winters (six months and a day) for the sunshine and the tax break once I hung up my microphone. I had my 401(k) and my pension and a $5 million life insurance policy that would provide tax-free income whenever I decided to cash in.

But when I started spending quality time with Kelly, I realized it was time to pivot. I'd been living in my bubble for a long time. She introduced me to a whole new set of people and places, sharing a world I hadn't seen or experienced before, and I wanted to be in that world with her forever.

Life with Kelly is charmed. I've never had so much fun with a partner. As corny as it might sound, Kelly and I were sharing love and laughter, in near-perfect sync with each other. We're cut from the same cloth, despite our very different backgrounds and experiences. She was the partner I'd always dreamed of.

I'd often said I'd never move to California, but when I met Kelly and realized the only way to be together was for me to do just that, I didn't hesitate for a second. Being apart for even a few days at a time was really difficult for both of us, and I knew we couldn't pull off a long-distance relationship. So, right around the time I proposed to Kelly, I asked for a meeting with Jay Wallace, who'd been promoted to president of Fox News Channel the year before.

Jay and I had been friends for more than fifteen years. He rose through the ranks at Fox, working in the newsroom and producing Shep's show and even doing time as the New York bureau chief, acting as my immediate supervisor. We played on a city league basketball team together (and won four championships), we competed against each other every fall in a Fox Fantasy Football League, and his vacation home was literally down the street from mine in Westhampton.

"A-1!" he said. He always called me that. My nickname from Chicago had followed me to New York.

I sat down across from him in his spacious second-floor office, with its high ceilings and massive windows facing the plaza out front and 6th Avenue beyond.

"I need your help," I told him. "Kelly is the woman of my dreams and we're getting married, and she can't move here."

Jay asked me if I was sure, and I told him I was.

He definitely wasn't happy about it.

"If I do this for you [transferring me to the LA Bureau] it opens the door for a bunch of other people to ask for the same thing," he told me.

"But it's been done before!" and I gave him examples of other correspondents who'd jumped from one bureau to another.

"I can make it happen but it's gonna take time," he warned me. "And if I move you, you're gonna have to stay in L.A. I won't be able to bring you back."

I wasn't worried about that. I was just worried about having to wait.

I kept checking in to find out if there was progress on my transfer. I spoke regularly with Nancy Harmeyer, the L.A. bureau chief, who respected my work and was happy to have me move there, but it wasn't her call. I got intel on other moves that were about to happen that would help to clear a path for me, and things were progressing, albeit slowly, and then the pandemic hit.

New York City was the epicenter in the early days, so I was busy covering the impact of the virus every day. It was the worst possible circumstances for me, trying to leave when there was this kind of news breaking daily in my backyard. I was a bit less concerned because Kelly was able to stay with me for much of the first half of 2020, but I had other pressures. We'd rented a house because her lease was up, and I moved her in and was paying the rent, along with the mortgage on my city apartment, the mortgage on my beach house, and the mortgage on the condo I bought in Florida.

This was a lot for me to carry. I had a tenant all lined up to rent the Florida condo for more than my mortgage, but when the lockdowns started, his plans to build a new home nearby got put on hold, and he couldn't commit to my place. It then became nearly impossible to rent or sell the place, because management wouldn't let anyone on the property who wasn't a resident. It took months before my realtor was allowed to show it. I knew I could sell my city apartment because I'd just gut-renovated the place and it looked fantastic, and the huge terrace made it a rare and still affordable property. My beach house practically rented itself, and still does, but at the time the financial pressures were real, and I was eager to start my new life.

I would gently nudge Jay from time to time and ask others in management if they'd heard anything about a change in my situation. I started getting more and more frustrated as the months went by, but finally, in late June, I got word that my last day in New York would be Friday, July 3.

I was free to book my flight!

I packed a bunch of suitcases, shipped the rest of my clothes in boxes, took that Friday off and got a seat up front on the

United flight that had been my best friend the past few months, direct from Newark to John Wayne International in Orange County, with the Polaris lay-flat seats and big flat-screen TVs. My life was changing in ways I'd never thought possible, and my career with Fox would be over in less than nine months.

A QUIET GOODBYE

I commuted to the LA office from our home in Newport Beach for about nine months, fifty miles each way, reporting early mornings, during prime time and anchoring overnight coverage of breaking news events. It was a busy stretch, but my passion for breaking news had evaporated. My heart was with Kelly, and after twenty-four years of being one email, text, or phone call away from packing my bag, I was ready for a break.

I officially left Fox in June 2021, at the end of my eighth three-year contract. Twenty-four years was a long time to spend in one place, but of course that one place took me to thousands of places. It was an incredible run and the greatest job I've ever had. I earned a great living, worked with bright, talented people, traveled to some of the best and worst spots on Earth and experienced things most could only dream of (and yes, some of those dreams would qualify as nightmares).

It was strange to leave without fanfare, from an office I'd barely worked in. There was no goodbye party with hundreds of colleagues. There was no party at all. I was promised one in the future, but we were still in a pandemic, and I was thousands of miles from the vast majority of my former colleagues.

The network took very good care of me on my way out the door, meaning I wouldn't have to worry about going back to work for a while, and my 401(k) and pension accounts were enough to insure my comfort in my even-more-golden years.

It was time to relax and spend quality time with Kelly and Jolie and the rest of our family and friends and not worry about traveling on a moment's notice to somewhere I didn't necessarily want to go. We began working on our own projects including our *Rick & Kelly Unmasked* (now called *The Rick & Kelly Show*) podcasts, buying and remodeling a house we bought in the desert, and writing about my greatest adventures.

It's been the best year of my life. I'm grateful for everything I have, and grateful to you for reading my book.

ACKNOWLEDGMENTS

This book highlights some of the most incredible adventures of my career, none of which would've been possible without the people I worked and traveled with for nearly thirty-five years.

There have been hundreds if not thousands of photographers, producers, engineers, editors, fixers, security guards, and other crew members I spent considerable time with, who helped get us to locations, find interview subjects, collect information and video, gain access to people and places, communicate with the network and show producers back home and make sure I got on the air and our content was properly edited and shared with viewers.

To each and every one of you talented, hardworking people I say thank you. Thank you for helping me tell my stories. Thank you for making me look as good as I could while doing it. And thank you for keeping me alive.

To Pat Butler, the engineer on the ground with me in lower Manhattan on 9/11 who got us on television and kept us there throughout the worst, most chaotic day I've ever experienced, you will always be my brother and will always have my utmost respect.

To Carlos Van Meek, my first producer at Fox News Channel, who I traveled with extensively and who helped guide me through the early years of my network career, I will always appreciate your knowledge, perspective, and support.

To Tamara Gitt, Lissa Kaplan, Kathleen Foster, Andrew Fone, and Ron Ralston, you will always be my favorite producers who helped ensure my facts were straight and my scripts were accurate and tight.

To Scott Wilder, John "Hollywood" Kisala, Paul Celeste, Rob Ginnane, Tommy Chiu, and the rest of the Fox cameramen, our journeys were always more meaningful because we shared them together.

To Christian Galdabini, you were my rock in Iraq. We endured the most difficult and challenging conditions ever and actually had fun doing it because of your incredible drive, poise, energy, and sense of humor.

To Richie Harlow, my photog in Libya, you are supremely talented, dedicated, and entertaining and made our journeys truly rewarding.

To former General Stacy Clardy, who led the Marines battalion we embedded with into Iraq, thank you for keeping us safe and informed and for being a true friend ever since.

To all of my friends and contacts in law enforcement who trusted me with inside information and shared facts and insights on developing stories, thank you for consistently helping me get out front with the best, most accurate reports possible.

To my family and friends who put up with my constant travels and frequent last minute cancellations of personal trips, dinners and events because of work, I'm sorry I missed so much and will always appreciate your understanding.

And finally, to Pierre Zakrzewski, a cameraman who I worked with many times overseas who was killed during the conflict in Ukraine, you will always have my utmost respect. You were one of the nicest and hardest working guys I ever met, fearless and relaxed in some of the most stressful environments and most dangerous places on earth. I was always amazed by you and always looked forward to working together. May you Rest In Peace.